Katey Niemer
3233 34th Ave. W.
Seattle, WA 98199

BORN TO RUN

BORN TO RUN

A HIDDEN TRIBE, SUPERATHLETES,

AND THE GREATEST RACE

THE WORLD HAS NEVER SEEN

Christopher McDougall

 **ALFRED A. KNOPF** · New York · 2009

THIS IS A BORZOI BOOK
PUBLISHED BY ALFRED A. KNOPF

www.aaknopf.com

Knopf, Borzoi Books, and colophon are registered trademarks of
Random House, Inc.

Library of Congress Control Number: 2009922861

ISBN 978-0-307-26630-9

Manufactured in the United States of America

Published May 7, 2009

Reprinted Six Times

Eighth Printing, July 2009

To John and Jean McDougall,

my parents,

who gave me everything

and keep on giving

The best runner leaves no tracks.

—*Tao Te Ching*

BORN TO RUN

To live with ghosts requires solitude.

—ANNE MICHAELS, *Fugitive Pieces*

FOR DAYS, I'd been searching Mexico's Sierra Madre for the phantom known as *Caballo Blanco*—the White Horse. I'd finally arrived at the end of the trail, in the last place I expected to find him—not deep in the wilderness he was said to haunt, but in the dim lobby of an old hotel on the edge of a dusty desert town.

"*Sí, El Caballo está,*" the desk clerk said, nodding. Yes, the Horse is here.

"For real?" After hearing that I'd *just* missed him so many times, in so many bizarre locations, I'd begun to suspect that Caballo Blanco was nothing more than a fairy tale, a local Loch Ness *monstruo* dreamed up to spook the kids and fool gullible gringos.

"He's always back by five," the clerk added. "It's like a ritual."

I didn't know whether to hug her in relief or high-five her in triumph. I checked my watch. That meant I'd actually lay eyes on the ghost in less than . . . hang on.

"But it's already after six."

The clerk shrugged. "Maybe he's gone away."

I sagged into an ancient sofa. I was filthy, famished, and defeated. I was exhausted, and so were my leads.

Some said Caballo Blanco was a fugitive; others heard he was a boxer who'd run off to punish himself after beating a man to death in the ring. No one knew his name, or age, or where he was from. He was like some Old West gunslinger whose only traces were tall tales and a whiff of cigarillo smoke. Descriptions and sightings were all over the map; villagers who lived impossible distances apart swore they'd seen him traveling on foot on the same day, and described him on a scale that swung wildly from "funny and *simpático*" to "freaky and gigantic."

But in all versions of the Caballo Blanco legend, certain basic details were always the same: He'd come to Mexico years ago and trekked deep into the wild, impenetrable Barrancas del Cobre—the Copper Canyons—to live among the Tarahumara, a near-mythical tribe of Stone Age superathletes. The Tarahumara (pronounced Spanish-style by swallowing the "h": Tara-oo-mara) may be the healthiest and most serene people on earth, and the greatest runners of all time.

When it comes to ultradistances, nothing can beat a Tarahumara runner—not a racehorse, not a cheetah, not an Olympic marathoner. Very few outsiders have ever seen the Tarahumara in action, but amazing stories of their superhuman toughness and tranquillity have drifted out of the canyons for centuries. One explorer swore he saw a Tarahumara catch a deer with his bare hands, chasing the bounding animal until it finally dropped dead from exhaustion, "its hoofs falling off." Another adventurer spent ten hours climbing up and over a Copper Canyon mountain by mule; a Tarahumara runner made the same trip in ninety minutes.

"Try this," a Tarahumara woman once told an exhausted explorer who'd collapsed at the base of a mountain. She handed him a gourd full of a murky liquid. He swallowed a few gulps, and was amazed to feel new energy pulsing in his veins. He got to his feet and scaled the peak like an overcaffeinated Sherpa. The Tarahumara, the explorer would later report, also guarded the recipe to a special energy food that leaves them trim, powerful, and unstoppable: a few mouthfuls packed enough nutritional punch to let them run all day without rest.

But whatever secrets the Tarahumara are hiding, they've hidden them well. To this day, the Tarahumara live in the side of cliffs higher than a hawk's nest in a land few have ever seen. The Barrancas are a lost world in the most remote wilderness in North America, a sort of a shorebound Bermuda Triangle known for swallowing the misfits and desperadoes who stray inside. Lots of bad things can happen down there, and probably will; survive the man-eating jaguars, deadly snakes, and blistering heat, and you've still got to deal with "canyon fever," a potentially fatal freak-out brought on by the Barrancas' desolate eeriness. The deeper you penetrate into the Barrancas, the more it feels like a crypt sliding shut around you. The walls tighten, shadows spread, phantom echoes whisper; every route out seems to end in sheer rock. Lost prospectors would be gripped by such madness and despair, they'd slash their own throats or hurl themselves off cliffs. Little surprise that few strangers have ever seen the Tarahumara's homeland—let alone the Tarahumara.

But somehow the White Horse had made his way to the depths of the Barrancas. And there, it's said, he was adopted by the Tarahumara as a friend and kindred spirit; a ghost among ghosts. He'd certainly mastered two Tarahumara skills—invisibility and extraordinary endurance—because even though he was spotted all over the canyons, no one seemed to know where he lived or when he might appear next. If anyone could translate the ancient secrets of the Tarahumara, I was told, it was this lone wanderer of the High Sierras.

I'd become so obsessed with finding Caballo Blanco that as I dozed on the hotel sofa, I could even imagine the sound of his voice. "Probably like Yogi Bear ordering burritos at Taco Bell," I mused. A guy like that, a wanderer who'd go anywhere but fit in nowhere, must live inside his own head and rarely hear his own voice. He'd make weird jokes and crack himself up. He'd have a booming laugh and atrocious Spanish. He'd be loud and chatty and . . . and . . .

Wait. I *was* hearing him. My eyes popped open to see a dusty cadaver in a tattered straw hat bantering with the desk clerk. Trail dust streaked his gaunt face like fading war paint, and the shocks of sun-bleached hair sticking out from under the hat could have been trimmed with a hunting knife. He looked like a castaway on a desert island, even to the way he seemed hungry for conversation with the bored clerk.

"Caballo?" I croaked.

The cadaver turned, smiling, and I felt like an idiot. He didn't look wary; he looked confused, as any tourist would when confronted by a deranged man on a sofa suddenly hollering "Horse!"

This wasn't Caballo. There was no Caballo. The whole thing was a hoax, and I'd fallen for it.

Then the cadaver spoke. "You know me?"

"Man!" I exploded, scrambling to my feet. "Am I glad to see you!"

The smile vanished. The cadaver's eyes darted toward the door, making it clear that in another second, he would as well.

CHAPTER 2

IT ALL BEGAN with a simple question that no one could answer.

It was a five-word puzzle that led me to a photo of a very fast man in a very short skirt, and from there it only got stranger. Soon, I was dealing with a murder, drug guerrillas, and a one-armed man with a cream-cheese cup strapped to his head. I met a beautiful blonde forest ranger who slipped out of her clothes and found salvation by running naked in the Idaho forests, and a young surfer babe in pigtails who ran straight toward her death in the desert. A talented young runner would die. Two others would barely escape with their lives.

I kept looking, and stumbled across the Barefoot Batman . . . Naked Guy . . . Kalahari Bushmen . . . the Toenail Amputee . . . a cult devoted to distance running and sex parties . . . the Wild Man of the Blue Ridge Mountains . . . and, ultimately, the ancient tribe of the Tarahumara and their shadowy disciple, Caballo Blanco.

In the end, I got my answer, but only after I found myself in the middle of the greatest race the world would never see: the Ultimate Fighting Competition of footraces, an underground showdown pitting some of the best ultradistance runners of our time against the best ultrarunners of *all* time, in a fifty-mile race on hidden trails only Tarahumara feet had ever touched. I'd be startled to discover that the ancient saying of the *Tao Te Ching*—"The best runner leaves no tracks"—wasn't some gossamer koan, but real, concrete, how-to, training advice.

And all because in January 2001 I asked my doctor this:
"How come my foot hurts?"

I'd gone to see one of the top sports-medicine specialists in the country because an invisible ice pick was driving straight up through the sole of my foot. The week before, I'd been out for an easy three-mile jog on a snowy farm road when I suddenly whinnied in pain, grabbing my right foot and screaming curses as I toppled over in the snow. When I got a grip on myself, I checked to see how badly I was bleeding. I must have impaled my foot on a sharp rock, I figured, or an old nail wedged in the ice. But there wasn't a drop of blood, or even a hole in my shoe.

"Running is your problem," Dr. Joe Torg confirmed when I limped into his Philadelphia examining room a few days later. He should know; Dr. Torg had not only helped create the entire field of sports medicine, but he also co-wrote *The Running Athlete*, the definitive radiographic analysis of every conceivable running injury. He ran me through an X-ray and watched me hobble around, then determined that I'd aggravated my cuboid, a cluster of bones parallel to the arch that I hadn't even known existed until it reengineered itself into an internal Taser.

"But I'm barely running at all," I said. "I'm doing, like, two or three miles every other day. And not even on asphalt. Mostly dirt roads."

Didn't matter. "The human body is not designed for that kind of abuse," Dr. Torg replied. "Especially not *your* body."

I knew exactly what he meant. At six feet four inches and two hundred thirty pounds, I'd been told many times that nature intended guys my size to post up under the hoop or take a bullet for the President, not pound our bulk down the pavement. And since I'd turned forty, I was starting to see why; in the five years since I'd stopped playing pickup hoops and tried turning myself into a marathoner, I'd ripped my hamstring (twice), strained my Achilles tendons (repeatedly), sprained my ankles (both, alternately), suffered aching arches (regularly), and had to walk down stairs backward on tiptoe because my heels were so sore. And now, apparently, the last docile spot on my feet had joined the rebellion.

The weird thing was, I seemed to be otherwise unbreakable. As a writer for *Men's Health* magazine and one of *Esquire* magazine's original "Restless Man" columnists, a big part of my job was experimenting with semi-extreme sports. I'd ridden Class IV rapids on a boogie board, surfed giant sand dunes on a snowboard, and mountain biked across the North Dakota Badlands. I'd also reported from three war zones for the Associated Press and spent months in some of the most lawless regions of Africa, all without a nick or a twinge. But jog a few miles down the street, and suddenly I'm rolling on the ground like I'd been gut shot in a drive-by.

Take any other sport, and an injury rate like mine would classify me as defective. In running, it makes me normal. The real mutants are the runners who *don't* get injured. Up to eight out of every ten runners are hurt *every year.* It doesn't matter if you're heavy or thin, speedy or slow, a marathon champ or a weekend huffer, you're just as likely as the other guy to savage your knees, shins, hamstrings, hips, or heels. Next time you line up for a Turkey Trot, look at the runners on your right and left: statistically, only one of you will be back for the Jingle Bell Jog.

No invention yet has slowed the carnage; you can now buy running shoes with steel bedsprings embedded in the soles and Adidas that adjust their cushioning by microchip, but the injury rate hasn't decreased a jot in thirty years. If anything, it's actually ebbed up; Achilles tendon blowouts have seen a 10 percent increase. Running seemed to be the fitness version of drunk driving: you could get away with it for a while, you might even have some fun, but catastrophe was waiting right around the corner.

"Big surprise," the sports-medicine literature sneers. Not exactly like that, though. More like this: "Athletes whose sport involves running put enormous strain on their legs." That's what the *Sports Injury Bulletin* has declared. "Each footfall hits one of their legs with a force equal to more than twice their body weight. Just as repeated hammering on an apparently impenetrable rock will eventually reduce the stone to dust, the impact loads associated with running can ultimately break down your bones, cartilage, muscles, tendons, and ligaments." A report by the American Association of Orthopedic Surgeons concluded that distance running is "an outrageous threat to the integrity of the knee."

And instead of "impenetrable rock," that outrage is banging down on one of the most sensitive points in your body. You know what kind of nerves are in your feet? The same ones that network into your genitals. Your feet are like a minnow bucket full of sensory neurons, all of them wriggling around in search of sensation. Stimulate those nerves just a little, and the impulse will rocket through your entire nervous system; that's why tickling your feet can overload the switch-board and cause your whole body to spasm.

No wonder South American dictators had a foot fetish when it came to breaking hard cases; the bastinado, the technique of tying victims down and beating the soles of their feet, was developed by the Spanish Inquisition and eagerly adopted by the world's sickest sadists. The Khmer Rouge and Saddam Hussein's sinister son Uday were big-time bastinado fans because they knew their anatomy; only the face and hands compare with the feet for instant-messaging capa-bility to the brain. When it comes to sensing the softest caress or tiniest grain of sand, your toes are as finely wired as your lips and fingertips.

"So isn't there anything I can do?" I asked Dr. Torg.

He shrugged. "You can keep running, but you'll be back for more of these," he said, giving a little *ting* with his fingernail to the giant needle full of cortisone he was about to push into the bottom of my foot. I'd also need custom-made orthotics ($400) to slip inside my motion-control running shoes ($150 and climbing, and since I'd need to rotate two pairs, make it $300). But that would just post-pone the real big-ticket item: my inevitable next visit to his waiting room.

"Know what I'd recommend?" Dr. Torg concluded. "Buy a bike."

I thanked him, promised I'd take his advice, then immediately went behind his back to someone else. Doc Torg was getting up in years, I realized; maybe he'd gotten a little too conservative with his advice and a little too quick with his cortisone. A physician friend recommended a sports podiatrist who was also a marathoner, so I made an appointment for the following week.

The podiatrist took another X-ray, then probed my foot with his thumbs. "Looks like you've got cuboid syndrome," he concluded. "I can blast the inflammation out with some cortisone, but then you're going to need orthotics."

"Damn," I muttered. "That's just what Torg said."

He'd started to leave the room for the needle, but then he stopped short. "You already saw Joe Torg?"

"Yes."

"You already got a cortisone shot?"

"Uh, yeah."

"So what are you doing here?" he asked, suddenly looking impatient and a little suspicious, as if he thought I really enjoyed having needles shoved into the tenderest part of my foot. Maybe he suspected I was a sadomasochistic junkie who was addicted to both pain *and* painkillers.

"You realize Dr. Torg is the godfather of sports medicine, right? His diagnoses are usually well respected."

"I know. I just wanted to double-check."

"I'm not going to give you another shot, but we can schedule a fitting for the orthotics. And you should really think about finding some other activity besides running."

"Sounds good," I said. He was a better runner than I'd ever be, and he'd just confirmed the verdict of a doctor he readily admitted was the sensei of sports physicians. There was absolutely no arguing with his diagnosis. So I started looking for someone else.

It's not that I'm all that stubborn. It's not that I'm even all that crazy about running. If I totaled all the miles I'd ever run, half were aching drudgery. But it does say something that even though I haven't read *The World According to Garp* in twenty years, I've never forgotten one minor scene, and it ain't the one you're thinking of: I keep thinking back to the way Garp used to burst out his door in the middle of the workday for a five-mile run. There's something so universal about that sensation, the way running unites our two most primal impulses: fear and pleasure. We run when we're scared, we run when we're ecstatic, we run away from our problems and run around for a good time.

And when things look worst, we run the most. Three times, America has seen distance-running skyrocket, and it's always in the midst of a national crisis. The first boom came during the Great Depression, when more than two hundred runners set the trend by racing forty miles a day across the country in the Great American Footrace. Running then went dormant, only to catch fire again in the early '70s, when we were struggling to recover from Vietnam, the

Cold War, race riots, a criminal president, and the murders of three beloved leaders. And the third distance boom? One year after the September 11 attacks, trail-running suddenly became the fastest-growing outdoor sport in the country. Maybe it was a coincidence. Or maybe there's a trigger in the human psyche, a coded response that activates our first and greatest survival skill when we sense the raptors approaching. In terms of stress relief and sensual pleasure, running is what you have in your life before you have sex. The equipment and desire come factory installed; all you have to do is let 'er rip and hang on for the ride.

That's what I was looking for; not some pricey hunk of plastic to stick in my shoe, not a monthly cycle of painkillers, just a way to let 'er rip without tearing myself up. I didn't love running, but I *wanted* to. Which is what brought me to the door of M.D. No. 3: Dr. Irene Davis, an expert in biomechanics and head of the Running Injury Clinic at the University of Delaware.

Dr. Davis put me on a treadmill, first in my bare feet and then in three different types of running shoes. She had me walk, trot, and haul ass. She had me run back and forth over a force plate to measure the impact shock from my footfalls. Then I sat in horror as she played back the video.

In my mind's eye, I'm light and quick as a Navajo on the hunt. That guy on the screen, however, was Frankenstein's monster trying to tango. I was bobbing around so much, my head was disappearing from the top of the frame. My arms were slashing back and forth like an ump calling a player safe at the plate, while my size 13s clumped down so heavily it sounded like the video had a bongo backbeat.

If that wasn't bad enough, Dr. Davis then hit slow-mo so we could all settle back and really appreciate the way my right foot twisted out, my left knee dipped in, and my back bucked and spasmed so badly that it looked as if someone ought to jam a wallet between my teeth and call for help. How the hell was I even moving forward with all that up-down, side-to-side, fish-on-a-hook flopping going on?

"Okay," I said. "So what's the right way to run?"

"That's the eternal question," Dr. Davis replied.

As for the eternal answer . . . well, that was tricky. I might straighten out my stride and get a little more shock absorption if I landed on my fleshy midfoot instead of my bony heel, *buuuuut* . . . I might just be swapping one set of problems for another. Tinkering with a new gait can suddenly load the heel and Achilles with unaccustomed stress and bring on a fresh batch of injuries.

"Running is tough on the legs," Dr. Davis said. She was so gentle and apologetic, I could tell what else she was thinking: "Especially *your* legs, big fella."

I was right back where I'd started. After months of seeing specialists and searching physiology studies online, all I'd managed was to get my question flipped around and fired back at me:

How come my foot hurts?

Because running is bad for you.

Why is running bad for me?

Because it makes your foot hurt.

But *why?* Antelope don't get shin splints. Wolves don't ice-pack their knees. I doubt that 80 percent of all wild mustangs are annually disabled with impact injuries. It reminded me of a proverb attributed to Roger Bannister, who, while simultaneously studying medicine, working as a clinical researcher, and minting pithy parables, became the first man to break the four-minute mile: "Every morning in Africa, a gazelle wakes up," Bannister said. "It knows it must outrun the fastest lion or it will be killed. Every morning in Africa, a lion wakes up. It knows it must run faster than the slowest gazelle, or it will starve. It doesn't matter whether you're a lion or a gazelle—when the sun comes up, you'd better be running."

So why should every other mammal on the planet be able to depend on its legs except us? Come to think of it, how could a guy like Bannister charge out of the lab every day, pound around a hard cinder track in thin leather slippers, and not only get faster, but never get hurt? How come some of us can be out there running all lionlike and Bannisterish every morning when the sun comes up, while the rest of us need a fistful of ibuprofen before we can put our feet on the floor?

These were very good questions. But as I was about to discover, the only ones who knew the answers—the only ones who *lived* the answers—weren't talking.

Especially not to someone like me.

In the winter of 2003, I was on assignment in Mexico when I began flipping through a Spanish-language travel magazine. Suddenly, a photo of Jesus running down a rock slide caught my eye.

Closer inspection revealed that while maybe not Jesus, it was definitely a man in a robe and sandals sprinting down a mountain of rubble. I started translating the caption, but couldn't figure out why it was in the present tense; it seemed to be some kind of wishful Atlantean legend about an extinct empire of enlightened superbeings. Only gradually did I figure out that I was right about everything except the "extinct" and "wishful" parts.

I was in Mexico to track down a missing pop star and her secret brainwashing cult for *The New York Times Magazine*, but the article I was writing suddenly seemed a snore compared with the one I was reading. Freakish fugitive pop stars come and go, but the Tarahumara seemed to live forever. Left alone in their mysterious canyon hideaway, this small tribe of recluses had solved nearly every problem known to man. Name your category—mind, body, or soul—and the Tarahumara were zeroing in on perfection. It was as if they'd secretly turned their caves into incubators for Nobel Prize winners, all toiling toward the end of hatred, heart disease, shin splints, and greenhouse gases.

In Tarahumara Land, there was no crime, war, or theft. There was no corruption, obesity, drug addiction, greed, wife-beating, child abuse, heart disease, high blood pressure, or carbon emissions. They didn't get diabetes, or depressed, or even old: fifty-year-olds could outrun teenagers, and eighty-year-old great-grandads could hike marathon distances up mountainsides. Their cancer rates were barely detectable. The Tarahumara geniuses had even branched into economics, creating a one-of-a-kind financial system based on booze and random acts of kindness: instead of money, they traded favors and big tubs of corn beer.

You'd expect an economic engine fueled by alcohol and freebies to spiral into a drunken grab-fest, everyone double-fisting for themselves like bankrupt gamblers at a casino buffet, but in Tarahumara Land, it works. Perhaps it's because the Tarahumara are industrious and inhumanly honest; one researcher went as far as to speculate that after so many generations of truthfulness, the Tarahumara brain was actually chemically incapable of forming lies.

And if being the kindest, happiest people on the planet wasn't enough, the Tarahumara were also the toughest: the only thing that rivaled their superhuman serenity, it seemed, was their superhuman tolerance for pain and *lechuguilla*, a horrible homemade tequila brewed from rattlesnake corpses and cactus sap. According to one of the few outsiders who'd ever witnessed a full-on Tarahumara rave, the partiers got so blitzed that wives began ripping each others' tops off in a bare-breasted wrestling match, while a cackling old man circled around trying to spear their butts with a corncob. The husbands, meanwhile, gazed on in glassy-eyed paralysis. Cancún at spring break had nothing on the Barrancas under a harvest moon.

The Tarahumara would party like this all night, then roust themselves the next morning to face off in a running race that could last not two miles, not two hours, but *two full days*. According to the Mexican historian Francisco Almada, a Tarahumara champion once ran 435 miles, the equivalent of setting out for a jog in New York City and not stopping till you were closing in on Detroit. Other Tarahumara runners reportedly went three hundred miles at a pop. That's nearly twelve full marathons, back to back to back, while the sun rose and set and rose again.

And the Tarahumara weren't cruising along smooth, paved roads, either, but scrambling up and down steep canyon trails formed only by their own feet. Lance Armstrong is one of the greatest endurance athletes of all time, and he could barely shuffle through his first marathon despite sucking down an energy gel nearly every mile. (Lance's text message to his ex-wife after the New York City Marathon: "Oh. My. God. Ouch. Terrible.") Yet these guys were knocking them out a dozen at a time?

In 1971, an American physiologist trekked into the Copper Canyons and was so blown away by Tarahumara athleticism that he had to reach back twenty-eight hundred years for a suitable scale to rank it on. "Probably not since the days of the ancient Spartans has a people achieved such a high state of physical conditioning," Dr. Dale Groom concluded when he published his findings in the *American Heart Journal*. Unlike the Spartans, however, the Tarahumara are benign as bodhisattvas; they don't use their superstrength to kick ass, but to live in peace. "As a culture, they're one of the great unsolved mysteries," says Dr. Daniel Noveck, a University of Chicago anthropologist who specializes in the Tarahumara.

The Tarahumara are so mysterious, in fact, they even go by an alias. Their real name is Rarámuri—the Running People. They were dubbed "Tarahumara" by conquistadores who didn't understand the tribal tongue. The bastardized name stuck because the Rarámuri remained true to form, running away rather than hanging around to argue the point. Answering aggression with their heels has always been the Rarámuri way. Ever since Cortés's armored invaders came jangling into their homeland and then through subsequent invasions by Pancho Villa's roughriders and Mexican drug barons, the Tarahumara have responded to attacks by running farther and faster than anyone could follow, retreating ever deeper into the Barrancas.

God, they must be unbelievably disciplined, I thought. *Total focus and dedication. The Shaolin monks of running.*

Well, not quite. When it comes to marathoning, the Tarahumara prefer more of a Mardi Gras approach. In terms of diet, lifestyle, and belly fire, they're a track coach's nightmare. They drink like New Year's Eve is a weekly event, tossing back enough corn beer in a year to spend every third day of their adult lives either buzzed or recovering. Unlike Lance, the Tarahumara don't replenish their bodies with electrolyte-rich sports drinks. They don't rebuild between workouts with protein bars; in fact, they barely eat any protein at all, living on little more than ground corn spiced up by their favorite delicacy, barbecued mouse. Come race day, the Tarahumara don't train or taper. They don't stretch or warm up. They just stroll to the starting line, laughing and bantering . . . then go like hell for the next forty-eight hours.

How come they're not crippled? I wondered. It's as if a clerical error entered the stats in the wrong columns: shouldn't *we*—the ones with state-of-the-art running shoes and custom-made orthotics—have the zero casualty rate, and the Tarahumara—who run way more, on way rockier terrain, in shoes that barely qualify as shoes—be constantly banged up?

Their legs are just tougher, since they've been running all their lives, I thought, before catching my own goof. *But that means they should be hurt* more, *not less: if running is bad for your legs, then running lots should be a lot worse.*

I shoved the article aside, feeling equal parts intrigued and annoyed. Everything about the Tarahumara seemed backward, taunting, as irritatingly ungraspable as a Zen master's riddles. The toughest guys were the gentlest; battered legs were the bounciest; the healthiest people had the crappiest diet; the illiterate race was the wisest; the guys working the hardest were having the most fun. . . .

And what did running have to do with all this? Was it a coincidence that the world's most enlightened people were also the world's most amazing runners? Seekers used to climb the Himalayas for that kind of wisdom—and all this time, I realized, it was just a hop across the Texas border.

CHAPTER 3

FIGURING OUT WHERE over the border, however, was going to be tricky.

Runner's World magazine assigned me to trek into the Barrancas in search of the Tarahumara. But before I could start looking for the ghosts, I'd need to find a ghost hunter. Salvador Holguín, I was told, was the only man for the job.

By day, Salvador is a thirty-three-year-old municipal administrator in Guachochi, a frontier town on the edge of the Copper Canyons. By night, he's a barroom mariachi singer, and he looks it; with his beer gut and black-eyed, rose-in-the-teeth good looks, he's the exact image of a guy who splits his life between desk chairs and bar stools. Salvador's brother, however, is the Indiana Jones of the Mexican school system; every year, he loads a burro with pencils and workbooks and bushwhacks into the Barrancas to resupply the canyon-bottom schools. Because Salvador is game for just about anything, he has occasionally blown off work to accompany his brother on these expeditions.

"*Hombre*, no problem," he told me once I'd tracked him down. "We can go see Arnulfo Quimare. . . ."

If he'd stopped right there, I'd have been ecstatic. While searching for a guide, I'd learned that Arnulfo Quimare was the greatest living Tarahumara runner, and he came from a clan of cousins, brothers, in-laws, and nephews who were nearly as good. The prospect of heading right to the hidden huts of the Quimare dynasty was better than I could have hoped for. The only problem was, Salvador was still talking.

"... I'm *pretty* sure I know the way," he continued. "I've never actually been there. *"Pues, lo que sea."* Well, whatever. "We'll find it. Eventually."

Ordinarily, that would sound a little ominous, but compared with everyone else I'd talked with, Salvador was wildly optimistic. Since fleeing into no-man's-land four hundred years ago, the Tarahumara have spent their time perfecting the art of invisibility. Many Tarahumara still live in cliffside caves reachable only by long climbing poles; once inside, they pull up the poles and vanish into the rock. Others live in huts so ingeniously camouflaged, the great Norwegian explorer Carl Lumholtz was once startled to discover he'd trekked right past an entire Tarahumara village without detecting a hint of homes or humans.

Lumholtz was a true backwoods badass who'd spent years living among headhunters in Borneo before heading into Tarahumara Land in the late 1890s. But you can sense even his fortitude grinding thin after he'd dragged himself through deserts and up death-defying cliffs, only to arrive at last in the heart of Tarahumara country to find ...

No one.

"To look at these mountains is a soul-inspiring sensation; but to travel over them is exhaustive to muscle and patience," Lumholtz wrote in *Unknown Mexico: A Record of Five Years' Exploration Among the Tribes of the Western Sierra Madre.* "Nobody except those who have travelled in the Mexican mountains can understand and appreciate the difficulties and anxieties attending such a journey."

And that's assuming you make it as far as the mountains in the first place. "On first encounter, the region of the Tarahumara appears inaccessible," the French playwright Antonin Artaud grumbled after he sweated and inched his way into the Copper Canyons in search of shamanic wisdom in the 1930s. "At best, there are a few poorly marked trails that every twenty yards seem to disappear under the ground." When Artaud and his guides finally did discover a path, they had to gulp hard before taking it: subscribing to the principle that the best trick for throwing off pursuers was to travel places where only a lunatic would follow, the Tarahumara snake their trails over suicidally steep terrain.

"A false step," an adventurer named Frederick Schwatka jotted in his notebook during a Copper Canyon expedition in 1888, "would send the climber two hundred to three hundred feet to the bottom of the canyon, perhaps a mangled corpse."

Schwatka was no prissy Parisian poet, either; he was a U.S. Army lieutenant who'd survived the frontier wars and later lived among the Sioux as an amateur anthropologist, so the man knew from mangled corpses. He'd also traveled the baddest of badlands in his time, including a hellacious two-year expedition to the Arctic Circle. But when he got to the Copper Canyons, he had to recalibrate his scoring table. Scanning the ocean of wilderness around him, Schwatka felt a quick pulse of admiration—"The heart of the Andes or the crests of the Himalayas contain no more sublime scenery than the wild, unknown fastnesses of the Sierra Madres of Mexico"—before being jerked back to morbid bewilderment: "How they can rear children on these cliffs without a loss of one hundred percent annually is to me one of the most mysterious things connected with these strange people."

Even today, when the Internet has shrunk the world into a global village and Google satellites let you spy on a stranger's backyard on the other side of the country, the traditional Tarahumara remain as ghostly as they were four hundred years ago. In the mid-1990s, an expeditionary group was pushing into the deep Barrancas when they were suddenly rattled by the feeling of invisible eyes:

"Our small party had been hiking for hours through Mexico's Barranca del Cobre—the Copper Canyon—without seeing a trace of any other human being," wrote one member of the expedition. "Now, in the heart of a canyon even deeper than the Grand Canyon, we heard the echoes of Tarahumara drums. Their simple beats were faint at first, but soon gathered strength. Echoing off stony ridges, it was impossible to tell their number or location. We looked to our guide for direction. '¿Quién sabe?' she said. 'Who knows? The Tarahumara can't be seen unless they want to be.'"

The moon was still high when we set off in Salvador's trusty four-wheel-drive pickup. By the time the sun came up, we'd left pavement far behind and were jouncing along a dirt track that was more like a creek bed than a road, grinding along in low, low gear as we pitched and rolled like a tramp steamer on stormy seas.

I tried keeping track of our location with a compass and map, but I sometimes couldn't tell if Salvador was making a deliberate turn or taking evasive action around a fallen boulder. Soon, it didn't matter—wherever we were, it wasn't part of the known world; we were still snaking along a narrow gash through the trees, but the map showed nothing but untouched forest.

"*Mucha mota por aquí,*" Salvador said, swirling a finger at the hills around us. Lots of marijuana around here.

Because the Barrancas are impossible to police, they've become a base for two rival drug cartels, Los Zetas and the New Bloods. Both were manned by ex–Army Special Forces and were absolutely ruthless; the Zetas were notorious for plunging uncooperative cops into burning barrels of diesel fuel and feeding captured rivals to the gang's mascot—a Bengal tiger. After the victims stopped screaming, their scorched and tiger-gnawed heads were carefully harvested as marketing tools; the cartels liked to mark their territory by, in one case, impaling the heads of two police officers outside a government building with a sign in Spanish reading LEARN SOME RESPECT. Later that same month, five heads were rolled onto the dance floor of a crowded nightclub. Even way out here on the fringes of the Barrancas, some six bodies were turning up a week.

But Salvador seemed totally unconcerned. He drove on through the woods, throatily butchering something about a bra full of bad news named Maria. Suddenly, the song died in his mouth. He snapped off the tape player, his eyes fixed on a red Dodge pickup with smoked-black glass that had just burst through the dust ahead of us.

"*Narcotraficantes,*" he muttered.

Drug runners. Salvador edged as close as he could to the cliff edge on our right and eased even further back on the gas, dropping deferentially from the ten miles per hour we'd been averaging down to a dead halt, granting the big red Dodge every bit of road he could spare.

No trouble here was the message he was trying to send. *Just minding our own, non-*mota *business. Just don't stop . . .* because what would we say if they cut us off and came piling out, demanding that we speak slowly and clearly into the barrels of their assault rifles while we explained what the hell we were doing way out here in the middle of Mexican marijuana country?

We couldn't even tell them the truth; if they believed us, we were dead. If Mexico's drug gangs hated anything as much as cops, it was singers and reporters. Not singers in any slang sense of snitches or stool pigeons; they hated real, guitar-strumming, love-song-singing crooners. Fifteen singers were executed by drug gangs in just eighteen months, including the beautiful Zayda Peña, the twenty-eight-year-old lead singer of Zayda y Los Culpables, who was gunned down after a concert; she survived, but the hit team tracked her to the hospital and blasted her to death while she was recovering from surgery. The young heartthrob Valentín Elizalde was killed by a barrage of bullets from an AK-47 just across the border from McAllen, Texas, and Sergio Gómez was killed shortly after he was nominated for a Grammy; his genitals were torched, then he was strangled to death and dumped in the street. What doomed them, as far as anyone could tell, was their fame, good looks, and talent; the singers challenged the drug lords' sense of their own importance, and so were marked for death.

The bizarre fatwa on balladeers was emotional and unpredictable, but the contract on reporters was all business. News articles about the cartels got picked up by American papers, which embarrassed American politicians, which put pressure on the Drug Enforcement Administration to crack down. Infuriated, the Zetas threw hand grenades into newsrooms, and even sent killers across the U.S. border to hunt down meddlesome journalists. After thirty reporters were killed in six years, the editor of the Villahermosa newspaper found the severed head of a low-level drug soldier outside his office with a note reading, "You're next." The death toll had gotten so bad, Mexico would eventually rank second only to Iraq in the number of killed or kidnapped reporters.

And now we'd saved the cartels a lot of trouble; a singer and a journalist had just driven smack into their backyard. I jammed my notebook down my pants and quickly scanned the front seat for more things to hide. It was hopeless; Salvador had his group's tapes scattered everywhere, a shiny red press pass was in my wallet, and right between my feet was a backpack full of tape recorders, pens, and a camera.

The red Dodge pulled alongside us. It was a glorious, sunny day with a cool, pine-scented breeze, but the truck's windows were all tightly shut, leaving the mysterious crew invisible behind their smoked-black glass. The truck slowed to a rumbling crawl.

Just keep going, I chanted inside my head. *Don't stop don'tstopdon't don'tdon't . . .*

The truck stopped. I cut my eyes hard left and saw Salvador was staring straight ahead, his hands frozen on the steering wheel. I darted my eyes forward again and didn't move a muscle.

We sat.

They sat.

We were silent.

They were silent.

Six murders a week, I was thinking. *Burned his balls off.* I could see my head rolling between panicky stilettos on a Chihuahua dance floor.

Suddenly, a roar split the air. My eyes slashed left again. The big red Dodge was spitting back to life and growling on past.

Salvador watched in the side-view mirror till the Deathmobile disappeared in a swirl of dust. Then he slapped the steering wheel and blasted his *ay-yay-yaying* tape again.

"*¡Bueno!*" he shouted. "*¡Ándale pues, a más aventuras!*" Excellent! On to more adventures!

Parts of me that had clenched tight enough to crack walnuts slowly began to relax. But not for long.

A few hours later, Salvador stomped on the brakes. He backed up, cut a hard right off the rutted path, and started winding between the trees. We wandered farther and farther into the woods, crunching over pine needles and bouncing into gullies so deep I was banging my head on the roll bar.

As the woods got darker, Salvador got quieter. For the first time since our encounter with the Deathmobile, he even turned off the music. I thought he was drinking in the solitude and stillness, so I tried to sit back and appreciate it with him. But when I finally broke the silence with a question, he grunted moodily back at me. I began to suspect what was going on: we were lost, and Salvador didn't want to admit it. I watched him more closely, and noticed he was slowing down to study the tree trunks, as if somewhere in the cuneiform bark was a decryptable road atlas.

"We're screwed," I realized. We had a one-in-four shot of this turning out well, which left three other possibilities: driving smack back into the Zetas, driving off a cliff in the dark, or driving around in the wilderness until the Clif Bars ran out and one of us ate the other.

And then, just as the sun set, we ran out of planet.

We emerged from the woods to find an ocean of empty space ahead—a crack in the earth so vast that the far side could be in a different time zone. Down below, it looked like a world-ending explosion frozen in stone, as if an angry god had been in the midst of destroying the planet, then changed his mind in mid-apocalypse. I was staring at twenty thousand square miles of wilderness, randomly slashed into twisting gorges deeper and wider than the Grand Canyon.

I walked to the edge of the cliff, and my heart started to pound. A sheer drop fell for about . . . ever. Far below, birds were swirling about. I could just make out the mighty river at the bottom of the canyon; it looked like a thin blue vein in an old man's arm. My stomach clenched. How the hell would we get down there?

"We'll manage," Salvador assured me. "The Rarámuri do it all the time."

When I didn't look any more cheerful, Salvador came up with a silver lining. "Hey, it's better this way," he said. "It's too steep for *narcotraficantes* to mess around down there."

I didn't know if he really believed it or was lying to buck me up. Either way, he should have known better.

TWO DAYS LATER, Salvador dropped his backpack, mopped his sweating face, and said, "We're here."

I looked around. There was nothing but rocks and cactus.

"We're where?"

"*Aquí mismo*," Salvador said. "Right here. This is where the Quimare clan lives."

I didn't get what he was talking about. As far as the eye could see, it was exactly like the dark side of a lost planet we'd been hiking over for days. After ditching the truck on the rim of the canyon, we'd slid and scrambled our way down to the bottom. It had been a relief to finally walk on level ground, but not for long; after striking out upstream the next morning, we found ourselves wedged tighter and tighter between the soaring stone walls. We pushed on, holding our backpacks on our heads as we shoved against water up to our chests. The sun was slowly eclipsed by the steep walls, until we were inching our way through gurgling darkness, feeling as if we were slowly walking to the bottom of the sea.

Eventually, Salvador spotted a gap in the slick wall and we climbed through, leaving the river behind. By midday, I was longing for the gloomy dark again; with a baking sun overhead and nothing but bare rock all around, pulling ourselves up that slope was like climbing a steel sliding board. Salvador finally stopped, and I dropped against a rock to rest.

CHAPTER 13

He who loves his body more than
dominion over the empire
can be given custody of the empire.

—LAO TZU, *Tao Te Ching*

DR. JOE VIGIL, a sixty-five-year-old army of one, warmed his
hands around his coffee as he waited for the first flashlight beams to
come stabbing toward him through the woods.

No other elite coach in the world was anywhere near Leadville,
because no other elite coach could give a hoot what was going on at
that giant outdoor insane asylum in the Rockies. Self-mutilators,
mean mothermuckers or whatever they called themselves—what did
they have to do with real running? With *Olympic* running? As a sport,
most track coaches ranked ultras somewhere between competitive
eating and recreational S&M.

Super, Vigil thought, as he stomped his feet against the chill. *Go
ahead and sleep, and leave the freaks to me*—because he knew the freaks
were onto something.

The secret to Vigil's success was spelled out right in his name: no
other coach was more vigilant about detecting the crucial little
details that everyone else missed. He'd been that way his entire competitive life, ever since he was a puny Latino kid trying to play high-
school football in a conference that didn't have many Latinos, let
alone puny ones. Joey Vigil couldn't outmuscle the meat slabs on the
other side of the line, so he out-scienced them; he studied the tricks

of leverage, propulsion, and timing, figuring out ways to position his feet so he popped up from a crouch like a spring-loaded anvil. By the time he graduated from college, the puny Latino kid was a first-team All-Conference guard. He then turned to track, and used that tireless bloodhound nose to become the greatest distance-running mind America has ever seen.

Besides his Ph.D. and two master's degrees, Vigil's pursuit of the lost art of distance running had taken him deep into the Russian outback, high into the mountains of Peru, and far across Kenya's Rift Valley highlands. He'd wanted to learn why Russian sprinters are forbidden to run a single step in training until they can jump off a twenty-foot ladder in their bare feet, and how sixty-year-old goatherds at Machu Picchu can possibly scale the Andes on a starvation diet of yogurt and herbs, and how Japanese runners trained by Suzuki-san and Koide-san could mysteriously alchemize slow walking into fast marathons. He'd tracked down the old masters and picked their brains, vacuuming up their secrets before they disappeared into the grave. His head was a Library of Congress of running lore, much of it vanished from every place on the planet except his memory.

His research paid off sensationally. At his alma mater, Adams State College in Alamosa, Colorado, Vigil took over the dying cross-country program and engineered it into an absolute terror. Adams State harriers won twenty-six national titles in thirty-three years, including the most awe-inspiring show of strength ever displayed in a national championship race: in 1992, Vigil's runners took the first five places in the NCAA Division II Championship meet, scoring the only shutout ever achieved at a national championship. Vigil also guided Pat Porter to *eight* U.S.A. Cross Country titles (twice as many as Olympic marathon gold medalist Frank Shorter, four times as many as silver medalist Meb Keflezighi), and was named College National Coach of the Year a record fourteen times. In 1988, Vigil was appointed the distance coach for American runners heading to the Seoul Olympics.

And that explained why, at that moment, old Joe Vigil was the only coach in America shivering in a freezing forest at four in the morning, waiting for a glimpse of a community-college science teacher and seven men in dresses. See, nothing about ultrarunning added up; and when Vigil couldn't do the math, he knew he was missing something big.

Take this equation: how come nearly all the women finish Leadville and fewer than half the men do? Every year, more than 90 percent of the female runners come home with a buckle, while 50 percent of the men come up with an excuse. Not even Ken Chlouber can explain the sky-high female finishing rate, but he can damn well exploit it: "All my pacers are women," Chlouber says. "They get the job done."

Or try this word problem: subtract the Tarahumara from last year's race, and what do you get?

Answer: a woman lunging for the tape.

In all the hubbub over the Tarahumara, few besides Vigil paid much attention to the remarkable fact that Christine Gibbons was just nosed out for third place. If Rick Fisher's van had blown a fan belt in Arizona, a woman would have been thirty-one seconds from winning the whole show.

How was that possible? No woman ranked among the top fifty in the world in the mile (the female world record for the mile, 4:12, was achieved a century ago by men and rather routinely now by high school boys). A woman *might* sneak into the top twenty in a marathon (in 2003, Paula Radcliffe's world-best 2:15:25 was just ten minutes off Paul Tergat's 2:04:55 men's record). But in ultras, women were taking home the hardware. Why, Vigil wondered, did the gap between male and female champions get smaller as the race got *longer*—shouldn't it be the other way around?

Ultrarunning seemed to be an alternative universe where none of planet Earth's rules applied: women were stronger than men; old men were stronger than youngsters; Stone Age guys in sandals were stronger than everybody. And the *mileage*! The sheer stress on their legs was off the charts. Running one hundred miles a week was supposed to be a straight shot to a stress injury, yet the ultrafreaks were doing one hundred miles in a *day*. Some of them were doing double that every week in training and still not getting hurt. Was ultrarunning self-selective, Vigil wondered—did it attract only runners with unbreakable bodies? Or had ultrarunners discovered the secret to megamileage?

So Joe Vigil had hauled himself stiffly out of bed, tossed a thermos of coffee in his car, and driven through the night to watch the body geniuses do their thing. The best ultrarunners in the world, he suspected, were on the verge of rediscovering secrets that the Tarahumara had never forgotten. Vigil's theory had brought him to the brink of a very important decision, one that would change his life and, he hoped, millions of others. He just needed to see the Tarahumara in person to verify one thing. It wasn't their speed; he probably knew more about their legs than they did. What Vigil was dying for was a look inside their heads.

Suddenly, he caught his breath. Something had just come floating out of the trees. Something that looked like ghosts . . . or magicians, appearing from a puff of smoke.

Right from the gun, Team Tarahumara caught everyone by surprise. Instead of hanging back as they had the last two years, they surged in a pack, hopping up on the Sixth Street sidewalk to patter around the crowd and take command of the front-running positions.

They were moving out fast—*Much too fast, it seemed*, thought Don Kardong, the 1976 Olympic marathoner and veteran *Runner's World* writer watching from the sidelines. Last year, Victoriano had shown shrewd restraint by steadily climbing along from last to first, gradually getting faster as he got closer to the finish line. *That's* how you run one hundred miles.

But Manuel Luna had spent a year reflecting on gringo-style racing, and he'd done a nice job of briefing his new teammates. The course is wide open under the streetlights, he told them, then suddenly funnels onto a dark single-track trail as it enters the woods. If you're not up front, you hit a solid wall of bodies as runners pause to fumble with flashlights and then caterpillar along in single file. Better to move out early and avoid the jam-up, Luna advised them, then ease back later.

Despite the dangerous pace, Johnny Sandoval of nearby Gypsum, Colorado, stuck tight with Martimano Cervantes and Juan Herrera. *Let everyone go nuts over Ann and the Tarahumara*, he thought, *while I stealth myself to a trophy*. After finishing ninth the previous year in 21:45, Sandoval had the best training year of his life. Quietly, he'd been coming to Leadville throughout the summer, running each segment of the course over and over until he'd memorized every twist, quirk, and creek crossing. A nineteen-hour run should win it, Sandoval figured, and he was ready to run one.

Ann Trason had expected to be in front, but an eight-minute mile right out of the box was just nuts. So she contented herself with staying within sight of Team Tarahumara's bobbing flashlights as they entered the woods around Turquoise Lake, confident she'd reel them in soon enough. The trail ahead was dark and knotted with rocks and roots, and that played to one of Ann's peculiar strengths: she absolutely loved night runs. Even back in college, midnight was her favorite time to grab a flashlight and a friend and trot through the silent campus, the world reduced to glitters and sparkles in a tiny orb of light. If anyone could make up time running blindly on a treacherous trail, it was Ann.

But by the first aid station, Sandoval and the Tarahumara had opened a good half-mile lead. Sandoval checked in, got his split—about 1:55 for 13.5 miles—and shot right back on the trail. The Tarahumara, however, veered into the parking lot and ran over to Rick Fisher's van. They began kicking off their yellow Rockports like they were crawling with fire ants. Rick and Kitty, as planned, were already standing by with their huaraches. So much for product endorsement.

The Tarahumara knelt, looping the leather thong around and around their ankles and high up on their calves, adjusting the tautness as carefully as you'd tune a guitar string. It's a fine art, custom-fitting a strip of rubber to the bottom of your foot with a single lash of leather so it doesn't shift or flop for eighty-seven miles of gritty, rocky trail. Then they were up and gone, hard on Johnny Sandoval's heels. By the time Ann Trason arrived at the aid station, Martimano Cervantes and Juan Herrera were out of sight.

Sick pace, Sandoval thought, as he shot a glance over his shoulder. Anyone tell these guys it had been raining here for the past two weeks? Sandoval knew they were heading straight into a world of slop around the Twin Lakes marshes and down the muddy back end of Hope Pass. The Arkansas River would be a roaring mess; they'd have to haul themselves hand over hand along a safety rope to cross, and then claw their way two thousand feet to the top of Hope Pass. Then spin around and do the same again coming home.

Okay, this is suicide, Sandoval decided after he came through mile

23.5 in three hours and twenty minutes. *I'll save my strength and cream those guys when their tires go flat.* He let Martimano Cervantes and Juan Herrera go—and almost immediately, he was passed by Ann Trason. *Where the hell did she come from?* Ann should know better; this was crash-and-burn speed.

At the thirty-mile mark in Half Moon campground, Martimano and Juan were ready for breakfast. Kitty Williams slapped thin bean burritos into their hands. They ran on, chomping contentedly, and were soon swallowed up by the thick woods around Mount Elbert.

Ann raced in a few minutes later, pissed off and shouting. "Where's Carl? *Where the hell is he?*" It was now 8:20 in the morning and she was ready to shuck weight by dumping her headlamp and jacket. But she was so far under record pace, her husband hadn't yet made it to the aid station.

To hell with him; Ann kept her night gear, and disappeared on the trail of the invisible Tarahumara.

At mile 40, the crowd milled around the ancient wood firehouse in the tiny cabin village of Twin Lakes, checking their watches. The first runners probably wouldn't show up for another, oh, about—

"There she is!"

Ann had just crested the hill. Last year, it took Victoriano seven hours and twelve minutes to get this far; Ann had done it in less than six. "No woman has ever led at this point in the race before," said an incredulous Scott Tinley, the two-time world champion Ironman triathlete who was doing TV commentary for *ABC's Wide World of Sports.* "We're witnessing the most incredible demonstration of raw courage in sports today."

Less than a minute later, Martimano and Juan popped out of the woods and came scrambling down the hill behind her. Tony Post of Rockport was so swept up in the drama, he didn't care for the moment that his boys were not only losing but had also shit-canned the shoes he was paying them to wear. "It was the most amazing thing," said Post, once a nationally ranked marathoner himself, with times in the low 2:20s. "We were just flipping out, watching this woman take control."

Luckily, Ann's husband was in position this time. He got a banana into Ann's hands, then ushered her into the little firehouse for her medical exam. All Leadville runners need to have their pulse and weight checked at the forty-mile mark, because shedding pounds too quickly is an early warning sign of dangerous dehydration. Only with Doc Perna's okay are they cleared to plunge into the meat grinder ahead: there, looming across the marsh, was the twenty-six-hundred-foot climb to the top of Hope Pass.

Ann munched the banana while a nurse named Cindy Corbin adjusted the scale. A moment later, Martimano stepped up on the scale beside Ann.

"*¿Cómo estás?*" Kitty Williams asked Martimano, laying an encouraging hand on his back. How are you feeling after nearly six straight hours of high-altitude hill running at impossibly fast speed?

"Ask him how it feels to get beat by a woman," Ann called out. Nervous laughter rippled through the room, but Ann wasn't smiling; she glared at Martimano as if she were a black belt and he was a stack of bricks. Kitty shot her an appalled look, but Ann ignored it and kept her eyes locked on Martimano. Martimano turned questioningly toward Kitty, but Kitty chose not to translate. In all her years of running ultras and pacing them for her dad, it was the first time Kitty had ever heard one runner taunt another.

Despite what most people in the room heard, a video of the incident would later suggest that what Ann actually said was, "Ask him how it feels to compete with a woman." But while her exact words were debatable, her attitude was unmistakable: Ann didn't just win by running hard; she won by *racing* hard. This thing was going to be a death match.

As Martimano got off the scale, Ann pushed past him and hurried out the door. She slung on her fanny pack—freshly loaded with carbohydrate gel, gloves, and a slicker in case she hit sleet or freezing winds above the timberline—and began trotting down the road toward the snow-capped mountain. She was outa there so fast, Martimano and Juan were still biting into slices of orange while Ann was heading around the corner and out of sight.

What was wrong with her? The trash talk, the hasty exit—Ann didn't even take time to slip on a dry shirt and socks, or get a few more calories down her neck. And why was she even in the lead at all? Mile 40 was only round one of a very long fight. Once you jump ahead, you're vulnerable; you surrender all element of surprise, and become a prisoner of your own pace. Even middle-school milers know that the smart tactic is to sit on the leader's shoulder, go only as fast as you have to, then jam 'er into gear and blow past on the bell lap.

Classic example: Steve Prefontaine. Pre came out too quickly *twice* in the same race in the '72 Olympics; both times, he was chased down. By the home stretch, Pre had nothing left and faded out of the medals to fourth. That historic defeat pounded home the lesson: nobody gives up the pursuit position if they don't have to. Not unless you're foolish, or reckless—or Garry Kasparov.

In the 1990 World Chess Championship, Kasparov made a horrible mistake and lost his queen right at the start of a decisive game. Chess grand masters around the world let out a pained groan; the bad boy of the chessboard was now road kill (a less-gracious observer for *The New York Times* visibly sneered). Except it wasn't a mistake; Kasparov had deliberately sacrificed his most powerful piece in exchange for an even more powerful psychological advantage. He was deadliest when swashbuckling, when he was chased into a corner and had to slash, scramble, and improvise his way out. Anatoly Karpov, his by-the-book opponent, was too conservative to pressure Kasparov early in the game, so Kasparov put the pressure on himself with a Queen's Gambit—and won.

That's what Ann was doing. Instead of hunting the Tarahumara, she'd hit on the risky, inspired strategy of letting the Tarahumara hunt her. Who's more committed to winning, after all: predator or prey? The lion can lose and come back to hunt another day, but the antelope gets only one mistake. To defeat the Tarahumara, Ann knew she needed more than willpower: she needed fear. Once she was out front, every cracking twig would spur her toward the finish.

"To move into the lead means making an act requiring fierceness and confidence," Roger Bannister once noted. "But fear must play some part . . . no relaxation is possible, and all discretion is thrown to the wind."

Ann had fierceness and confidence to burn. Now she was deep-sixing discretion and letting fear play its part. Ultrarunning was about to see its first Queen's Gambit.

CHAPTER 14

SHE'S INSANE! She's . . . awesome.

Coach Vigil was a hard-data freak, but as he watched Ann plunge into the Rockies with her ballsy do-or-die game plan, he loved the fact that ultrarunning had no science, no playbook, no training manual, no conventional wisdom. That kind of freewheeling self-invention is where big breakthroughs come from, as Vigil knew (and Columbus, the Beatles, and Bill Gates would happily agree). Ann Trason and her compadres were like mad scientists messing with beakers in the basement lab, ignored by the rest of the sport and free to defy every known principle of footwear, food, biomechanics, training intensity . . . *everything.*

And whatever breakthroughs they came up with, they'd be legit. With ultrarunners, Vigil had the refreshing peace of mind of dealing with pure lab specimens. He wasn't being hoodwinked by a phony superperformance, like the "miraculous" endurance of Tour de France cyclists, or the gargantuan power of suddenly melon-headed home-run hitters, or the blazing speed of female sprinters who win five medals in one Olympics before going to jail for lying to the feds about steroids. "Even the brightest smile," one observer would say of disgraced wondergirl Marion Jones, "can hide a lie."

So whose could you trust? Easy; the smiles on the oddballs in the woods.

Ultrarunners had no reason to cheat, because they had nothing to gain: no fame, no wealth, no medals. No one knew who they were, or cared who won their strange rambles through the woods. They didn't even get prize money; all you get for winning an ultra is the same belt buckle as the guy who comes in last. So, as a scientist, Vigil could rely on the data from an ultramarathon; as a fan, he could enjoy the show without scorn or skepticism. There's no EPO in Ann Trason's blood, no smuggled blood in her fridge, no ampules of Eastern European anabolics on her FedEx account.

Vigil knew that if he could understand Ann Trason, he'd grasp what one amazing person could do. But if he could understand the Tarahumara, he'd know what *everyone* could do.

Ann sucked air with deep, shuddering gasps. The final push up Hope Pass was agony, but she kept reminding herself that ever since the time Carl cursed her out, no one had beaten her on a big climb. About two years earlier, she and Carl were running on a rainy day when Ann began grousing about the endless, slippery hill ahead. Carl got tired of hearing her kvetch, so he blistered her with the most obscene name he could think of.

"A wimp!" Ann would later say. "The big W! Right then, I decided I was going to work to be a better hill climber than he was." Not only better than Carl, but better than everybody; Ann developed into such a relentless mountain goat that hills became her favorite place to drop the hammer and leave the competition behind.

But now, as she approached the Hope Pass peak, she could glance back and see Martimano and Juan steadily closing the gap, looking as light and breezy as the capes that swirled around them.

"God," Ann panted. She was so hunched over, she could almost pull herself up the slope with her hands. "I don't know how they do it."

A little farther down the mountain, Manuel Luna and the rest of Team Tarahumara were also catching up. They'd gotten scattered in the early miles by the startlingly fast pace, but now—like an alien protoplasm that re-forms and gets stronger every time you blast it to bits—they were tightening back into a pack behind Manuel Luna.

"God!" Ann exclaimed again.

She finally reached the peak. The view was spectacular; if Ann turned around, she could see all forty-five miles of tumbling green wilderness between her and Leadville. But she didn't even pause for a slurp of water. She had an ace in her hand, and she had to play it now. She was woozy from the thin air and her hamstrings were screaming, but Ann pushed straight over the top and started chop-stepping downhill.

This was a Trason specialty: using terrain to recharge on the move. After a steep first drop, the backside descent quickly softens into long, gently sloped switchbacks, so Ann could lean back, make her legs go limp, and let gravity do the work. After a bit, she could feel the knots easing in her calves and the strength creeping back into her thighs. By the time she reached bottom, her head was up and the glint was back in her cougar eyes.

Time to fire the jets. Ann veered off the muddy trail and onto hard-packed road, her legs spinning fast and loose from the hip as she accelerated into the last three miles to the turnaround.

Juan and Martimano, meanwhile, had gotten a little sidetracked. As soon as they'd broken past the tree line above, they were startled to see a giant herd of strange, woolly beasts—and among them, some animals. "SOUP'S ON, FELLAS," a hoarse voice bellowed to the uncomprehending Tarahumara from somewhere inside the herd. The Tarahumara had just made first contact with another wilderness tribe: the Hopeless Crew.

Twelve years earlier, Ken Chlouber had mustered enough of his neighbors to staff a good half-dozen aid stations, but he refused to put anyone at the top of Hope Pass; even the tough-guy miner who delighted in his race's high hospitalization rate considered that inhumane. A volunteer on Hope Pass would have to haul enough supplies up the mountain to feed, water, and bandage an endless parade of battered runners, and then camp out for two nights on a snowy peak with gale-force gusts. Nothin' doin'; if Ken sent anyone up there, he'd have hell to pay when they didn't come back down.

Luckily, a group of Leadville llama farmers shrugged and said, Eh, what the hell. Sounded like a party. They loaded their llamas with enough food and booze to make it through the weekend, and hammered in tent stakes at 12,600 feet. Since then, the Hopeless Crew has grown into an army eighty-some strong of llama owners and friends. For two days, they endure fierce winds and frostbitten fingers while dispensing first aid and hot soup, packing injured runners out by llama and partying in between like a tribe of amiable yetis. "Hope Pass is a bad son of a bitch on a *good* day," Ken says. "If it weren't for those llamas, we'd have lost a good many lives."

Juan and Martimano shyly returned high fives as they jogged through the raucous Hopeless gauntlet. They stopped to drink in the sight of the weird gypsy camp (as well as cups of some really tasty noodle soup someone shoved into their hands), then began quick-stepping down the back side of the mountain. Ann was nowhere to be seen.

Ann hit the fifty-mile mark at 12:05 p.m., nearly two hours ahead of Victoriano's time from the previous year. Carl loaded her up with sports drink and Cytomax carbohydrate gel, then snapped on his own fanny pack and gave his shoelaces a tug. According to Leadville rules, a "mule" can run alongside a racer for the last fifty miles, which meant Ann would now have a personal pit crew by her side all the way to the finish.

A good pacer is a huge help during an ultra, and Ann had one of the best: not only was Carl fast enough to push her, but experienced enough to take over if Ann's brain fritzed out. After twenty or so hours of nonstop running, an ultrarunner can get too mind numb to replace flashlight batteries, or comprehend trail markers, or even, in the unfortunate true case of a Badwater runner in 2005, distinguish between an imminent bowel movement and an occurring one.

And those are the runners who are really keeping it together. Hallucinations are no strangers to the rest; one ultrarunner kept screaming and leaping into the woods whenever he saw a flashlight, convinced it was an oncoming train. One runner enjoyed the company of a smokin' young hottie in a silver bikini who Rollerbladed by his side for miles across Death Valley until, to his regret, she dissolved into heat shimmers. Six out of twenty Badwater runners reported hallucinations that year, including one who saw rotting corpses along the road and "mutant mice monsters" crawling over the asphalt. One pacer got a little freaked out after she saw her runner stare into space for a while and then tell the empty air, "I know you're not real."

A tough pacer, consequently, can save your race; a sharp one can save your life. Too bad for Martimano, then, that the best he could hope for was that the shaggy goofball he'd met in town would actually show up—and could actually run.

The night before, Rick Fisher had brought the Tarahumara to a prerace spaghetti dinner at the Leadville VFW hall to see if he could recruit a few pacers. It wouldn't be easy; pacing is so grueling and thankless, usually only family, fools, and damn good friends let themselves get talked into it. The job means shivering in the middle of nowhere for hours until your runner shows up, then setting off at sunset for an all-night run through wind-whistling mountains. You'll get blood on your shins, vomit on your shoes, and not even a T-shirt for completing two marathons in a single night. Other job requirements can include staying awake while your runner catches a nap in the mud; popping a blood blister between her butt cheeks with your fingernails; and surrendering your jacket, even though your teeth are chattering, because her lips have gone blue.

At the spaghetti dinner, Martimano locked eyes with some long-haired local who, for some bizarre reason, immediately began cracking up. Martimano started laughing, too; he found the shaggy guy totally cool and hilarious. "It's you and me, brother," Shaggy said. "You follow? *Tú* and *yo*. If you want a mule, I'm your man."

"Whoa, whoa, hang on," Fisher interjected. "You sure you're fast enough for these guys?"

"You're not doing me any favor," Shaggy shrugged. "Who else you got lined up?"

"Yeah," Fisher said. "Okay, then."

And just as he'd promised, Shaggy was hollering and waving by the aid station the next afternoon when Juan and Martimano came running into the fifty-mile turnaround. They took a long, cool drink of water and grabbed some *pinole* and thin bean burritos from Kitty Williams. Rick Fisher had also roped in another pacer, an elite ultrarunner from San Diego who'd been a longtime student of Tarahumara lore. The four runners traded Tarahumara handshakes—that soft caressing of fingertips—and turned toward Hope Pass. Ann was already out of sight.

"Saddle up, guys," Shaggy said. "Let's go get the *bruja*."

Juan and Martimano barely understood anything the guy said, but they caught that all right: Shaggy was calling Ann a witch. They looked closely to see if he was serious, decided he wasn't, and started laughing. This guy was going to be a kick.

"Yeah, she's a *bruja*, but that's cool," Shaggy went on. "We've got stronger mojo. You understand that, mojo? No? Doesn't matter. We're gonna run the *bruja* down like a deer. Like a *venado*. Yeah, a *venado*. Got it? We're gonna run the *bruja* down like a *venado*. *Poco a poco*—little bit at a time."

But the bruja wasn't backing off. By the time she summited Hope Pass for the second time, Ann had widened her lead from four minutes to seven. "I was heading up Hope Pass, and she just blew by me going the other direction—*vroo-o-o-om!*" a Leadville runner named Glen Vaassen later told *Runner's World.* "She was *cruisin'.*"

She threaded her way to the bottom of the switchbacks and plunged back through the Arkansas River, fighting to keep from being swept downstream in the waist-deep water. It was 2:31 p.m. when she and Carl arrived back at the Twin Lakes fire station at mile 60. Ann checked in, got her medical clearance, and trudged up the twenty-foot dirt ramp to the trailhead. By the time Shaggy and the Tarahumara arrived, Ann had been gone for twelve minutes.

Coincidentally, Ken Chlouber was just arriving at the Twin Lakes aid station heading outbound when Juan and Martimano came through on their return trip. Everyone in the firehouse was buzzing about Ann's record pace and ever-growing lead, but as Ken watched Juan and Martimano exit the firehouse, he was struck by something else: when they hit the dirt ramp, they hit it laughing.

"Everybody else walks that hill," Chlouber thought, as Juan and Martimano churned up the slope like kids playing in a leaf pile. "*Everybody.* And they sure as hell ain't laughin' about it."

CHAPTER 15

The flesh about my body felt soft and relaxed, like an
experiment in functional background music.

—RICHARD BRAUTIGAN, *Trout Fishing in America*

"SUCH A SENSE of joy!" marveled Coach Vigil, who'd never
seen anything like it, either. "It was quite remarkable." Glee and
determination are usually antagonistic emotions, yet the Tarahumara
were brimming with both at once, as if running to the death made
them feel more alive.

Vigil had been furiously taking mental notes (*Look how they point
their toes down, not up, like gymnasts doing the floor exercise. And their
backs! They could carry water buckets on their heads without spilling a drop!
How many years have I been telling my kids to straighten up and run from
the gut like that?*). But it was the smiles that really jolted him.

That's it! Vigil thought, ecstatic. *I found it!*

Except he wasn't sure what "it" was. The revelation he'd been
hoping for was right in front of his eyes, but he couldn't quite grasp
it; he could only catch the glim around the edges, like spotting the
cover of a rare book in a candlelit library. But whatever "it" was, he
knew it was exactly what he was looking for.

Over the previous few years, Vigil had become convinced that the
next leap forward in human endurance would come from a dimen-
sion he dreaded getting into: character. Not the "character" other
coaches were always rah-rah-rah-ing about; Vigil wasn't talking
about "grit" or "hunger" or "the size of the fight in the dog." In fact,

he meant the exact opposite. Vigil's notion of character wasn't toughness. It was compassion. Kindness. Love.

That's right: love.

Vigil knew it sounded like hippie-dippy drivel, and make no mistake, he'd have been much happier sticking to good, hard, quantifiable stuff like VO_2 max and periodized-training tables. But after spending nearly fifty years researching performance physiology, Vigil had reached the uncomfortable conclusion that all the easy questions had been answered; he was now learning more and more about less and less. He could tell you exactly how much of a head start Kenyan teenagers had over Americans (eighteen thousand miles run in training). He'd discovered why those Russian sprinters were leaping off ladders (besides strengthening lateral muscles, the trauma teaches nerves to fire more rapidly, which decreases the odds of training injuries). He'd parsed the secret of the Peruvian peasant diet (high altitude has a curious effect on metabolism), and he could talk for hours about the impact of a single percentage point in oxygen-consumption efficiency.

He'd figured out the body, so now it was on to the brain. Specifically: How do you make anyone actually want to do any of this stuff? How do you flip the internal switch that changes us all back into the Natural Born Runners we once were? Not just in history, but in our own lifetimes. Remember? Back when you were a kid and you had to be yelled at to slow down? Every game you played, you played at top speed, sprinting like crazy as you kicked cans, freed all, and attacked jungle outposts in your neighbors' backyards. Half the fun of doing anything was doing it at record pace, making it probably the last time in your life you'd ever be hassled for going too fast.

That was the real secret of the Tarahumara: they'd never forgotten what it felt like to love running. They remembered that running was mankind's first fine art, our original act of inspired creation. Way before we were scratching pictures on caves or beating rhythms on hollow trees, we were perfecting the art of combining our breath and mind and muscles into fluid self-propulsion over wild terrain. And when our ancestors finally did make their first cave paintings, what were the first designs? A downward slash, lightning bolts through the bottom and middle—behold, the Running Man.

Distance running was revered because it was indispensable; it was the way we survived and thrived and spread across the planet. You ran to eat and to avoid being eaten; you ran to find a mate and impress her, and with her you ran off to start a new life together. You had to love running, or you wouldn't live to love anything else. And like everything else we love—everything we sentimentally call our "passions" and "desires"—it's really an encoded ancestral necessity. We were born to run; we were born *because* we run. We're all Running People, as the Tarahumara have always known.

But the American approach—*ugh*. Rotten at its core. It was too artificial and grabby, Vigil believed, too much about getting stuff and getting it now: medals, Nike deals, a cute butt. It wasn't art; it was business, a hard-nosed quid pro quo. No wonder so many people hated running; if you thought it was only a means to an end—an investment in becoming faster, skinnier, richer—then why stick with it if you weren't getting enough quo for your quid?

It wasn't always like that—and when it wasn't, we were awesome. Back in the '70s, American marathoners were a lot like the Tarahumara; they were a tribe of isolated outcasts, running for love and relying on raw instinct and crude equipment. Slice the top off a '70s running shoe, and you had a sandal: the old Adidas and Onitsuka Tigers were just a flat sole and laces, with no motion control, no arch support, no heel pad. The guys in the '70s didn't know enough to worry about "pronation" and "supination"; that fancy running-store jargon hadn't even been invented yet.

Their training was as primitive as their shoes. They ran way too much: "We ran twice a day, sometimes three times," Frank Shorter would recall. "All we did was run—run, eat, and sleep." They ran way too hard: "The modus operandi was to let a bunch of competitive guys have at each other every day in a form of road rage," one observer put it. And they were *waaay* too buddy-buddy for so-called competitors: "We liked running together," recalled Bill Rodgers, a chieftain of the '70s tribe and four-time Boston Marathon champ. "We had fun with it. It wasn't a grind."

They were so ignorant, they didn't even realize they were supposed to be burned out, overtrained, and injured. Instead, they were fast; *really* fast. Frank Shorter won the '72 Olympic marathon gold and the '76 silver, Bill Rodgers was the No. 1 ranked marathoner in the world for three years, and Alberto Salazar won Boston, New

York, *and* the Comrades ultramarathon. By the early '80s, the Greater Boston Track Club had half a dozen guys who could run a 2:12 marathon. That's six guys, in one amateur club, in one city. Twenty years later, you couldn't find a single 2:12 marathoner anywhere in the country. The United States couldn't even get one runner to meet the 2:14 qualifying standard for the 2000 Olympics; only Rod DeHaven squeaked into the games under the 2:15 "B" standard. He finished sixty-ninth.

So what happened? How did we go from leader of the pack to lost and left behind? It's hard to determine a single cause for any event in this complex world, of course, but forced to choose, the answer is best summed up as follows:

$

Sure, plenty of people will throw up excuses about Kenyans having some kind of mutant muscle fiber, but this isn't about why other people got faster; it's about why we got *slower*. And the fact is, American distance running went into a death spiral precisely when cash entered the equation. The Olympics were opened to professionals after the 1984 Games, which meant running-shoe companies could bring the distance-running savages out of the wilderness and onto the payroll reservation.

Vigil could smell the apocalypse coming, and he'd tried hard to warn his runners. "There are two goddesses in your heart," he told them. "The Goddess of Wisdom and the Goddess of Wealth. Everyone thinks they need to get wealth first, and wisdom will come. So they concern themselves with chasing money. But they have it backwards. You have to give your heart to the Goddess of Wisdom, give her all your love and attention, and the Goddess of Wealth will become jealous, and follow you." Ask nothing from your running, in other words, and you'll get more than you ever imagined.

Vigil wasn't beating his chest about the purity of poverty, or fantasizing about a monastic order of moneyless marathoners. Shoot, he wasn't even sure he had a handle on the problem, let alone the solution. All he wanted was to find one Natural Born Runner—someone who ran for sheer joy, like an artist in the grip of inspiration—and study how he or she trained, lived, and thought. Whatever that thinking was, maybe Vigil could transplant it back into American culture like an heirloom seedling and watch it grow wild again.

Vigil already had the perfect prototype. There was this Czech soldier, a gawky dweeb who ran with such horrendous form that he looked "as if he'd just been stabbed through the heart," as one sportswriter put it. But Emil Zatopek loved running so much that even when he was still a grunt in army boot camp, he used to grab a flashlight and go off on twenty-mile runs through the woods at night.

In his combat boots.

In winter.

After a full day of infantry drills.

When the snow was too deep, Zatopek would jog in the tub on top of his dirty laundry, getting a resistance workout along with clean tighty whities. As soon as it thawed enough for him to get outside, he'd go nuts; he'd run four hundred meters as fast as he could, over and over, for ninety repetitions, resting in between by jogging two hundred meters. By the time he was finished, he'd done more than thirty-three miles of speedwork. Ask him his pace, and he'd shrug; he never timed himself. To build explosiveness, he and his wife, Dana, used to play catch with a javelin, hurling it back and forth to each other across a soccer field like a long, lethal Frisbee. One of Zatopek's favorite workouts combined all his loves at once: he'd jog through the woods in his army boots with his ever-loving wife riding on his back.

It was all a waste of time, of course. The Czechs were like the Zimbabwean bobsled team; they had no tradition, no coaching, no native talent, no chance of winning. But being counted out was liberating; having nothing to lose left Zatopek free to try any way to win. Take his first marathon: everyone knows the best way to build up to 26.2 miles is by running long, slow distances. Everyone, that is, except Emil Zatopek; he did hundred-yard dashes instead.

"I already know how to go slow," he reasoned. "I thought the point was to go fast." His atrocious, death-spasming style was punchline heaven for track scribes ("The most frightful horror spectacle since Frankenstein." . . . "He runs as if his next step would be his last." . . . "He looks like a man wrestling with an octopus on a conveyor belt"), but Zatopek just laughed along. "I'm not talented enough to run and smile at the same time," he'd say. "Good thing it's not figure skating. You only get points for speed, not style."

And dear God, was he a Chatty Cathy! Zatopek treated competition like it was speed dating. Even in the middle of a race, he liked to natter with other runners and try out his smattering of French and English and German, causing one grouchy Brit to complain about Zatopek's "incessant talking." At away meets, he'd sometimes have so many new friends in his hotel room that he'd have to give up his bed and sleep outside under a tree. Once, right before an international race, he became pals with an Australian runner who was hoping to break the Australian 5,000-meter record. Zatopek was only entered in the 10,000-meter race, but he came up with a plan; he told the Aussie to drop out of his race and line up next to Zatopek instead. Zatopek spent the first half of the 10,000-meter race pacing his new buddy to the record, then sped off to attend to his own business and win.

That was pure Zatopek, though; races for him were like a pub crawl. He loved competing so much that instead of tapering and peaking, he jumped into as many meets as he could find. During a manic stretch in the late '40s, Zatopek raced nearly every other week for three years *and never lost*, going 69–0. Even on a schedule like that, he still averaged up to 165 miles a week in training.

Zatopek was a bald, self-coached thirty-year-old apartment-dweller from a decrepit Eastern European backwater when he arrived for the 1952 Olympics in Helsinki. Since the Czech team was so thin, Zatopek had his choice of distance events, so he chose them all. He lined up for the 5,000 meters, and won with a new Olympic record. He then lined up for the 10,000 meters, and won his second gold with another new record. He'd never run a marathon before, but what the hell; with two golds already around his neck, he had nothing to lose, so why not finish the job and give it a bash?

Zatopek's inexperience quickly became obvious. It was a hot day, so England's Jim Peters, then the world-record holder, decided to use the heat to make Zatopek suffer. By the ten-mile mark, Peters was already ten minutes under his own world-record pace and pulling away from the field. Zatopek wasn't sure if anyone could really sustain such a blistering pace. "Excuse me," he said, pulling alongside Peters. "This is my first marathon. Are we going too fast?"

"No," Peters replied. "Too slow." If Zatopek was dumb enough to ask, he was dumb enough to deserve any answer he got.

Zatopek was surprised. "You say too slow," he asked again. "Are you sure the pace is too slow?"

"Yes," Peters said. Then he got a surprise of his own.

"Okay. Thanks." Zatopek took Peters at his word, and took off.

When he burst out of the tunnel and into the stadium, he was met with a roar: not only from the fans, but from athletes of every nation who thronged the track to cheer him in. Zatopek snapped the tape with his third Olympic record, but when his teammates charged over to congratulate him, they were too late: the Jamaican sprinters had already hoisted him on their shoulders and were parading him around the infield. "Let us live so that when we come to die, even the undertaker will be sorry," Mark Twain used to say. Zatopek found a way to run so that when he won, even other teams were delighted.

You can't pay someone to run with such infectious joy. You can't bully them into it, either, which Zatopek would unfortunately have to prove. When the Red Army marched into Prague in 1968 to crush the pro-democracy movement, Zatopek was given a choice: he could get on board with the Soviets and serve as a sports ambassador, or he could spend the rest of his life cleaning toilets in a uranium mine. Zatopek chose the toilets. And just like that, one of the most beloved athletes in the world disappeared.

At the same time, coincidentally, his rival for the title of world's greatest distance runner was also taking a beating. Ron Clarke, a phenomenally talented Australian with Johnny Depp's dark, dreamy beauty, was exactly the kind of guy that Zatopek, by all rights, should hate. While Zatopek had to teach himself to run in the snow at night after sentry duty, the Australian pretty boy was enjoying sunny morning jogs along the beaches of Mornington Peninsula and expert coaching. Everything Zatopek could wish for, Clarke had to spare: Freedom. Money. Elegance. Hair.

Ron Clarke was a star—but still a loser in the eyes of his nation. Despite breaking nineteen records in every distance from the half-mile to six miles, "the bloke who choked" never managed to win the big ones. In the summer of '68, he blew his final chance: in the 10,000-meter finals at the Mexico City Games, Clarke was knocked out by altitude sickness. Anticipating a barrage of abuse back home, Clarke delayed his return by stopping off in Prague to pay a courtesy call to the bloke who never lost. Toward the end of their visit, Clarke glimpsed Zatopek sneaking something into his suitcase.

"I thought I was smuggling some message to the outside world for him, so I did not dare to open the parcel until the plane was well away," Clarke would say. Zatopek sent him off with a strong embrace. "Because you deserved it," he said, which Clarke found cute and very touching; the old master had far worse problems of his own to deal with, but was still playful enough to grant a victory-stand hug to the young punk who'd missed his chance to mount one.

Only later would he discover that Zatopek wasn't talking about the hug at all: in his suitcase, Clarke found Zatopek's 1952 Olympic 10,000-meters gold medal. For Zatopek to give it to the man who'd replaced his name in the record books was extraordinarily noble; to give it away at precisely the moment in his life when he was losing everything else was an act of almost unimaginable compassion.

"His enthusiasm, his friendliness, his love of life, shone through every movement," an overcome Ron Clarke said later. "There is not, and never was, a greater man than Emil Zatopek."

So here's what Coach Vigil was trying to figure out: was Zatopek a great man who happened to run, or a great man *because* he ran? Vigil couldn't quite put his finger on it, but his gut kept telling him that there was some kind of connection between the capacity to love and the capacity to love *running*. The engineering was certainly the same: both depended on loosening your grip on your own desires, putting aside what you wanted and appreciating what you got, being patient and forgiving and undemanding. Sex and speed—haven't they been symbiotic for most of our existence, as intertwined as the strands of our DNA? We wouldn't be alive without love; we wouldn't have survived without running; maybe we shouldn't be surprised that getting better at one could make you better at the other.

Look, Vigil was a scientist, not a swami. He hated straying into this Buddha-under-the-lotus-tree stuff, but he wasn't going to ignore it, either. He'd made his bones by finding connections where everyone else saw coincidence, and the more he examined the compassion

Team Jerker wasn't quite as well oiled. One of Scott's pacers was fanning him with a sweatshirt, unaware that Scott was too exhausted to complain that the zipper was slashing his back. Scott's wife and his best friend, meanwhile, were at each other's throats. Dusty was annoyed by the way Leah kept trying to motivate Scott by giving him fake pacing splits, while Leah wasn't too pleased with Dusty's habit of calling her husband a fucking pussy.

By mile 60, Scott was vomiting and shaky. His hands dropped to his knees, then his knees dropped to the pavement. He collapsed by the side of the road, lying in his own sweat and spittle. Leah and his friends didn't bother trying to help him up; they knew there was no voice in the world more persuasive than the one inside Scott's own mind.

Scott lay there, thinking about how hopeless it all was. He wasn't even halfway done, and Sweeney was already too far ahead for him to see. Ferg Hawke was halfway up to the Father Crowley lookout, and Scott hadn't even started the climb yet. And the wind! It was like running into the blast of a jet engine. A couple of miles back, Scott had tried to cool off by sinking his entire head and torso into a giant cooler full of ice and holding himself underwater until his lungs were screaming. As soon as he got out, he was roasting again.

There's no way, Scott told himself. *You're done. You'd have to do something totally sick to win this thing now.*

Sick like what?

Like starting all over again. Like pretending you just woke up from a great night's sleep and the race hasn't even started yet. You'd have to run the next eighty miles as fast as you've ever run eighty miles in your life.

No chance, Jerker.

Yeah. I know.

For ten minutes, Scott lay like a corpse. Then he got up and did it, shattering the Badwater record with a time of 24:36.

King of the trails, king of the road. That 2005 doubleheader was one of the greatest performances in ultraracing history, and it couldn't have come at a better moment: just when Scott was becoming the greatest star in ultrarunning, ultrarunning was getting sexy. There was Dean Karnazes, shucking his shirt for magazine covers and telling David Letterman how he ordered pizzas on his cell phone in the middle of a 250-mile run. And check out Pam Reed; when Dean announced he was preparing for a 300-mile run, Pam went straight out and ran 301, landing her own Letterman appearance, and a book contract, and one of the greatest magazine headlines ever written: DESPERATE HOUSEWIFE STALKS MALE SUPERMODEL IN SPORTS DEATH MARCH.

Soooooo—where was the Scott Jurek memoir? The marketing campaign? The bare-chested treadmill run above Times Square, à la Karnazes? "If you're talking about hundred-mile races, or longer, on trails, there's no one in history who comes close to him. If you want to say he's the greatest all-time ultrarunner, a case could be made for it," came the judgment from *UltraRunning* editor Don Allison. "He's got the talent to put him up against anyone."

So where was he?

Long gone. Instead of promoting himself after his glorious summer, Scott and Leah immediately vanished into the deep woods to celebrate in solitude. Scott could give a crap about talk shows; he didn't even own a TV. He'd read Dean's book and Pam's book and all the magazine articles, and they turned his stomach. "Stunts," he muttered; they were taking this beautiful sport, this great gift of flight, and turning it into a freak show.

When he and Leah finally got back to their tiny apartment, Scott found another one of those crazy e-mails waiting for him. He'd been getting them on and off for about two years from some guy who kept signing off with different names: Caballo Loco . . . Caballo Confuso . . . Caballo Blanco. Something about a race, could he come, power to the people, blah blah blah. . . . Usually, Scott gave them a quick scan and clicked them into the trash, but this time, one word caught his eye: *Chingón*.

Whoa. Wasn't that a Spanish F-bomb? Scott didn't know much Spanish, but he recognized curse words when he saw them. Was this crazy Horse guy badmouthing him? Scott read the message again, more carefully this time:

> *I've been telling the Raramuri that my Apache friend Ramon*
> *Chingon says he's going to beat everybody. The tarahumara are more*
> *or less good runners compared to the Apaches, the Quimares a little*
> *more than less. But the question is, who's more chingon than Ramon?*

Deciphering Caballo-speak wasn't easy, but as best Scott could make out, it seemed that he—Scott—was supposed to be Ramón Chingón, the Mean Mutha who was going to come down and whomp Tarahumara butt. So this guy he'd never even met was trying to whip up a grudge match between the Tarahumara and their ancient Apache enemies, and he wanted Scott to play the role of masked villain? *Psycho-o-o-o-o . . .*

Scott fingered the delete button, then paused. On the other hand . . . wasn't that exactly what Scott had set out to do? Find the best runners and the toughest courses in the world and conquer them all? Someday no one, not even ultrarunners, would remember the names Pam Reed or Dean Karnazes. But if Scott was as good as he thought he was—if he was as good as he *dared* to be—then he'd run like no one ever had. Scott wasn't settling for best in the world; he was out to be the best of all time.

But like every champion, he was up against the Curse of Ali: he could beat everyone alive and still lose to guys who were dead (or at least, long retired). Every heavyweight boxer has to hear: "Yeah, you're good, but you'd never a' beat Ali in his prime." Likewise, no matter how many records Scott set, there would always be one unanswered question: what would have happened if he'd been in Leadville in 1994? Could he have whipped Juan Herrera and Team Tarahumara, or would they have run him down like a deer, just like they did the Bruja?

The heroes of the past are untouchable, protected forever by the fortress door of time—unless some mysterious stranger magically turns up with a key. Maybe Scott, thanks to this Caballo character, was the one athlete who could turn back the clock and test himself against the immortals.

Who's more chingón *than Ramón?*

CHAPTER 20

NINE MONTHS LATER, I found myself back on the Mexican border with a ticking clock and zero margin for error. It was Saturday evening, February 25, 2006, and I had twenty-four hours to find Caballo again.

As soon as he got a reply from Scott Jurek, Caballo began setting up a trapeze act of logistics. He only had a tiny window of opportunity, since the race couldn't take place during the fall harvest, the winter rainy season, or the blistering heat of summer, when many of the Tarahumara migrate toward cooler caves higher in the canyons. Caballo also had to avoid Christmas, Easter Week, the Fiesta Guadalupana and at least a half-dozen traditional wedding weekends.

Caballo finally figured he could wedge the race in on Sunday, March 5. Then the real tricky work began: because he'd barely have enough time to Paul Revere from village to village to announce the race logistics, he had to figure out exactly where and when the Tarahumara runners should meet up with us on the hike to the race-course. If he miscalculated, it was over; it was already a tremendous long shot that any Tarahumara would show up, and if they got to the meeting spot and we were a no-show, they'd be gone.

Caballo made his best-guess estimates, then set off into the canyons to spread the word, as he messaged me a few weeks later:

Ran 30 some miles out to Tarahumara country and back today, like the messenger that I am. The message fueled me more than the bag of

pinole in my pocket. Was lucky enough to see both Manuel Luna and
Felipe Quimare on the same loop, the same day. When I spoke to each
of them, I could sense excitement even in the Geronimo like solemnness
that is the face of Manuel.

But while things were looking up for Caballo, my end of the operation was maddeningly difficult. Once word hit the grapevine that
Jurek might be going toe-to-toe with the Tarahumara, other ultra
aces suddenly wanted a piece of the action. But there was no telling
how many would really show up—and that included the star attraction himself.

In true Jurek fashion, Scott had told almost no one what he was up
to, so word of his plans only began to spread a little more than a
month before the race. He'd even kept me guessing, and I was pretty
much his point man; Scott e-mailed me a few times with travel questions, but as crunch time approached, he dropped off the radar. Two
weeks before race day, I was startled to see a posting on the *Runner's
World* message board from a runner in Texas who'd gotten a jolt of
his own that morning when he arrived at the starting line of the
Austin Marathon and found himself standing next to America's
greatest (and contender for most reclusive) ultrarunner.

Austin? Last I'd heard, Scott was supposed to be two thousand
miles away at that very moment, crossing Baja with his wife to catch
the Chihuahua-Pacific train to Creel. And what was the deal with the
urban marathon—why was Scott flying across the country for a
junior varsity road race, when he was supposed to be fine-tuning for
the showdown of a lifetime on trails? He was up to something, no
doubt about it; and as usual, whatever strategy he was developing
remained locked in his own head.

So, until the moment I arrived in El Paso, Texas, that Saturday, I
had no idea if I was leading a platoon or hucking solo. I checked into
the airport Hilton, made arrangements for a ride across the border at
five the next morning, then doubled back to the airport. I was pretty
sure I was wasting my time, but there was a chance I'd be picking up
Jenn "Mookie" Shelton and Billy "Bonehead" Barnett, a pair of
twenty-one-year-old hotshots who'd been electrifying the East
Coast ultra circuit, at least whenever they weren't otherwise occupied surfing, partying, or posting bail for simple assault (Jenn), disor-

derly conduct (Billy), or public indecency (both, for a burst of trail-side passion that resulted in an arrest and community service).

Jenn and Billy had only started running two years before, but Billy was already winning some of the toughest 50ks on the East Coast, while "the young and beautiful Jenn Shelton," as the ultrarace blogger Joey Anderson called her, had just clocked one of the fastest 100-mile times in the country. "If this young lady could swing a tennis racket as well as she runs," Anderson wrote, "she would be one of the richest women in sports with all the sponsors she would attract."

I'd spoken to Jenn once on the phone, and while she and Billy were wildly eager to join the trek into the Copper Canyons, I didn't see any way they'd pull it off. She and the Bonehead had no money, no credit cards, and no time off from school: they were both still in college and Caballo's race was smack in the middle of midterms, meaning they'd flunk the semester if they skipped out. But two days before my flight to El Paso, I suddenly got this frantic e-mail:

> *Wait for us! we can get in by 8:10 pm.*
> *El Paso is texas, right?*

After that—silence. On the slim chance that Jenn and Billy had actually found the right city and finagled their way onto a flight, I headed over to the airport for a look around. I'd never met them, but their outlaw reputation created a pretty vivid mental image. When I got to baggage claim, I immediately locked in on a couple who looked like teenage runaways hitchhiking to Lollapalooza.

"Jenn?" I asked.

"Right on!"

Jenn was wearing flip-flops, surf shorts, and a tie-dyed T-shirt. Her summer-wheat hair was in braids, giving her the look of a blonder, lesser-known Longstocking. She was pretty and petite enough to pass for a figure skater, an image she'd tried in the past to scruff up by shaving her head down to stubble and getting a big, black vampire bat tattooed on her right forearm, only discovering later that it was a dead ringer for the Bacardi rum logo. "Whatever," Jenn said with a shrug. "Truth in advertising."

Billy shared Jenn's raw good looks and beach-bum wardrobe. He had a tribal tattoo across the back of his neck and thick sideburns that blended into shaggy, sun-streaked hair. With his flowery board shorts and ripped surfer's build, he looked—to Jenn, at least—"like some little yeti who raided your underwear drawer."

"I can't believe you guys made it," I said. "But there's been a change of plans. Scott Jurek isn't going to be meeting us in Mexico."

"Oh, fuck me," Jenn said. "I knew this was too good to be true."

"He came here instead." On my way to the airport, I'd spotted two guys jogging across the parking lot. They were too far away for me to see their faces, but their smooth-glide strides gave them away. After quick introductions, they'd headed to the bar while I continued to the airport.

"Scott's here?"

"Yup. I just saw him on the way over. He's back at the hotel bar with Luis Escobar."

"Scott *drinks*?"

"Looks that way."

"Suh-*weet*!!"

Jenn and Billy grabbed their gear—a Nike shopping bag with a chiropractic stick jutting out the top and a duffel with the tail of a sleeping bag stuck in the zipper—and we began heading across the parking lot.

"So what's Scott like?" Jenn asked. Ultrarunning, like rap music, was split by geography; as East Coast playas, Jenn and Billy had done most of their racing close to home and hadn't yet crossed paths (or swords) with many of the West Coast elites. To them—to just about all ultrarunners, actually—Scott was as much of a mythic figure as the Tarahumara.

"I only caught a glimpse of him myself," I said. "Pretty tough guy to read, I can tell you that much."

Right there, I should have shut my stupid mouth. But who can predict when the trivial will become tragic? How could I have known that a friendly gesture, like giving Caballo my running shoes, would nearly cost him his life? Likewise, I never suspected that the next ten words out of my mouth would snowball into disaster:

"Maybe," I suggested, "you can get him drunk and loosen him up."

CHAPTER 21

"PREPARE TO MEET your god," I said as we entered the hotel bar. "Sucking down a cold one."

Scott was on a stool, sipping a Fat Tire Ale. Billy dropped his duffel and stuck out his hand, while Jenn hung behind me. She'd barely let Billy get a word in the whole way across the parking lot, but now, in Scott's presence, she was starstruck. At least I thought she was, till I saw the look in her eye. She wasn't bashful; she was sizing him up. Scott might be hunting the Tarahumara, but he'd better watch who was hunting him.

"Is this all of us?" Scott asked.

I looked around the bar and did a head count. Jenn and Billy were ordering beers. Beside them was Eric Orton, an adventure-sports coach from Wyoming and longtime student of the Tarahumara who'd made me his personal disaster reconstruction project; over the past nine months, we'd been in weekly contact, sometimes daily, as Eric attempted to transform me from a splintery wreck into an unbreakable ultramarathon man. He was the one guy I'd been sure would turn up; even though he'd be leaving his wife behind with their newborn daughter in the middle of a fierce Wyoming winter, there was no way he'd be sitting at home while I was putting his art to the test. I'd flat-out told him he was wrong and there was no way I could run fifty miles; now, we'd both see if he was right.

Sandwiching Scott were Luis Escobar and his father, Joe Ramírez.

Luis was not only an ultrastud who'd won the H.U.R.T. 100 and raced Badwater, but also one of the top race photographers in the sport (his artistry aided, of course, by the fact that his legs could take him places no other shooters could reach). Just by chance, Luis had recently called Scott to make sure they'd be seeing each other at Coyote Fourplay, a semi-secret, invitation-only free-for-all described as "a four-day orgy of idiocy involving severed coyote heads, poisoned snacks, panties in trees, and one hundred twenty miles of trails you'll wish you'd missed."

Fourplay is held at the end of February every year in the back-woods of Oxnard, California, and it exists to give a small band of ultrarunners a chance to whip each other's butts and then glue said butts to toilet seats. Every day, the Fourplayers race anywhere from thirty to fifty miles on trails marked by mummified coyote skulls and women's underwear. Every night, they face off with bowling tourna-ments and talent shows and endless guerrilla pranks, like replacing ProBars with frozen cat food and gluing the wrappers back shut. Fourplay was a battle royal for amateurs who loved to run hard and play rough; it wasn't really for pros who had to worry about their rac-ing schedules and sponsorship commitments. Naturally, Scott never missed it.

Until 2006, that is. "Sorry, something came up," Scott told Luis. When Luis heard what it was, his heart skipped a beat. No one had ever gotten photos of Tarahumara runners in full flight on their home turf, and for good reason: the Tarahumara run for fun, and having white devils around wasn't any fun. Their races were sponta-neous and secretive and absolutely hidden from outside eyes. But if Caballo pulled this thing off, then a few lucky devils would get the chance to cross over to the Tarahumara side. For the first time, they'd all be Running People together.

Luis's dad, Joe, has the chiseled-oak face, gray ponytail, and turquoise rings of a Native American sage, but he's actually a former migrant worker who, in his hard-scrapping sixty-plus years, made himself into a California highway patrolman, then a chef, and finally an artist with a flair for the colors and culture of his native Mexico. When Joe heard his kid was heading into the homeland to see their ancestral heroes in action, he set his jaw and insisted he was going, too. The hike alone could, quite literally, kill him, but Joe wasn't worried. Even more than the ultrastuds around him, this son of the picking fields was a survivor.

"How about that barefoot guy?" I asked. "Is he still coming?"

A few months before, someone who called himself "Barefoot Ted" began blitzing Caballo with a torrent of messages. He seemed to be the Bruce Wayne of barefoot running, the wealthy heir of a California amusement-park fortune who devoted himself to battling the worst crime ever committed against the human foot: the invention of the running shoe. Barefoot Ted believed we could abolish foot injuries by throwing away our Nikes, and he was willing to prove it on himself: he ran the Los Angeles and Santa Clarita marathons in his bare feet and finished fast enough to qualify for the elite Boston Marathon. He was rumored to train by running barefoot in the San Gabriel Mountains, and by pulling his wife and daughter through the streets of Burbank in a rickshaw. Now, he was coming to Mexico to commune with the Tarahumara and explore whether the key to their amazing resilience was their nearly bare feet.

"He left a message that he'd be getting here later," Luis said.

"I guess that's everyone, then. Caballo is going to be psyched."

"So what's the story with this guy?" Scott asked.

I shrugged. "I don't really know much. I only met him once."

Scott's eyes narrowed. Billy and Jenn turned from the bar and cocked their heads, suddenly more interested in me than the beers they were ordering. The atmosphere of the whole group instantly changed. Seconds ago, everyone was drinking and chatting, but now, it was quiet and a little tense.

"What?" I asked.

"I thought you were really good buddies," Scott said.

"Buddies? Not even close," I said. "He's a total mystery. I don't even know where he lives. I don't even know his real name."

"So how do you know he's legit?" Joe Ramírez asked. "Shit, he may not even know any Tarahumara."

"They know him," I said. "All I can tell you is what I wrote. He's kind of strange, he's a hell of a runner, and he's been down there for a long time. That's all I found out about him."

Everyone sat for a sec and drank that in, myself included. So why were we trusting Caballo? I'd gotten so carried away with training for the race, I'd forgotten that the real challenge was surviving the trip. I had no clue who Caballo really was, or where he was leading us. He could be totally demented or merrily inept, and the result would be the same: out there in the Barrancas, we'd be cooked.

"So!" Jenn blurted. "What are you guys up for tonight? I promised Billy some big-ass margaritas."

If the rest of the crew had hit a crossroad of doubt, they'd put it behind them. Scott and Luis and Eric and Joe all agreed to pile into the hotel courtesy van with Jenn and Billy and head downtown for drinks. Not me, though. We had a lot of hard miles ahead, and I wanted all the rest I could get. Unlike the rest of them, I'd been down there before. I knew what we were heading into.

Sometime in the middle of the night, I was jerked awake by shouting nearby. Very nearby—like, in my room. Then, a *BANG* shook the bathroom.

"Billy, get up!" someone yelled.

"Leemee here. I'm fine."

"You've got to get up!"

I snapped on a light, and saw Eric Orton, the adventure-sports coach, standing in the doorway. "The kids," he said, shaking his head. "I don't know, man."

"Is everyone all right?"

"I don't know, man."

I sat up, still groggy, and went to the door of the bathroom. Billy was sprawled in the tub with his eyes closed. Pink vomit was splattered all over his shirt . . . and the toilet . . . and the floor. Jenn had lost her clothes and found a shiner; she was wearing only shorts and a purple bra, and her left eye was swelling shut. She had Billy by the arm and was trying to haul him to his feet.

"Can you help me lift him?" Jenn asked.

"What happened to your eye?"

"Whaddaya mean?"

"JUST LEAVE ME HERE!" Billy was shouting. He cackled like an archvillain, then passed out cold.

Jesus. I squatted over him in the tub and looked for nonsticky places to get a grip. I got him under the arms, but couldn't find any soft flesh to grab hold of; Billy was so muscular, trying to hoist him was like lifting a side of lean beef. I finally managed to drag him out of the tub and into the sitting room. Eric and I had planned to share a room, but when Jenn and Billy showed up with no reservation or, it seemed, any money for a room, we said they could crash with us.

And crash they did. As soon as Eric yanked out the fold-out sofa, Jenn dropped like a sack of laundry. I stretched Billy out beside her with his head hanging over the edge. I got a wastebasket under his face just before another pink river gushed out. He was still retching when I hit the lights.

Back in the adjoining bedroom, Eric filled me in. They'd gone to a Tex-Mex place, and while everyone else was eating, Jenn and Billy had had a drinking contest with fishbowl-sized margaritas. At some point, Billy wandered off in search of a bathroom and never returned. Jenn, meanwhile, entertained herself by snatching Scott's cell phone while he was saying good night to his wife and shouting, "Help! I'm surrounded by penises!"

Luckily, that's when Barefoot Ted turned up. When he got to the hotel and heard that his traveling companions were out drinking, he commandeered the courtesy van and convinced the driver to shuttle him around till he found them. At the first stop, the driver spotted Billy asleep in the parking lot. The driver hauled Billy into the van while Barefoot Ted gathered the others. Whatever Billy was lacking in pep, Jenn made up for; during the ride back to the hotel, she did backflips over the seats until the driver slammed on the brakes and threatened to throw her out if she didn't sit the hell down.

The driver's jurisdiction, however, only extended as far as the van door. When he pulled up in front of the hotel, Jenn burst loose. She ran into the hotel, skidded across the lobby, and crashed into a giant fountain full of water plants, smashing her face against the marble and blackening her eye. She emerged soaking wet, waving fists full of foliage overhead like a Kentucky Derby winner.

"Miss! Miss!" the appalled desk clerk pleaded, before remembering that pleading doesn't work on drunks in fountains. "Get her under control," she warned the others, "or you're all out of here."

Gotcha. Luis and Barefoot Ted smothered Jenn in a tackle, then wrestled her into an elevator. Jenn kept wriggling, trying to break free while Scott and Eric were dragging Billy aboard. "Let me gooooo!" the hotel staff could hear Jenn wailing as the doors slid shut. "I'll be good! I promiiiiiiissse. . . ."

maybe that design wasn't such a big deal after all. From then on, he only bought cheap dime-store sneaks.

"Here he is, running more than most people, with the wrong shoe on the wrong foot and not having any problems," Ken Learman says. "That experiment taught us all something. Taught us that when it comes to running shoes, all that glitters isn't gold."

FINAL PAINFUL TRUTH: Even Alan Webb Says "Human Beings
Are Designed to Run Without Shoes"

BEFORE Alan Webb became America's greatest miler, he was a flat-footed frosh with awful form. But his high school coach saw potential, and began rebuilding Alan from—no exaggeration—the ground up.

"I had injury problems early on, and it became apparent that my biomechanics could cause injury," Webb told me. "So we did foot-strengthening drills and special walks in bare feet." Bit by bit, Webb watched his feet transform before his eyes. "I was a size twelve and flat-footed, and now I'm a nine or ten. As the muscles in my feet got stronger, my arch got higher." Because of the barefoot drills, Webb also cut down on his injuries, allowing him to handle the kind of heavy training that would lead to his U.S. record for the mile and the fastest 1,500-meter time in the world for the year 2007.

"Barefoot running has been one of my training philosophies for years," said Gerard Hartmann, Ph.D., the Irish physical therapist who serves as the Great and Powerful Oz for the world's finest distance runners. Paula Radcliffe never runs a marathon without seeing Dr. Hartmann first, and titans like Haile Gebrselassie and Khalid Khannouchi have trusted their feet to his hands. For decades, Dr. Hartmann has been watching the explosion of orthotics and ever-more-structured running shoes with dismay.

"The deconditioned musculature of the foot is the greatest issue leading to injury, and we've allowed our feet to become badly deconditioned over the past twenty-five years," Dr. Hartmann said. "Pronation has become this very bad word, but it's just the natural movement of the foot. The foot is *supposed* to pronate."

To see pronation in action, kick off your shoes and run down the driveway. On a hard surface, your feet will briefly unlearn the habits they picked up in shoes and automatically shift to self-defense mode: you'll find yourself landing on the outside edge of your foot, then gently rolling from little toe over to big until your foot is flat. That's pronation—just a mild, shock-absorbing twist that allows your arch to compress.

But back in the '70s, the most respected voice in running began expressing some doubts about all that foot twisting. Dr. George Sheehan was a cardiologist whose essays on the beauty of running had made him the philosopher-king of the marathon set, and he came up with the notion that excessive pronation might be the cause of runner's knee. He was both right and very, very wrong. You have to land on your heel to overpronate, and you can only land on your heel if it's cushioned. Nevertheless, the shoe companies were quick to respond to Dr. Sheehan's call to arms and came up with a nuclear response; they created monstrously wedged and superengineered shoes that wiped out virtually all pronation.

"But once you block a natural movement," Dr. Hartmann said, "you adversely affect the others. We've done studies, and only two to three percent of the population has real biomechanical problems. So who is getting all these orthotics? Every time we put someone in a corrective device, we're creating new problems by treating ones that don't exist." In a startling admission in 2008, *Runner's World* confessed that for years it had accidentally misled its readers by recommending corrective shoes for runners with plantar fasciitis: "But recent research has shown stability shoes are unlikely to relieve plantar fasciitis *and may even exacerbate the symptoms*" (italics mine).

"Just look at the architecture," Dr. Hartmann explained. Blueprint your feet, and you'll find a marvel that engineers have been trying to match for centuries. Your foot's centerpiece is the arch, the greatest weight-bearing design ever created. The beauty of any arch is the way it gets stronger under stress; the harder you push down, the tighter its parts mesh. No stonemason worth his trowel would ever stick a support *under* an arch; push up from underneath, and you weaken the whole structure. Buttressing the foot's arch from all sides is a high-tensile web of twenty-six bones, thirty-three joints, twelve rubbery tendons, and eighteen muscles, all stretching and flexing like an earthquake-resistant suspension bridge.

"Putting your feet in shoes is similar to putting them in a plaster cast," Dr. Hartmann said. "If I put your leg in plaster, we'll find forty to sixty percent atrophy of the musculature within six weeks. Something similar happens to your feet when they're encased in shoes." When shoes are doing the work, tendons stiffen and muscles shrivel. Feet live for a fight and thrive under pressure; let them laze around, as Alan Webb discovered, and they'll collapse. Work them out, and they'll arc up like a rainbow.

"I've worked with over a hundred of the best Kenyan runners, and one thing they have in common is marvelous elasticity in their feet," Dr. Hartmann continued. "That comes from never running in shoes until you're seventeen." To this day, Dr. Hartmann believes that the best injury-prevention advice he's ever heard came from a coach who advocated "running barefoot on dewy grass three times a week."

He's not the only medical professional preaching the Barefoot Doctrine. According to Dr. Paul W. Brand, chief of rehab at the U.S. Public Health Service Hospital in Carville, Louisiana, and a professor of surgery at Louisiana State University Medical School, we could wipe out every common foot ailment within a generation by kicking off our shoes. As far back as 1976, Dr. Brand was pointing out that nearly every case in his waiting room—corns, bunions, hammertoes, flat feet, fallen arches—was nearly nonexistent in countries where most people go barefoot.

"The barefoot walker receives a continuous stream of information about the ground and about his own relationship to it," Dr. Brand has said, "while a shod foot sleeps inside an unchanging environment."

Drumbeats for the barefoot uprising were growing. But instead of doctors leading the charge for a muscular foot, it was turning into a class war pitting podiatrists against their own patients. Barefoot advocates like Drs. Brand and Hartmann were still rare, while traditional podiatric thinking still saw human feet as Nature's Mistake, a work in progress that could always be improved by a little scalpel-sculpting and orthotic reshaping.

That born-broken mentality found its perfect expression in *The Runners' Repair Manual*. Written by Dr. Murray Weisenfeld, a leading sports podiatrist, it's one of the top-selling foot-care books of all time, and begins with this dire pronouncement:

"Man's foot was not originally designed for walking, much less running long distances."

So what, according to the *Manual*, was our foot designed for? Well, at first swimming ("The modern foot evolved out of the fin of some primordial fish and these fins pointed backward"). After that, climbing ("The grasping foot permitted the creature to squat on branches without falling out").

And then . . . ?

And then, according to the podiatric account of evolution, we got stuck. While the rest of our bodies adapted beautifully to solid earth, somehow the only part of our body that actually touched the earth got left behind. We developed brains and hands deft enough to perform intravascular surgery, yet our feet never made it past the Paleolithic era. "Man's foot is not yet completely adapted to the ground," the *Manual* laments. "Only a portion of the population has been endowed with well ground-adapted feet."

So who are these lucky few with well-evolved feet? Come to think of it, nobody: "Nature has not yet published her plan for the perfect modern runner's foot," Dr. Weisenfeld writes. "Until the perfect foot comes along, my experience has shown me that we've all got an excellent chance at having some kind of injury." Nature may not have published her blueprint, but that didn't stop some podiatrists from trying to come up with one of their own. And it was exactly that kind of overconfidence—the belief that four years of podiatric training could trump two million years of natural selection—that led to a catastrophic rash of operations in the '70s.

"Not too many years ago, runner's knee was treated by surgery," Dr. Weisenfeld acknowledges. "That didn't work too well, since you need that cushioning when you run." Once the patients came out from under the knife, they discovered that their nagging ache had turned into a life-changing mutilation; without cartilage in their knees, they'd never be able to run without pain again. Despite the podiatric profession's checkered history of attempting to one-up nature, *The Runners' Repair Manual* never recommends strengthening feet; instead, the treatment of choice is always tape, orthotics, or surgery.

It even took Dr. Irene Davis, whose credentials and open-mindedness are hard to beat, until 2007 to take barefooting seriously, and only then because one of her patients flat-out defied her. He was so frustrated by his chronic plantar fasciitis, he wanted to try blasting it away by running in thin-soled, slipperlike shoes. Dr. Davis told him he was nuts. He did it anyway.

"To her surprise," as *BioMechanics* magazine would later report, "the plantar fasciitis symptoms abated and the patient was able to run short distances in the shoes."

"This is how we often learn things, when patients don't listen to us," Dr. Davis graciously responded. "I think perhaps the widespread plantar fasciitis in this country is partly due to the fact that we really don't allow the muscles in our feet to do what they are designed to do." She was so impressed by her rebellious patient's recovery that she even began adding barefoot walks to her own workouts.

Nike doesn't earn $17 billion a year by letting the Barefoot Teds of the world set the trends. Soon after the two Nike reps returned from Stanford with news that the barefoot uprising had even spread to elite college track, Nike set to work to see if it could make a buck from the problem it had created.

Blaming the running injury epidemic on big, bad Nike seems too easy—but that's okay, because it's largely their fault. The company was founded by Phil Knight, a University of Oregon runner who could sell anything, and Bill Bowerman, the University of Oregon coach who thought he knew everything. Before these two men got together, the modern running shoe didn't exist. Neither did most modern running injuries.

For a guy who told so many people how to run, Bowerman didn't do much of it himself. He only started to jog a little at age fifty, after spending time in New Zealand with Arthur Lydiard, the father of fitness running and the most influential distance-running coach of all time. Lydiard had begun the Auckland Joggers Club back in the late '50s to help rehab heart-attack victims. It was wildly controversial at the time; physicians were certain that Lydiard was mobilizing a mass suicide. But once the formerly ill men realized how great they felt after a few weeks of running, they began inviting their wives, kids, and parents to come along for the two-hour trail rambles.

By the time Bill Bowerman paid his first visit in 1962, Lydiard's Sunday morning group run was the biggest party in Auckland. Bowerman tried to join them, but was in such lousy shape that he had to be helped along by a seventy-three-year-old man who'd survived three coronaries. "God, the only thing that kept me alive was the hope that I would die," Bowerman said afterward.

But he came home a convert, and soon penned a best-selling book whose one-word title introduced a new word and obsession to the American public: *Jogging*. Between writing and coaching, Bowerman was busy ruining his nervous system and his wife's waffle iron by tinkering in the basement with molten rubber to invent a new kind of footwear. His experiments left Bowerman with a debilitating nerve condition, but also the most cushioned running shoe ever created. In a stroke of dark irony, Bowerman named it the Cortez—after the conquistador who plundered the New World for gold and unleashed a horrific smallpox epidemic.

Bowerman's deftest move was advocating a new style of running that was only possible in his new style of shoe. The Cortez allowed people to run in a way no human safely could before: by landing on their bony heels. Before the invention of a cushioned shoe, runners through the ages had identical form: Jesse Owens, Roger Bannister, Frank Shorter, and even Emil Zatopek all ran with backs straight, knees bent, feet scratching back under their hips. They had no choice: the only shock absorption came from the compression of their legs and their thick pad of midfoot fat. Fred Wilt verified as much in 1959 in his classic track text, *How They Train*, which detailed the techniques of more than eighty of the world's top runners. "The forward foot moves toward the track in a downward, backward, 'stroking' motion (not punching or pounding) and the outer edge of the ball of the foot makes first contact with the track," Wilt writes. "Running progression results from these forces pushing behind the center of gravity of the body. . . ."

In fact, when the biomedical designer Van Phillips created a state-of-the-art prosthetic for amputee runners in 1984, he didn't even bother equipping it with a heel. As a runner who lost his left leg below the knee in a water-skiing accident, Phillips understood that the heel was needed only for standing, not motion. Phillips's C-shaped "Cheetah foot" mimics the performance of an organic leg so effectively, it allowed the South African double amputee Oscar Pistorius to compete with the world's greatest sprinters.

But Bowerman had an idea: maybe you could grab a little extra distance if you stepped *ahead* of your center of gravity. Stick a chunk of rubber under the heel, he mused, and you could straighten your leg, land on your heel, and lengthen your stride. In *Jogging*, he compared the styles: with the time-tested "flat foot" strike, he acknowledged, "the wide surface area pillows the footstrike and is easy on the rest of the body." Nevertheless, he still believed a "heel-to-toe" stride would be "the least tiring over long distances." *If* you've got the shoe for it.

Bowerman's marketing was brilliant. "The same man created a market for a product and then created the product itself," as one Oregon financial columnist observed. "It's genius, the kind of stuff they study in business schools." Bowerman's partner, the runner-turned-entrepreneur Phil Knight, set up a manufacturing deal in Japan and was soon selling shoes faster than they could come off the assembly line. "With the Cortez's cushioning, we were in a monopoly position probably into the Olympic year, 1972," Knight would gloat. By the time other companies geared up to copy the new shoe, the Swoosh was a world power.

Delighted with the reaction to his amateur designs, Bowerman let his creativity take off. He contemplated a waterproof shoe made of fish skin, but let that one die on the drawing board. He did come out with the LD-1000 Trainer, a shoe with a sole so wide it was like running on pie plates. Bowerman figured it would kill pronation in its tracks, overlooking the fact that unless the runner's foot was perfectly straight, the flared heel would wrench his leg. "Instead of stabilizing, it accelerated pronation and hurt both feet and ankles," former Oregon runner Kenny Moore reported in his biography of Bowerman. The shoe that was supposed to give you a perfect stride, in other words, only worked if you already had one. When Bowerman realized he was causing injuries instead of preventing them, he had to backtrack and narrow the heel in later versions.

Back in New Zealand, meanwhile, an appalled Arthur Lydiard was watching the flashy exports flooding out of Oregon and wondering what in the world his friend was up to. Compared with Bowerman, Lydiard was by far the superior track mind; he'd coached many more Olympic champions and world-record holders, and he'd created a training program that remains the gold standard. Lydiard liked Bill Bowerman and respected him as a coach, but good God! What was this junk he was selling?

Lydiard knew all this pronation stuff was just marketing gibberish. "If you told the average person of any age to take off his or her shoes and run down the hallway, you would almost always discover the foot action contains no hint of pronation or supination," Lydiard complained. "Those sideways flexings of the ankles begin only when people lace themselves into these running shoes because the construction of many of the shoes immediately alters the natural movement of the feet.

"We ran in canvas shoes," Lydiard went on. "We didn't get plantar fascia, we didn't pronate or supinate, we might have lost a bit of skin from the rough canvas when we were running marathons, but, generally speaking, we didn't have foot problems. Paying several hundred dollars for the latest in high-tech running shoes is no guarantee you'll avoid any of these injuries and can even guarantee that you will suffer from them in one form or another."

Eventually, even Bowerman was stricken by doubt. As Nike steamrolled along, churning out a bewildering variety of shoes and changing models every year for no reason besides having something else to sell, Bowerman felt his original mission of making an honest shoe had been eroded by a new ideology, which he summed up in two words: "Make money." Nike, he griped in a letter to a colleague, was "distributing a lot of crap." Even to one of Nike's founding partners, it seemed, the words of the social critic Eric Hoffer were ringing true: "Every great cause begins as a movement, becomes a business, and turns into a racket."

Bowerman had died by the time the barefoot uprising was taking hold in 2002, so Nike went back to Bowerman's old mentor to see if this shoeless stuff really had merit. "Of course!" Arthur Lydiard reportedly snorted. "You support an area, it gets weaker. Use it extensively, it gets stronger. . . . Run barefoot and you don't have all those troubles.

"Shoes that let your foot function like you're barefoot—they're the shoes for me," Lydiard concluded.

Nike followed up that blast with its own hard data. Jeff Pisciotta, the senior researcher at Nike Sports Research Lab, assembled twenty runners on a grassy field and filmed them running barefoot. When he zoomed in, he was startled by what he found: instead of each foot clomping down as it would in a shoe, it behaved like an animal with a mind of its own—stretching, grasping, seeking the ground with splayed toes, gliding in for a landing like a lake-bound swan.

"It's beautiful to watch," a still spellbound Pisciotta later told me. "That made us start thinking that when you put a shoe on, it starts to take over some of the control." He immediately deployed his team to gather film of every existing barefoot culture they could find. "We found pockets of people all over the globe who are still running barefoot, and what you find is that during propulsion and landing, they have far more range of motion in the foot and engage more of the toe. Their feet flex, spread, splay, and grip the surface, meaning you have less pronation and more distribution of pressure."

Faced with the almost inescapable conclusion that it had been selling lemons, Nike shifted into make-lemonade mode. Jeff Pisciotta became head of a top-secret and seemingly impossible project: finding a way to make a buck off a naked foot.

It took two years of work before Pisciotta was ready to unveil his masterpiece. It was presented to the world in TV ads that showed so many barefoot athletes—Kenyan marathoners padding along a dirt trail, swimmers curling their toes around a starting block, gymnasts and Brazilian capoeira dancers and rock climbers and wrestlers and karate masters and beach soccer players—that after a while, it was hard to remember who *does* wear shoes, or why.

Flashing over the images were motivational messages: "Your feet are your foundation. Wake them up! Make them strong! Connect with the ground. . . . Natural technology allows natural motion. . . . Power to your feet." Across the sole of a bare foot is scrawled "Performance Starts Here." Then comes the grand finale: as "Tiptoe Through the Tulips" crescendos in the background, we cut back to those Kenyans, whose bare feet are now sporting some kind of thin little shoe. It's the new Nike Free, a swooshed slipper even thinner than the old Cortez.

And its slogan?

"Run Barefoot."

CHAPTER 26

Baby, this town rips the bones from your back;
It's a death trap, it's a suicide rap . . .

—BRUCE SPRINGSTEEN, *"Born to Run"*

CABALLO BLANCO'S face was pink with pride, so I tried to think of something nice to say.

We'd just arrived in Batopilas, an ancient mining town tucked eight thousand feet below the lip of the canyon. It was founded four hundred years ago when Spanish explorers discovered silver ore in the stony river, and it hasn't changed much since then. It's still a tiny strip of houses hugging the riverbank, a place where burros are as common as cars and the first telephone was installed when the rest of the world was programming iPods.

Getting down there took a cast-iron stomach and supreme faith in your fellow man, the man in question being the one driving the bus. The only way into Batopilas is a dirt road that corkscrews along the sheer face of a cliff, dropping seven thousand feet in less than ten miles. As the bus strained around hairpin turns, we hung on tight and looked far below at the wrecks of cars whose drivers had miscalculated by a few inches. Two years later, Caballo would make his own contribution to the steel cemetery when the pickup truck he was driving caught the lip of the cliff and tumbled over. Caballo managed to dive out just in time and watched as the truck exploded far below. Later, chunks of the scorched carcass were scavenged as good-luck charms.

After the bus pulled over on the edge of town, we climbed down stiffly, our faces as war-painted with dust and sweat salt as Caballo's had been the first the time I met him. "There she is!" Caballo hollered. "That's my place."

We looked around, but the only thing in sight was the ancient ruin of an old mission across the river. Its roof was gone and its red-stone walls were collapsing into the ruddy canyon they'd been carved from, looking like a sand castle dissolving back into sand. It was perfect; Caballo had found the ideal home for a living ghost. I could only imagine how freaky it must be to pass here at night and see his monstrous shadow dancing around behind his campfire as he wandered the ruins like Quasimodo.

"Wow, that's really something, uh . . . else," I said.

"No, man," he said. "Over here." He pointed behind us, toward a faint goat trail disappearing into the cactus. Caballo began to climb, and we fell in behind him, grabbing at brush for balance as we slipped and scrabbled up the stony path.

"Damn, Caballo," Luis said. "This is the only driveway in the world that needs trail markers and an aid station at mile two."

After a hundred yards or so, we came through a thicket of wild lime trees and found a small, clay-walled hut. Caballo had built it by hauling up rocks from the river, making the round-trip over that treacherous path hundreds of times with river-slick stones in his hands. As a home, it suited Caballo even better than the ruined mission; here in his handmade fortress of solitude, he could see everything in the river valley and remain unseen.

We wandered inside, and saw Caballo had a small camp bed, a pile of trashed sports sandals, and three or four books about Crazy Horse and other Native Americans on a shelf next to a kerosene lamp. That was it; no electricity, no running water, no toilet. Out back, Caballo had cut away the cactus and smoothed a little place to kick back after a run, smoke something relaxing, and gaze off at the prehistoric wilderness. Whatever Barefoot Ted's heavy Heidegger word was, no one was ever more an expression of their place than Caballo was of his hut.

Caballo was anxious to get us fed and off his hands so he could catch up on sleep. The next few days were going to take everything we had, and none of us had gotten much rest since El Paso. He led us

back down his hidden driveway and up the road to a tiny shop oper-
ating from the front window of a house; you poked your head in and
if shopkeeper Mario had what you wanted, you got it. Upstairs,
Mario rented us a few small rooms with a cold-water shower at the
end of the hall.

Caballo wanted us to dump our bags and head off immediately for
food, but Barefoot Ted insisted on stripping down and padding off to
the shower to sluice away the road grime. He came out screaming.

"Jesus! The shower's got loose wires. I just got the shit shocked
out of me!"

Eric looked at me. "You think Caballo did it?"

"Justifiable homicide," I said. "No jury would convict." The Barefoot Ted–Caballo Blanco storm front hadn't improved a bit since
we'd left Creel. During one rest stop, Caballo climbed down from
the roof and squeezed his way into the back of the bus to escape.
"That guy doesn't know what silence is," Caballo fumed. "He's from
L.A., man; he thinks you've got to fill every space with noise."

After we'd gotten settled at Mario's, Caballo brought us to
another of his Mamás. We didn't even have to order; as soon as we
arrived, Doña Mila began pulling out whatever she had in the fridge.
Soon, platters were being handed around of guacamole, frijoles,
sliced cactus and tomatoes doused in tangy vinegar, Spanish rice, and
a fragrant beef stew thickened with chicken liver.

"Pack it in," Caballo had said. "You're going to need it tomorrow." He was taking us on a little warm-up hike, Caballo said. Just a
jaunt up a nearby mountain to give us a taste of the terrain we'd be
tackling on the trek to the racecourse. He kept saying it was no big
deal, but then he'd warn us we'd better pound down the food and get
right to bed. I became even more apprehensive after a white-haired
old American ambled in and joined us.

"How's the giddyup, Hoss?" he greeted Caballo. His name was
Bob Francis. He had first wandered down to Batopilas in the '60s,
and part of him had never left. Even though he had kids and grand-
kids back in San Diego, Bob still spent most of the year wandering
the canyons around Batopilas, sometimes guiding trekkers, sometimes just visiting Patricio Luna, a Tarahumara friend who was
Manuel Luna's uncle. They met thirty years before, when Bob got

lost in the canyons. Patricio found him, fed him, and brought him back to his family's cave for the night.

Because of his long friendship with Patricio, Bob is one of the only Americans to have ever attended a Tarahumara *tesgüinada*—the marathon drinking party that precedes and occasionally prevents the ball races. Even Caballo hasn't reached that level of trust with the Tarahumara, and after listening to Bob's stories, he wasn't sure he wanted to.

"All of a sudden, Tarahumara I've been friends with for years, guys I knew as shy, gentle amigos, are in my face, butting against me with their chests, spitting insults at me, ready to fight," Bob said. "Meanwhile, their wives are in the bushes with other men, and their grown-up daughters are wrestling naked. They keep the kids away from these deals; you can imagine why."

Anything goes at a *tesgüinada*, Bob explained, because everything is blamed on the peyote, moonshine tequila, and *tesgüino*, the potent corn beer. As wild as these parties get, they actually serve a noble and sober purpose: they act as a pressure valve to vent explosive emotions. Just like the rest of us, the Tarahumara have secret desires and grievances, but in a society where everyone relies on one another and there are no police to get between them, there has to be a way to satisfy lusts and grudges. What better than a booze-fest? Everyone gets ripped, goes wild, and then, chastened by bruises and hangovers, they dust themselves off and get on with their lives.

"I could have been married or murdered twenty times before the night was over," Bob said. "But I was smart enough to put down the gourd and get myself out of there before the real shenanigans started." If one outsider knew the Barrancas as well as Caballo, it was Bob, which was why, even though he was liquored up and in a bit of a ranting mood, I paid careful attention when he got into it with Ted.

"Those fucking things are going to be dead tomorrow," Bob said, pointing at the FiveFingers on Ted's feet.

"I'm not going to wear them," Ted said.

"Now you're talking sense," Bob said.

"I'm going barefoot," Ted said.

Bob turned to Caballo. "He messing with us, Hoss?"

Caballo just smiled.

―――――――

Early the next morning, Caballo came for us as dawn was breaking over the canyon. "That's where we're headed tomorrow," Caballo said, pointing through the window of my room toward a mountain rearing in the distance. Between us and the mountain was a sea of rolling foothills so thickly overgrown that it was hard to see how a trail could punch through. "We'll run one of those little guys this morning."

"How much water do we need?" Scott asked.

"I only carry this," Caballo said, waving a sixteen-ounce plastic bottle. "There's a freshwater spring up top to refill."

"Food?"

"Nah," Caballo shrugged as he and Scott left to check on the others. "We'll be back by lunch."

"I'm bringing the big boy," Eric said to me, gurgling springwater into the bladder on his ninety-six-ounce hydration backpack. "I think you should, too."

"Really? Caballo says we're only going about ten miles."

"Can't hurt to carry the max when you go off-road," Eric said. "Even if you don't need it, it's training for when you do. And you never know—something happens, you could be out there longer than you think."

I put down my handheld bottle and reached for my hydration pack. "Bring iodine pills in case you need to purify water. And shove in some gels, too," Eric added. "On race day, you're going to need two hundred calories an hour. The trick is learning how to take in a little at a time, so you've got a steady drip of fuel without overwhelming your stomach. This'll be good practice."

We walked through Batopilas, past shopkeepers hand-sprinkling water on the stones to keep the dust down. Schoolkids in spotless white shirts, their black hair sleek with water, interrupted their chatter to politely wish us *"Buenos días."*

"Gonna be a hot one," Caballo said, as we ducked into a storefront with no sign out front. *"¿Hay teléfono?"* he asked the woman who greeted us. Are the phones working?

"Todavía no," she said, shaking her head in resignation. Not yet. Clarita had the only two public phones in all Batopilas, but service

had been knocked out for the past three days, leaving shortwave radio the only form of communication. For the first time, it hit me how cut off we were; we had no way of knowing what was going on in the outside world, or letting the outside world know what was happening to us. We were putting a hell of a lot of trust in Caballo, and once again, I had to wonder why; as knowledgeable as Caballo was, it still seemed crazy to put our lives in the hands of a guy who didn't seem too concerned about his own.

But for the moment, the grumble of my stomach and the aroma of Clarita's breakfast managed to push those thoughts aside. Clarita served up big plates of huevos rancheros, the fried eggs smothered in homemade salsa and freshly chopped cilantro and sitting atop thick, hand-patted tortillas. The food was too delicious to wolf down, so we lingered, refilling our coffee a few times before getting up to go. Eric and I followed Scott's example and tucked an extra tortilla in our pockets for later.

Only after we finished did I realize that the Party Kids hadn't shown up. I checked my watch; it was already pushing 10 a.m.

"We're leaving them," Caballo said.

"I'll run back for them," Luis offered.

"No," Caballo said. "They could still be in bed. We've got to hit it if we're going to dodge the afternoon heat."

Maybe it was for the best; they could use a day to rehydrate and power up for the hike tomorrow. "No matter what, don't let them try to follow us," Caballo told Luis's father, who was staying behind. "They get lost out there, we'll never see them again. That's no joke."

Eric and I cinched tight our hydration packs, and I pulled a bandanna over my head. It was already steamy. Caballo slid through a gap in the retaining wall and began picking his way over the boulders to the edge of the river. Barefoot Ted pushed ahead to join him, showing off how nimbly he could hop from rock to rock in his bare feet. If Caballo was impressed, he wasn't showing it.

"YOU GUYS! HOLD UP!" Jenn and Billy were sprinting down the street behind us. Billy had his shirt in his hand, and Jenn's shoelaces were untied.

"You sure you want to come?" Scott asked when they panted up. "You haven't even eaten anything."

Jenn tore a PowerBar in two and gave half to Billy. They were each carrying a skinny water bottle that couldn't have held more than six swallows. "We're good," Billy said.

We followed the stony riverbank for a mile, then turned into a dry gully. Without a word, we all spontaneously broke into a trot. The gully was wide and sandy, leaving plenty of room for Scott and Bare-foot Ted to flank Caballo and run three abreast.

"Check out their feet," said Eric. Even though Scott was in the Brooks trail shoe he'd helped design and Caballo was in sandals, they both skimmed their feet over the ground just the way Ted did in his bare feet, their foot strikes in perfect sync. It was like watching a team of Lipizzaner stallions circle the show ring.

After about a mile, Caballo veered onto a steep, rocky washout that climbed up into the mountain. Eric and I eased back to a walk, obeying the ultrarunner's creed: "If you can't see the top, walk." When you're running fifty miles, there's no dividend in bashing up the hills and then being winded on the way down; you only lose a few seconds if you walk, and then you can make them back up by flying downhill. Eric believes that's one reason ultrarunners don't get hurt and never seem to burn out: "They know how to train, not strain."

As we walked, we caught up with Barefoot Ted. He'd had to slow down to pick his way over the jagged, fist-sized stones. I squinted up at the trail ahead: we had at least another mile of crumbly rock to climb before the trail leveled and, hopefully, smoothed.

"Ted, where are your FiveFingers?" I asked.

"Don't need 'em," he said. "I made a deal with Caballo that if I handled this hike, he wouldn't get mad anymore if I went barefoot."

"He rigged the bet," I said. "This is like running up the side of a gravel pit."

"Humans didn't invent rough surfaces, Oso," Ted said. "We invented the *smooth* ones. Your foot is perfectly happy molding itself around rocks. All you've got to do is relax and let your foot flex. It's like a foot massage. Oh, hey!" he called after us as Eric and I pulled ahead. "Here's a great tip. Next time your feet are sore, walk on slippery stones in a cold creek. Unbelievable!"

Eric and I left Ted singing to himself as he hopped and trotted along. The glare off the stones was blinding and heat kept rising, making it feel as if we were climbing straight into the sun. In a way, we were; after two miles, I checked the altimeter on my watch and saw we'd climbed over a thousand feet. Soon, though, the trail plateaued and softened from stones to footworn dirt.

The others were a few hundred yards ahead, so Eric and I started to run to close the gap. Before we caught them, Barefoot Ted came whisking by. "Time for a drink," he said, waving his empty water bottle. "I'll wait for you guys at the spring."

The trail veered abruptly upward again, jagging back and forth in lightning-bolt switchbacks. Fifteen hundred feet . . . two thousand . . . We bent into the slope, feeling as though we only gained a few inches every step. After three hours and six miles of hard climbing, we hadn't hit the spring; we hadn't seen shade since we left the riverbank.

"See?" Eric said, waving the nozzle of his hydration pack. "Those guys have got to be parched."

"And starving," I added, ripping open a raw-food granola bar.

At thirty-five hundred feet, we found Caballo and the rest of the crew waiting in a hollow under a juniper tree. "Anyone need iodine pills?" I asked.

"Don't think so," Luis said. "Take a look."

Under the tree was a natural stone basin carved out by centuries of cool, trickling spring water. Except there was no water.

"We're in a drought," Caballo said. "I forgot about that."

But there was a chance another spring might be flowing a few hundred feet higher up the mountain. Caballo volunteered to run up and check. Jenn, Billy, and Luis were too thirsty to wait and went with him. Ted gave his bottle to Luis to fill up for him and sat to wait in the shade with us. I gave him a few sips from my pack, while Scott shared some pita and hummus.

"You don't use goos?" Eric asked.

"I like real food," Scott said. "It's just as portable and you get real calories, not just a fast burn." As a corporate-sponsored elite athlete, Scott had the worldwide buffet of nutrition at his fingertips, but after experimenting with the entire spectrum—everything from deer meat to Happy Meals to organic raw-food bars—he'd ended up with a diet a lot like the Tarahumara.

"Growing up in Minnesota, I used to be a total junk eater," he said. "Lunch used to be two McChickens and large fries." When he was a

Nordic skier and cross-country runner in high school, his coaches were always telling him he needed plenty of lean meat to rebuild his muscles after a tough workout, yet the more Scott researched traditional endurance athletes, the more vegetarians he found.

Like the Marathon Monks in Japan he'd just been reading about; they ran an ultramarathon *every day for seven years,* covering some twenty-five thousand miles on nothing but miso soup, tofu, and vegetables. And what about Percy Cerutty, the mad Australian genius who coached some of the greatest milers of all time? Cerutty believed food shouldn't even be cooked, let alone slaughtered; he put his athletes through triple sessions on a diet of raw oats, fruit, nuts, and cheese. Even Cliff Young, the sixty-three-year-old farmer who stunned Australia in 1983 by beating the best ultrarunners in the country in a 507-mile race from Sydney to Melbourne, did it all on beans, beer, and oatmeal ("I used to feed the calves by hand and they thought I was their mother," Young said. "I couldn't sleep too good those nights when I knew they would get slaughtered." He switched to grains and potatoes, and slept a whole lot better. Ran pretty good, too).

Scott wasn't sure why meatless diets worked for history's great runners, but he figured he'd trust the results first and figure out the science later. From that point on, no animal products would pass his lips—no eggs, no cheese, not even ice cream—and not much sugar or white flour, either. He stopped carrying Snickers and PowerBars during his long runs; instead, he loaded a fanny pack with rice burritos, pita stuffed with hummus and Kalamata olives, and home-baked bread smeared with adzuki beans and quinoa spread. When he sprained his ankle, he eschewed ibuprofen and relied instead on wolfsbane and whomping portions of garlic and ginger.

"Sure, I had my doubts," Scott said. "Everyone told me I'd get weaker, I wouldn't recover between workouts, I'd get stress fractures and anemia. But I found that I actually feel better, because I'm eating foods with more high-quality nutrients. And after I won Western States, I never looked back."

By basing his diet on fruits, vegetables, and whole grains, Scott is deriving maximum nutrition from the lowest possible number of calories, so his body isn't forced to carry or process any useless bulk.

Weird, Bramble thought. *How come we acquired all this specialized running stuff, and other walkers didn't?* For a walking animal, the Achilles would just be a liability. Moving on two legs is like walking on stilts; you plant your foot, pivot your body weight over the leg, and repeat. The last thing you'd want would be stretchy, wobbly tendons right at your base of support. All an Achilles tendon does is stretch like a rubber band—

A rubber band! Dr. Bramble felt twin surges of pride and embarrassment. Rubber bands . . . There he'd been, thumping his chest about not being like all those other morphologists who "tick off the things they expect to see," when all along, he'd been just as misguided by myopia; he hadn't even thought about the rubber-band factor. When David started talking about running, Dr. Bramble assumed he meant speed. But there are *two* kinds of great runners: sprinters and marathoners. Maybe human running was about going *far,* not fast. That would explain why our feet and legs are so dense with springy tendons—because springy tendons store and return energy, just like the rubber-band propellers on balsa-wood airplanes. The more you twist the rubber band, the farther the plane flies; likewise, the more you can stretch the tendons, the more free energy you get when that leg extends and swings back.

And if I were going to design a long-distance running machine, Dr. Bramble thought, that's exactly what I'd load it with—lots of rubber bands to maximize endurance. Running is really just jumping, springing from one foot to another. Tendons are irrelevant to walking, but great for energy-efficient jumping. So forget speed; maybe we were born to be the world's greatest marathoners.

"And you've got to ask yourself why only one species in the world has the urge to gather by the tens of thousands to run twenty-six miles in the heat for fun," Dr. Bramble mused. "Recreation has its reasons."

Together, Dr. Bramble and David Carrier began putting their World's Greatest Marathoner model to the test. Soon, evidence was turning up all over, even in places they weren't looking. One of their first big discoveries came by accident when David took a horse for a jog. "We wanted to videotape a horse to see how its gait coordinated with its breathing," Dr. Bramble says. "We needed someone to keep the gear from getting tangled, so David ran alongside it." When they played back the tape, something seemed strange, although Bramble couldn't figure out what it was. He had to rewind a few times before it hit him: even though David and the horse were moving at the same speed, David's legs were moving more slowly.

"It was astonishing," Dr. Bramble explains. "Even though the horse has long legs and four of them, David had a longer stride." David was in great shape for a scientist, but as a medium-height, medium-weight, middle-of-the-pack runner, he was perfectly average. That left only one explanation: as bizarre as it may seem, the average human has a longer stride than a horse. The horse looks like it's taking giant lunges forward, but its hooves swing back before touching the ground. The result: even though biomechanically smooth human runners have short strides, they still cover more distance per step than a horse, making them more efficient. With equal amounts of gas in the tank, in other words, a human can theoretically run farther than a horse.

But why settle for theory when you can put it to the test? Every October, a few dozen runners and riders face off in the 50-mile Man Against Horse Race in Prescott, Arizona. In 1999, a local runner named Paul Bonnet passed the lead horses on the steep climb up Mingus Mountain and never saw them again till after he'd crossed the finish line. The following year, Dennis Poolheco began a remarkable streak: he beat every man, woman, and steed for the next six years, until Paul Bonnet wrested the title back in 2006. It would take eight years before a horse finally caught up with those two and won again.

Discoveries like these, however, were just happy little extras for the two Utah scientists as they tunneled closer to their big breakthrough. As David had suspected on the day he peered into a rabbit's carcass and saw the history of life staring back at him, evolution seemed to be all about air; the more highly evolved the species, the better its carburetor. Take reptiles: David put lizards on a treadmill, and found they can't even run and breathe at the same time. The best they can manage is a quick scramble before stopping to pant.

Dr. Bramble, meanwhile, was working a little higher up the evolutionary ladder with big cats. He discovered that when many quadrupeds run, their internal organs slosh back and forth like water in a bathtub. Every time a cheetah's front feet hit the ground, its guts slam forward into the lungs, forcing out air. When it reaches out for the next stride, its innards slide rearward, sucking air back in. Adding that extra punch to their lung power, though, comes at a cost: it limits cheetahs to just one breath per stride.

Actually, Dr. Bramble was surprised to find that *all* running mammals are restricted to the same cycle of take-a-step, take-a-breath. In the entire world, he and David could only find one exception:

You.

"When quadrupeds run, they get stuck in a one-breath-per-locomotion cycle," Dr. Bramble said. "But the human runners we tested *never* went one to one. They could pick from a number of different ratios, and generally preferred two to one." The reason we're free to pant to our heart's content is the same reason you need a shower on a summer day: we're the only mammals that shed most of our heat by sweating. All the pelt-covered creatures in the world cool off primarily by breathing, which locks their entire heat-regulating system to their lungs. But humans, with our millions of sweat glands, are the best air-cooled engine that evolution has ever put on the market.

"That's the benefit of being a naked, sweating animal," David Carrier explains. "As long as we keep sweating, we can keep going." A team of Harvard scientists had once verified exactly that point by sticking a rectal thermometer in a cheetah and getting it to run on a treadmill. Once its temperature hit 105 degrees, the cheetah shut down and refused to run. That's the natural response for all running mammals; when they build up more heat in their bodies than they can puff out their mouths, they have to stop or die.

Fantastic! Springy legs, twiggy torsos, sweat glands, hairless skin, vertical bodies that retain less sun heat—no wonder we're the world's greatest marathoners. But so what? Natural selection is all about two things—eating and not getting eaten—and being able to run twenty miles ain't worth a damn if the deer disappears in the first twenty seconds and a tiger can catch you in ten. What good is endurance on a battlefield built on speed?

That's the question Dr. Bramble was mulling in the early '90s when he was on sabbatical and met Dr. Dan Lieberman during a visit to Harvard. At the time, Lieberman was working on the other end of the animal Olympics; he had a pig on a treadmill and was trying to figure out why it was such a lousy runner.

"Take a look at its head," Bramble pointed out. "It wobbles all over the place. Pigs don't have a nuchal ligament."

Lieberman's ears perked up. As an evolutionary anthropologist, he knew that nothing on our bodies has changed as much as the shape of our skulls, or says more about who we are. Even your breakfast burrito plays a role; Lieberman's investigations had revealed that as our diet shifted over the centuries from chewy stuff like raw roots and wild game and gave way to mushy cooked staples like spaghetti and ground beef, our faces began to shrink. Ben Franklin's face was chunkier than yours; Caesar's was bigger than his.

The Harvard and Utah scientists got along right from the start, mostly because of Lieberman's eyes: they didn't roll when Bramble briefed him on the Running Man theory. "No one in the scientific community was willing to take it seriously," Bramble said. "For every one paper on running, there were four thousand on walking. Whenever I'd bring it up at conferences, everyone would always say, 'Yeah, but we're slow.' They were focused on speed and couldn't understand how endurance could be an advantage."

Well, to be fair, Bramble hadn't really figured that one out yet, either. As biologists, he and David Carrier could decipher how the machine was designed, but they needed an anthropologist to determine what that design could actually do. "I knew a lot about evolution and a little about locomotion," Lieberman says. "Dennis knew a shitload about locomotion, but not so much about evolution."

As they traded stories and ideas, Bramble could tell that Lieberman was his kind of lab partner. Lieberman was a scientist who believed that being hands-on meant being prepared to soak them in blood. For years, Lieberman had organized a Cro-Magnon barbecue on a Harvard Yard lawn as part of his human evolution class. To demonstrate the dexterity necessary to operate primitive tools, he'd get his students to butcher a goat with sharpened stones, then cook it in a pit. As soon as the aroma of roasting goat spread and the post-butchering libations began flowing, homework turned into a house party. "It eventually evolved into a kind of bacchanalian feast," Lieberman told the *Harvard University Gazette*.

But there was an even more important reason that Lieberman was the perfect guy to tackle the Running Man mystery: the solution seemed to be linked to his specialty, the head. Everyone knew that at some point in history, early humans got access to a big supply of protein, which allowed their brains to expand like a thirsty sponge in a bucket of water. Our brains kept growing until they were seven times larger than the brains of any comparable mammal. They also sucked up an ungodly number of calories; even though our brains account for only 2 percent of our body weight, they demand 20 percent of our energy, compared with just 9 percent for chimps.

Dr. Lieberman threw himself into Running Man research with his usual creative zeal. Soon, students dropping by Lieberman's office on the top floor of Harvard's Peabody Museum were startled to find a sweat-drenched one-armed man with an empty cream-cheese cup strapped to his head running on a treadmill. "We humans are weird," Lieberman said as he punched buttons on the control panel. "No other creature has been found with a neck like ours." He paused to shout a question to the man on the treadmill. "How much faster can you go, Willie?"

"Faster than this thing!" Willie called back, his steel left hand clanging against the treadmill rail. Willie Stewart lost his arm when he was eighteen after a steel cable he was carrying on a construction job got caught in a whirling turbine, but he recovered to become a champion triathlete and rugby player. In addition to the cream-cheese cup, which was being used to secure a gyroscope, Willie also had electrodes taped to his chest and legs. Dr. Lieberman had recruited him to test his theory that the human head, with its unique position directly on top of the neck, acts like the roof weights used to prevent skyscrapers from pitching in the wind. Our heads didn't just expand because we got better at running, Lieberman believed; we got better at running because our heads were expanding, thereby providing more ballast.

"Your head works with your arms to keep you from twisting and swaying in midstride," Dr. Lieberman said. The arms, meanwhile, also work as a counterbalance to keep the head aligned. "That's how bipeds solved the problem of how to stabilize a head with a movable neck. It's yet another feature of human evolution that only makes sense in terms of running."

But the big mystery continued to be food. Judging by the

Godzilla-like growth of our heads, Lieberman could pinpoint the exact moment when the caveman menu changed: it had to be two million years ago, when apelike *Australopithecus*—with his tiny brain, giant jaw, and billy-goat diet of tough, fibrous plants—evolved into *Homo erectus*, our slim, long-legged ancestor with the big head and small, tearing teeth perfectly suited for raw flesh and soft fruits. Only one thing could have sparked such a dramatic makeover: a diet no primate had ever eaten before, featuring a reliable supply of meat, with its high concentrations of calories, fat, and protein.

"So where the fuck did they get it?" Lieberman asks, with all the gusto of a man who's not squeamish about hacking into goats with a rock. "The bow and arrow is twenty thousand years old. The spear-head is two hundred thousand years old. But *Homo erectus* is around two *million* years old. That means that for most of our existence—*for nearly two million years!*—hominids were getting meat with their bare hands."

Lieberman began playing the possibilities out in his mind. "Maybe we pirated carcasses killed by other predators?" he asked himself. "Scooting in and grabbing them while the lion was sleeping?"

No; that would give us an appetite for meat but not dependable access. You'd have to get to a kill site before the vultures, who can strip an antelope in minutes and "chew bones like crackers," as Lieberman likes to say. Even then, you might only tear off a few mouthfuls before the lion opened a baleful eye or a pack of hyenas drove you away.

"Okay, maybe we didn't have spears. But we could have jumped on a boar and throttled it. Or clubbed it to death."

Are you kidding? With all that thrashing and goring, you'd get your feet crushed, your testicles torn, your ribs broken. You'd win, but you'd pay for it; break an ankle in the prehistoric wilderness while hunting for dinner, and you might become dinner yourself.

There's no telling how long Lieberman would have remained stumped if his dog hadn't finally given him the answer. One summer afternoon, Lieberman took Vashti, his mutty half border collie, for a five-mile jog around Fresh Pond. It was hot, and after a few miles, Vashti plopped down under a tree and refused to move. Lieberman got impatient; yeah, it was a little warm, but not *that* bad. . . .

As he waited for his panting dog to cool off, Lieberman's mind flashed back to his time doing fossil research in Africa. He recalled the shimmering waves across the sun-scorched savannah, the way the dry clay soaked up the heat and beamed it right back up through the soles of his boots. Ethnographers' reports he'd read years ago began flooding his mind; they told of African hunters who used to chase antelope across the savannahs, and Tarahumara Indians who would race after a deer "until its hooves fell off." Lieberman had always shrugged them off as tall tales, fables of a golden age of heroes who'd never really existed. But now, he started to wonder. . . .

So how long would it take to actually run an animal to death? he asked himself. Luckily, the Harvard bio labs have the best locomotive research in the world (as their willingness to insert a thermometer in a cheetah's butt should make clear), so all the data Lieberman needed was right at his fingertips. When he got back to his office, he began punching in numbers. *Let's see,* he began. A jogger in decent shape averages about three to four meters a second. A deer trots at almost the identical pace. But here's the kicker: when a deer wants to accelerate to four meters a second, it has to break into a heavy-breathing gallop, *while a human can go just as fast and still be in his jogging zone.* A deer is way faster at a sprint, but we're faster at a jog; so when Bambi is already edging into oxygen debt, we're barely breathing hard.

Lieberman kept looking, and found an even more telling comparison: the top galloping speed for most horses is 7.7 meters a second. They can hold that pace for about ten minutes, then have to slow to 5.8 meters a second. But an elite marathoner can jog for hours at 6 meters a second. The horse will erupt away from the starting line, as Dennis Poolheco had discovered in the Man Against Horse Race, but with enough patience and distance, you can slowly close the gap.

You don't even have to go fast, Lieberman realized. *All you have to do is keep the animal in sight, and within ten minutes, you're reeling him in.*

Lieberman began calculating temperatures, speed, and body weight. Soon, there it was before him: the solution to the Running Man mystery. To run an antelope to death, Lieberman determined, all you have to do is scare it into a gallop on a hot day. "If you keep just close enough for it to see you, it will keep sprinting away. After about ten or fifteen kilometers' worth of running, it will go into hyperthermia and collapse." Translation: if you can run six miles on a summer day, then you, my friend, are a lethal weapon in the animal kingdom. We can dump heat on the run, but animals can't pant while they gallop.

"We can run in conditions that no other animal can run in," Lieberman realized. "And it's not even hard. If a middle-aged professor can outrun a dog on a hot day, imagine what a pack of motivated hunter-gatherers could do to an overheated antelope."

It's easy to picture the scorn on the faces of those Masters of the Universe, the Neanderthals, as they watched these new Running Men puffing along behind bouncy little Bambis, or jogging all day under a hot sun to return with nothing but an armload of yams. The Running Men could get a load of meat by running, but they couldn't run with a belly load of meat, so most of the time they carbo-loaded on roots and fruits, saving the antelope chops for special, calorie-boosting occasions. Everyone scavenged together—Running Men, Running Women, Running Kids, and Grampies—but despite all that team activity, they were more likely to dine on grubs than wild game.

Bleh. Neanderthals wouldn't touch bugs and dirt food; they ate meat and only meat, and not gristly little antelopes, either. Neanderthals went Grade A all the way: bears, bison, and elk marbled with juicy fat, rhinos with livers rich in iron, mammoths with luscious, oily brains and bones dripping with lip-smacking marrow. Try chasing monsters like those, though, and they'll be chasing you. Instead, you've got to outsmart and outfight them. The Neanderthals would lure them into ambushes and launch a pincer attack, storming from all sides with eight-foot wooden lances. Hunting like that isn't for the meek; Neanderthals were known to suffer the kind of injuries you find on the rodeo circuit, neck and head trauma from getting thrown by bucking beasts, but they could count on their band of brothers to care for their wounds and bury their bodies. Unlike our true ancestors, those scampering Running Men, the Neanderthals were the mighty hunters we like to imagine we once were; they stood shoulder to shoulder in battle, a united front of brains and bravery, clever warriors armored with muscle but still refined enough to slow-cook their meat to tenderness in earth ovens and keep their women and children away from the danger.

Neanderthals ruled the world—till it started getting nice outside. About forty-five thousand years ago, the Long Winter ended and a hot front moved in. The forests shrank, leaving behind parched grasslands stretching to the horizon. The new climate was great for the Running Men; the antelope herds exploded and feasts of plump roots were pushing up all over the savannah.

The Neanderthals had it tougher; their long spears and canyon ambushes were useless against the fleet prairie creatures, and the big game they preferred was retreating deeper into the dwindling forests. Well, why didn't they just adopt the hunting strategy of the Running Men? They were smart and certainly strong enough, but that was the problem; they were *too* strong. Once temperatures climb above 90 degrees Fahrenheit, a few extra pounds of body weight make a huge difference—so much so that to maintain heat balance, a 160-pound runner would lose nearly three minutes *per mile* in a marathon against a one hundred-pound runner. In a two-hour pursuit of a deer, the Running Men would leave the Neanderthal competition more than ten miles behind.

Smothered in muscle, the Neanderthals followed the mastodons into the dying forest, and oblivion. The new world was made for runners, and running just wasn't their thing.

Privately, David Carrier knew the Running Man theory had a fatal flaw. The secret gnawed until it nearly turned him into a killer.

"Yeah, I was kind of obsessed," he admitted when I met him at his lab in the University of Utah, twenty-five years and three academic degrees since his moment of inspiration at the dissecting table in 1982. He was now David Carrier, Ph.D., professor of biology, with gray in his push-broom mustache and rimless round glasses over his intense brown eyes. "I was dying to just grab something with my own two hands and say, 'Look! Satisfied now?' "

The problem was this: Chasing an animal to death is evolution's version of the perfect crime. Persistence hunting (as it's known to anthropologists) leaves behind no forensics—no arrowheads, no spear-nicked deer spines—so how do you build a case that a killing took place when you can't produce a corpse, a weapon, or witnesses? Despite Dr. Bramble's physiological brilliance and Dr. Lieberman's fossil expertise, there was no way they could prove that our legs were once lethal weapons if they couldn't show that *someone*, somewhere, had actually run an animal to death. You can spout any theory you want about human performance ("We can suspend our own heartbeats! We can bend spoons with our brains!") but in the end, you can't make the shift from appealing notion to empirical fact if you don't come up with the goods.

"The frustrating thing is, we were finding stories all over the place," David Carrier said. Throw a dart at the map, and chances are you'll bull's-eye the site of a persistence-hunting tale. The Goshutes and Papago tribes of the American West told them; so did the Kalahari Bushmen in Botswana, the Aborigines in Australia, Masai warriors in Kenya, the Seri and Tarahumara Indians in Mexico. The trouble was, those legends were fourth- or fifth-hand at best; there was as much evidence to support them as there was that Davy Crockett kilt him a b'ar when he was only three.

"We couldn't find anyone who'd done a persistence hunt," David said. "We couldn't find someone who'd even *seen* one." No wonder the scientific community remained skeptical. If the Running Man theory was right, then at least one person on this planet of six billion should still be able to catch quarry on foot. We may have lost the tradition and necessity, but we should still have the native ability: our DNA hasn't changed in centuries and is 99.9 percent identical across the globe, meaning we've all got the same stock parts as any ancient hunter-gatherer. So how come none of us could catch a stinking deer?

"That's why I decided to do it myself," David said. "As an undergrad, I got into mountain races and had a lot of fun at those. So when it came to how humans breathe differently when we run, I think it was easier for me to see how it could affect us as a species. The idea didn't seem as strange to me as it would for someone who never left the lab."

Nor did it seem strange to him that if he couldn't find a caveman, he could become one. In the summer of 1984, David persuaded his brother, Scott, a freelance writer and reporter for National Public Radio, to go to Wyoming and help him catch a wild antelope. Scott wasn't much of a runner, but David was in great shape and fiercely motivated by the lure of scientific immortality. Between him and his light and loose, even more springy and energized than I had before the start.

"Way to go, Oso!" Bob Francis was calling from the opposite bank. "Little bitty hill ahead. Nothing to worry about."

I scrambled out of the water and up the sand dune, growing more hopeful with every step. Sure, I still had forty-eight more miles, but the way it was going, I might be able to steal the first dozen or so before I had to make any real effort. I started climbing the dirt trail just as the sun was slanting over the top of the canyon. Instantly, everything lit up: the glittering river, the shimmering green forest, the coral snake coiled at my feet. . . .

I yelped and leaped off the trail, sliding down the steep slope and grabbing at scrub brush to stop my fall. I could see the snake above me, silent and curled, ready to strike. If I climbed back up, I risked a fatal bite; if I climbed down toward the river, I could plunge off the side of the cliff. The only way out was to maneuver sideways, working my way from one scrub-brush handhold to the next.

The first clump held, then the next. When I'd made it ten feet away, I cautiously hauled myself back onto the trail. The snake was still blocking the trail, and for good reason—it was dead. Someone had already snapped its back with a stick. I wiped the dirt out of my eyes and checked the damage: rock rash down both shins, thorns in my hands, heart pounding through my chest. I pulled the thorns with my teeth, then cleaned my gashes, more or less, with a squirt from my water bottle. Time to get going. I didn't want anyone to come across me bleeding and panicky over a rotting snake.

The sun got stronger the higher I climbed, but after the early-morning chill, it was more exhilarating than exhausting. I kept thinking about Eric's advice—"If it feels like work, you're working too hard"—so I decided to get outside my head and stop obsessing about my stride. I began drinking in the view of canyon around me, watching the sun turn the top of the foothill across the river to gold. Pretty soon, I realized, I'd be nearly as high as that peak.

Moments later, Scott burst around a bend in the trail. He flashed me a grin and a thumbs-up, then vanished. Arnulfo and Silvino were right behind him, their blouses rippling like sails as they flew past. I must be close to the five-mile turnaround, I realized. I climbed around the next curve, and there it was: Guadalupe Coronado. It was little more than a whitewashed schoolhouse, a few small homes, and a tiny shop selling warm sodas and dusty packs of cookies, but even from a mile away, I could already hear cheers and drumbeats.

A pack of runners was just pulling out of Guadalupe and setting off in pursuit of Scott and the Quimares. Leading them, all by herself, was the Brujita.

The second Jenn saw her chance, she pounced. On the hike over from Batopilas, she'd noticed that the Tarahumara run downhill the same way they run up, with a controlled, steady flow. Jenn, on the other hand, loves to pound the descents. "It's the only strength I've got," she says, "so I milk it for all I'm worth." So instead of exhausting herself by dueling with Herbolisto, she decided to let him set the pace for the climb. As soon as they reached the turnaround and started the long downhill, she broke out of the chase pack and began speeding off.

This time, the Tarahumara let her go. She pulled so far ahead that by the time she hit the next uphill—a rocky single track climbing to the second branch of the Y at mile 15—Herbolisto and the pack couldn't get close enough to swarm her. Jenn was feeling so confident that when she reached the turnaround, she stopped to take a breather and refill her bottle. Her luck with water so far had been fabulous; Caballo had asked Urique villagers to fan out through the canyons with jugs of purified water, and it seemed that every time Jenn took her last swallow, she came across another volunteer.

She was still gurgling her full bottle when Herbolisto, Sebastiano, and the rest of the chase pack finally caught her. They spun around without stopping, and Jenn let them go. Once she was rewatered, she began pounding down the hill. Within two miles, she'd once again reeled them in and left them behind. She began mentally scanning the course ahead to calculate how long she could keep pulling away. Let's see . . . upcoming was two miles of descent, then four flat miles back into the village, then—

Wham! Jenn landed facedown on the rocks, bouncing and sliding on her chest before coming to a stunned stop. She lay there, blinded with pain. Her kneecap felt broken and an arm was smeared with blood. Before she could gather herself to try getting to her feet, Herbolisto and the chase pack came storming down the trail. One by one, they hurdled Jenn and disappeared, never looking back.

They're thinking, That's what you get for not knowing how to run on the rocks, Jenn thought. *Well, they've got a point.* Gingerly, she pulled herself to her feet to assess the damage. Her shins looked like pizza, but her kneecap was only bruised and the blood she thought was pouring from her hand turned out to be chocolaty goo from an exploded PowerGel packet she'd stashed in her handheld. Jenn walked a few cautious steps, then jogged, and felt better than she expected. She felt so good, in fact, that by the time she reached the bottom of the hill, she'd caught and passed every one of the Tarahumara who'd jumped over her.

"*¡BRUJITA!*" The crowd in Urique went crazy when Jenn came racing back through the village, bloody but smiling as she hit the twenty-mile mark. She paused at the aid station to dig a fresh goo out of her drop bag, while a deliriously happy Mamá Tita dabbed at Jenn's gory shins with her apron and kept shouting "*¡Cuarto! ¡Estás en cuarto lugar!*"

"I'm a what? A room?" Jenn was halfway out of town again before her rickety Spanish let her figure out what Mama Tita was talking about: she was in fourth place. Only Scott, Arnulfo, and Silvino were still ahead of her, and she was nibbling steadily at their lead. Caballo had picked her spirit name perfectly: twelve years after Leadville, the Bruja was back with a vengeance.

But only if she could handle the heat. The temperature was nearing 100 degrees just as Jenn was entering the furnace—the jagged up-and-down climb to the Los Alisos settlement. The trail hugged a sheer rock wall that plunged and soared and plunged again, gaining and losing some three thousand feet. Any of the hills in the Los Alisos stretch would rank among the hardest Jenn had ever seen, and there were at least half a dozen of them, strung one behind the other. The heat shimmering off the rocks felt as if it was blistering her skin, but she had to stick tight to the canyon wall to avoid slipping off the edge and into the gorge below.

Jenn had just reached the top of one of the hills when she suddenly had to leap against the wall: Arnulfo and Silvino were *blazing* toward her, running shoulder to shoulder. The Deer hunters had taken everyone by surprise; we'd expected the Tarahumara to haunt

Scott's heels all day and then try to blast past him at the finish, but instead, the Deer hunters had pulled a fast one and jumped out first.

Jenn pressed her back against the hot rock to let them pass. Before she had time to wonder where Scott was, she was leaping back against the wall again. "Scott is running up this goddamn thing with the most intensity I've ever seen in a human being," Jenn said later. "He's *booking*, going, '*Huh-Huh-Huh-Huh.*' I'm wondering if he's even going to acknowledge me, he's so in the zone. Then he looks up and starts screaming, 'Yaaaah, Brujita, *whooooo!*' "

Scott stopped to brief Jenn on the trail ahead and let her know where to expect water drops. Then he quizzed her about Arnulfo and Silvino: How far ahead were they? How did they look? Jenn figured they were maybe three minutes out and pushing hard.

"Good," Scott nodded. He swatted her on the back and shot off.

Jenn watched him go, and noticed he was running on the very edge of the trail and sticking tight to the turns. That was an old Marshall Ulrich trick: it made it harder for the guy in the lead to glance back and see you sneak up from behind. Scott hadn't been surprised by Arnulfo's big move after all. The Deer was hunting the hunters.

"Just beat the course," I told myself. "No one else. Just the course."

Before I tackled the climb to Los Alisos, I stopped to get myself under control. I ducked my head in the river and held it there, hoping the water would cool me off and the oxygen debt would snap me back to reality. I'd just hit the halfway point, and it had only taken me about four hours. Four hours, for a hard trail marathon in desert heat! I was so far ahead of schedule, I'd started getting competitive: *How hard can it be to pick off Barefoot Ted? He's got to be hurting on those stones. And Porfilio looked like he was struggling. . . .*

Luckily, the head-dunking worked. The reason I was feeling so much stronger today than I had on the long haul over from Batopilas, I realized, was because I was running like the Kalahari Bushmen. I wasn't trying to overtake the antelope; I was just keeping it in sight. What had killed me during the Batopilas hike was keeping pace with Caballo & Co. So far today, I'd only competed against the race-course, not the racers.

Before I got too ambitious, it was time to try another Bushman tactic and give myself a systems check. When I did, I noticed I was in rougher shape than I'd thought. I was thirsty, hungry, and down to just half a bottle of water. I hadn't taken a leak in over an hour, which wasn't a good sign considering all the water I'd been drinking. If I didn't rehydrate soon and get some calories down my neck, I'd be in serious trouble in the roller coaster of hills ahead. As I started sloshing the fifty yards across the river, I filled the bladder of my empty hydration pack with river water and dropped in a few iodine pills. I'd give that a half hour to purify, while I washed down a ProBar—a chewy raw-food blend of rolled oats, raisins, dates, and brown rice syrup—with the last of my clean water.

Good thing I did. "Brace yourself," Eric called as we passed each other on the far side of the river. "It's a lot rougher up there than you remember." The hills were so tough, Eric admitted, that he'd been on the verge of dropping out himself. A bad-news burst like that could come across as a punch in the gut, but Eric believes the worst thing you can give a runner midrace is false hope. What causes you to tense up is the unexpected; but as long as you know what you're in for, you can relax and chip away at the job.

Eric hadn't exaggerated. For over an hour, I climbed up and down the foothills, convinced I was lost and on the way to disappearing into the wilderness. There was only one trail and I was on it—but where the hell was the little grapefruit orchard at Los Alisos? It was only supposed to be four miles from the river, but I'd felt as if I'd covered ten and I still couldn't see it. Finally, when my thighs were burning and twitching so badly I thought I was going to collapse, I spotted a cluster of grapefruit trees on a hill ahead. I made it to the top, and dropped down next to a group of the Urique Tarahumara. They'd heard they were disqualified and decided to cool off in the shade before walking back to the village.

"*No hay problema*," one of them said. It's not a problem. "I was too tired to keep going anyway." He handed me an old tin cup. I scooped into the communal *pinole* pot, giardia be damned. It was cool and deliciously grainy, like a popcorn Slushee. I gulped down a cupful, then another, as I looked back at the trail I'd just covered. Far below, the river was faint as fading sidewalk chalk. I couldn't believe I'd run here from there. Or that I was about to do it again.

––––––

"It's *unbelievable*!" Caballo gasped.

He was slick with sweat and bug-eyed with excitement. As he struggled to catch his breath, he sluiced sweat off his dripping chest and flung it past me, the shower of droplets sparkling in the blazing Mexican sun. "We've got a world-class event going on!" Caballo panted. "Out here in the middle of nowhere!"

By the forty-two-mile mark, Silvino and Arnulfo were still ahead of Scott, while Jenn was creeping up behind all three. On her second pass through Urique, Jenn had dropped into a chair to drink a Coke, but Mamá Tita grabbed her under the arms and hauled her to her feet.

"*¡Puedes, cariño, puedes!*" Tita cried. You can do it, sweetie!

"I'm not dropping out," Jenn tried to protest. "I just need a drink."

But Tita's hands were in Jenn's back, pushing her back into the street. Just in time, too; Herbolisto and Sebastiano had taken advantage of the flat road into town to move back within a quarter mile of Jenn, while Billy Bonehead had broken free of Luis to move within a quarter mile of *them*.

"This is anybody's day!" Caballo said. He was trailing the leaders by about a half hour, and it was driving him batty. Not because he was losing; because he was in danger of missing the finish. The suspense was so unbearable, Caballo finally decided to drop out of his own race and cut back to Urique to see if he could get there in time for the final showdown.

I watched him run off, desperate to follow. I was so tired, I couldn't find my way to the skinny cable bridge over the river and somehow ended up under it, forcing me to splash through the river for the fourth time. My soaked feet felt too heavy to lift as I shuffled through the sand on the far side. I'd been out here all day, and now I was at the bottom of that same endless Alpine climb I'd almost fallen off this morning when I'd gotten spooked by the dead snake. There was no way I'd get down before sunset, so this time, I'd be stumbling back in the dark.

I dropped my head and started trudging. When I looked up again, Tarahumara kids were all around me. I closed my eyes, then opened them again. The kids were still there. I was so glad they weren't a hallucination, I was almost weepy. Where they'd come from and why they'd chosen to tag along with me, I had no idea. Together, we made our way higher and higher up the hill.

After we'd gone about half a mile, they darted up a nearly invisible side trail and waved for me to follow.

"I can't," I told them regretfully.

They shrugged, and ran off into the brush. "*¡Gracias!*" I rasped, missing them already. I kept pushing up the hill, shambling along at a trot that couldn't have been faster than a walk. When I hit a short plateau, the kids were sitting there, waiting. So *that's* how the Urique Tarahumara were able to break open such big leads. The kids hopped up and ran alongside me until, once again, they vanished into the brush. A half mile later, they popped out again. This was turning into a nightmare: I kept running and running, but nothing changed. The hill stretched on forever, and everywhere I looked, Children of the Corn appeared.

What would Caballo do? I wondered. He was always getting himself into hopeless predicaments out here in the canyons, and he always found a way to run his way out. *He'd start with easy*, I told myself. *Because if that's all you get, that's not so bad. Then he'd work on light. He'd make it effortless, like he didn't care how high the hill is or how far he had got to go—*

"OSO!" Heading toward me was Barefoot Ted, and he looked frantic.

"Some boys gave me some water and it felt so cold, I figured I'd use it to cool down," Barefoot Ted said. "So I'm squirting myself all over, spraying it around . . ."

I had trouble following Barefoot Ted's story, because his voice was fading in and out like a badly tuned radio. My blood sugars were so low, I realized, I was on the verge of bonking.

". . . and then I'm going, 'Crap, oh crap, I'm out of water—' "

From what I could make out from Barefoot Ted's yammering, it was maybe a mile to the turnaround. I listened impatiently, desperate to push on to the aid station so I could chow down an energy bar and take a break before tackling the final five miles.

". . . So I tell myself if I've got to pee, I'd better pee into one of these bottles in case I'm down to the last, you know, the last of the last. So I pee into this bottle and it's like, *orange*. It's not looking good. And it's *hot*. I think people were watching me pee in my bottle and thinking, 'Wow, these gringos are really tough.' "

"Wait," I said, starting to understand. "You're not drinking piss?"

"It was the *worst!* The worst-tasting urine I've ever tasted in my entire life. You could bottle this stuff and sell it to bring people back from the dead. I know you can drink urine, but not if it's been heated and shaken in your kidneys for forty miles. It was a failed experiment. I wouldn't drink that urine if it was the last liquid on planet Earth."

"Here," I said, offering the last of my water. I had no idea why he hadn't just gone back to the aid station and refilled if he was so worried, but I was too exhausted to ask any more questions. Barefoot Ted dumped his whiz, refilled his bottle, and padded off. Odd as he was, there was no denying his resourcefulness and determination; he was less than five miles from finishing a 50-mile race in his rubber toe slippers, and he'd been willing to drink bodily waste to get there.

Only after I arrived at the Guadalupe turnaround did it finally penetrate my woozy mind why Barefoot was dry in the first place: all the water was gone. All the people, too. Everyone in the village had trooped into Urique for the postrace party, closing up the little shop and leaving no one behind to point out the wells. I slumped down on a rock. My head was reeling, and my mouth was too cottony to let me chew food. Even if I managed to choke down a few bites, I was way too dehydrated to make the hour-long run to the finish. The only way to get back to Urique was on foot, but I was too wasted to walk.

"So much for compassion," I muttered to myself. "I give something away, and what do I get? Screwed."

As I sat, defeated, my heavy breathing from the hard climb slowed enough for me to become aware of another sound—a weird, warbling whistle that seemed to be getting closer. I pulled myself up for a look, and there, heading up this lost hill, was old Bob Francis.

"Hey, amigo," Bob called, fishing two cans of mango juice out of his shoulder bag and shaking them over his head. "Thought you could use a drink."

I was stunned. Old Bob had hiked five miles of hard trails in 95-degree heat to bring me juice? But then I remembered: a few days before, Bob had admired the knife I'd lent Barefoot Ted to make his sandals. It was a memento from expeditions in Africa, but Bob had been so kind to all of us that I had to give it to him. Maybe Bob's miracle delivery was just a lucky coincidence, but as I gulped the juice and got ready to run to the finish, I couldn't help feeling that the last piece of the Tarahumara puzzle had just snapped into place.

Caballo and Tita were jammed into the crowd at the finish line, craning their necks for the first glimpse of the leaders. Caballo pulled an old, broken-strapped Timex out of his pocket and checked the time. Six hours. That was probably way too fast, but there was a chance that—

"*¡Vienen!*" someone shouted. They're coming!

Caballo's head jerked up. He squinted down the straight road, peering through the bobbing heads of dancers. False alarm. Just a cloud of dust and—no, there it was. Bouncing dark hair and a crimson blouse. Arnulfo still had the lead.

Silvino was in second, but Scott was closing fast. With a mile to go, Scott ran Silvino down. But instead of blowing past, Scott slapped him on the back. "C'mon!" Scott shouted, waving for Silvino to come with him. Startled, Silvino reached deep and managed to match Scott stride for stride. Together, they bore down on Arnulfo.

Screams and cheers drowned out the mariachi band as the three runners made their last push toward the finish. Silvino faltered, surged again, but couldn't hold Scott's pace. Scott drove on. He'd been in this spot before, and he'd always found something left. Arnulfo glanced back and saw the man who'd beaten the best in the world coming after him with everything he had. Arnulfo blazed through the heart of Urique, the screams building as he got closer and closer to the tape. When he snapped it, Tita was in tears.

The crowd had already swallowed Arnulfo by the time Scott crossed the line in second. Caballo rushed over to congratulate him, but Scott pushed past him without a word. Scott wasn't used to losing, especially not to some no-name guy in a pickup race in the middle of nowhere. This had never happened to him before—but he knew what to do about it.

Scott walked up to Arnulfo and bowed.

The crowd went crazy. Tita rushed over to hug Caballo and found him wiping his eyes. In the midst of this pandemonium, Silvino struggled across the finish line, followed by Herbolisto and Sebastiano.

And Jenn? Her decision to win or die trying had finally caught up with her.

By the time she arrived at Guadalupe, Jenn was ready to faint. She slumped down against a tree and dropped her dizzy head between her knees. A group of Tarahumara clustered around, trying to encourage Jenn back to her feet. She lifted head and mimed drinking.

"¿*Agua?*" she asked. "¿*Agua purificada?*"

Someone shoved a warm Coke into her hand.

"Even better," she said, and smiled wearily.

She was still sipping the soda when a shout went up. Sebastiano and Herbolisto were running into the village. Jenn lost sight of them when the crowd thronged around to offer congratulations and *pinole*. Then Herbolisto was standing over her, stretching out his hand. With the other, he pointed toward the trail. Was she coming? Jenn shook her head. "Not yet," she said. Herbolisto started to run, then stopped and walked back. He put out his hand again. Jenn smiled and waved him off. "Get going, already!" Herbolisto waved good-bye.

Soon after he disappeared down the trail, the shouting began again. Someone relayed Jenn the information: the Wolf was coming.

Bonehead! Jenn saved him a long sip of her Coke, and pulled herself to her feet while he downed it. For all the times they'd paced each other and all the sunset runs they'd done on Virginia Beach, they'd never actually finished a race side by side.

"Ready?" Billy said.

"You're toast, dude."

Together, they flew down the long hill and thundered across the swaying bridge. They came into Urique whooping and hollering, redeeming themselves magnificently; despite Jenn's bloody legs and Billy's narcoleptic approach to prerace prep, they'd beaten all but four of the Tarahumara as well as Luis and Eric, two highly experienced ultrarunners.

Manuel Luna had dropped out halfway. Though he'd done his best to come through for Caballo, the ache of his son's death left him too leaden to compete. But while he couldn't get his heart into the racing, he was fully committed to one of the racers. Manuel prowled up and down the road, watching for Barefoot Ted. Soon, he was joined by Arnulfo . . . and Scott . . . and Jenn and Billy. Something odd began to happen: as the runners got slower, the cheers got wilder. Every time a racer struggled across the finish—Luis and Porfilio, Eric and Barefoot Ted—they immediately turned around and began calling home the runners still out there.

From high on the hill, I could see the twinkle of the red and green lights strung above the road to Urique. The sun had set, leaving me running through that silvery-gray dusk of the deep canyons, a moon-like glow that lingers, unchanging, until you feel everything is frozen in time except you. And then, from out of those milky shadows, emerged the lone wanderer of the High Sierras.

"Want some company?" Caballo said.

"Love it."

Together, we clattered across the swaying bridge, the cool air off the river making me feel oddly weightless. When we hit the last stretch into town, trumpets began blasting. Side by side, stride for stride, Caballo and I ran into Urique.

I don't know if I actually crossed a finish line. All I saw was a pig-tailed blur as Jenn came flying out of the crowd, knocking me staggering. Eric caught me before I hit the ground and pushed a cold bottle of water against the back of my neck. Arnulfo and Scott, their eyes already bloodshot, pushed a beer into each of my hands.

"You were amazing," Scott said.

"Yeah," I said. "Amazingly slow." It had taken me over twelve hours, meaning that Scott and Arnulfo could have run the course all over again and still beaten me.

"That's what I'm saying," Scott insisted. "I've been there, man. I've been there *a lot*. It takes more guts than going fast."

I limped over toward Caballo, who was sprawled under a tree as the party raged around him. Soon, he'd get to his feet and give a wonderful speech in his wacky Spanish. He'd bring forward Bob Francis, who'd walk back into town just in time to present Scott with a ceremonial Tarahumara belt and Arnulfo with a pocketknife of his own. Caballo would hand out prize money, and get choked up when the Party Kids, who could barely pay for the bus back to El Paso, immediately gave their cash to the Tarahumara runners who'd finished behind them. Caballo would roar with laughter as Herbolisto and Luis danced the Robot.

But that would all come later. For now, Caballo was content to just sit alone under a tree, smiling and sipping a beer, watching his dream play out before his eyes.

CHAPTER 32

That head of his has been occupied with contemporary
society's insoluble problems for so long, and he is
still battling on with his good-heartedness and boundless
energy. His efforts have not been in vain, but he will
probably not live to see them come to fruition.

—THEO VAN GOGH, 1889

"YOU'VE GOT TO HEAR THIS," Barefoot Ted said, grabbing my arm.

Damn. He caught me just as I was trying to slink away from the
madness of the street party and limp off to the hotel to collapse. I'd
already heard Barefoot Ted's entire postrace commentary, including
his observation that human urine is both nutrient-rich and an effective tooth whitener, and I couldn't imagine anything he could possibly say that would be more compelling than a deep sleep in a soft
bed. But it wasn't Ted telling stories this time. It was Caballo.

Barefoot Ted pulled me back into Mamá Tita's garden, where
Caballo was holding Scott and Billy and a few of the others spellbound. "You ever wake up in an emergency room," Caballo was saying, "and wondered whether you wanted to wake up at all?" With
that, he launched into the story I'd been waiting nearly two years to
hear. It didn't take me long to grasp why he'd chosen that moment.
At dawn, we'd all be scattering and heading home. Caballo didn't
want us to forget what we shared, so for the first time, he was revealing who he was.

He was born Michael Randall Hickman, son of a Marine Corps gunnery sergeant whose postings moved the family up and down the West Coast. As a skinny loner who constantly had to defend himself in new schools, young Mike's first priority every time they moved was to find the nearest Police Athletic League and sign up for boxing lessons.

Brawny kids would smirk and pound their gloves together as they watched the geek with the silky hippie hair gangle his way into the ring, but their grins died as soon as that long left arm began snapping jabs into their eyes. Mike Hickman was a sensitive kid who hated hurting people, but that didn't stop him from getting really good at it. "The guys I liked best were the big, muscular ones, 'cause they'd keep coming after me," he recalled. "But the first time I ever knocked out a guy, I cried. For a long time after that, I didn't knock out anybody."

After high school, Mike went off to Humboldt State to study Eastern religions and Native American history. To pay tuition, he began fighting in backroom smokers, billing himself as the Gypsy Cowboy. Because he was fearless about walking into gyms that rarely saw a white face, much less a vegetarian white face spouting off about universal harmony and wheatgrass juice, the Cowboy soon had all the action he could handle. Small-time Mexican promoters loved to pull him aside and whisper deals in his ear.

"*Oye, compay,*" they'd say. "Listen up, my friend. We're going to start a *chisme*, a little whisper, that you're a top amateur from back east. The gringos are gonna love it, man. Every *gabacho* in the house is going to bet their kids on you."

The Gypsy Cowboy shrugged. "Fine by me."

"Just dance around so you don't get slaughtered till the fourth," they'd warn him—or the third, or the seventh, whichever round the fix had been set for. The Cowboy could hold his own against gigantic black heavyweights by dodging and clinching up until it was time for him to hit the canvas, but against the speedy Latino middleweights, he had to fight for his life. "Man, sometimes they had to haul my bleeding butt out of there," he'd say. But even after leaving school, he stuck with it. "I just wandered the country fighting. Taking dives, winning some, losing but really winning others, mostly putting on good shows and learning how to fight and not get hurt."

After a few years of scrapping along in the fight game's underworld, the Cowboy took his winnings and flew to Maui. There, he turned his back on the resorts and headed east, toward the damp, dark side of the island and the hidden shrines of Hana. He was looking for a purpose for his life. Instead, he found Smitty, a hermit who lived in a hidden cave. Smitty led Mike to a cave of his own, then began guiding him to Maui's hidden sacred sites.

"Smitty is the guy who first got me into running," Caballo told us. Sometimes, they'd set out in the middle of the night to run the twenty miles up the Kaupo Trail to the House of the Sun at the top of 10,000-foot Mount Haleakala. They'd sit quietly as the first rays of morning sparkled on the Pacific, then run back down again, fueled only by wild papayas they'd knocked from the trees. Gradually, the backroom brawler named Mike Hickman disappeared. In his place arose Micah True, a name inspired by "the courageous and fearless spirit" of the Old Testament prophet Micah and the loyalty of an old mutt called True Dog. "I don't always live up to True Dog's example," Caballo would say. "But it's something to shoot for."

During one of his vision-seeking runs through the rain forest, the newly reborn Micah True met a beautiful young woman from Seattle who was visiting on vacation. They couldn't have been more different—Melinda was a psychology grad student and the daughter of a wealthy investment banker, while Micah was, quite literally, a caveman—but they fell in love. After a year in the wilderness, Micah decided it was time to return to the world.

Wham! The Gypsy Cowboy knocked out his third opponent . . .
. . . and his fourth . . .
. . . and his fifth . . .

With Melinda in his corner and those rain-forest runs powering his legs, Micah was virtually untouchable; he could dance and shuffle until the other fighter's arms felt like cement. Once his fists drooped, Micah would dart in and hammer him to the canvas. "I was inspired by love, man," Micah said. He and Melinda settled in Boulder, Colorado, where he could run the mountain trails and get bouts in Denver arenas.

"He sure didn't look like a fighter," Don Tobin, then the Rocky Mountain lightweight kickboxing champion, later told me. "He had real long hair and was carrying this crusty old pair of gloves, like they were handed down from Rocky Graziano." Don Tobin became the Cowboy's friend and occasional sparring partner, and to this day, he marvels at the Cowboy's work ethic. "He was doing unbelievable training on his own. For his thirtieth birthday, he went out and ran thirty miles. *Thirty miles!*" Few American marathoners were putting up those numbers.

By the time his unbeaten streak reached 12–0, the Cowboy's reputation was formidable enough to land him on the cover of Denver's weekly newspaper, *Westword*. Under the headline FIST CITY was a full-page photo of Micah, bare-chested and sweaty, fists cocked and hair swinging, his eyes in the same glower I saw twenty years later when I surprised him in Creel. "I'll fight anybody for the right amount of money," the Cowboy was quoted as saying.

Anybody, eh? That article fell into the hands of an ESPN kick-boxing promoter, who quickly tracked down the Cowboy and made an offer. Even though Micah was a boxer, not a kickboxer, she was willing to put him in the ring for a nationally televised bout against Larry Shepherd, America's fourth-ranked light heavyweight. Micah loved the publicity and the big payday, but smelled a rat. Just a few months before, he had been a homeless hippie meditating on a mountaintop; now, they were pitting him against a martial artist who could break cinder blocks with his head. "It was all a big joke to them, man," Micah says. "I was this long-haired hippie they wanted to shove into the ring for laughs."

What happened next summarizes Caballo's entire life story: the easiest choices he ever had to make were the ones between prudence and pride. When the bell clanged on ESPN's *Superfight Night*, the Gypsy Cowboy abandoned his usual canny strategy of dodging and dancing. Instead, he sprinted self-righteously across the ring and battered Shepherd with a furious barrage of lefts and rights. "He didn't know what I was doing, so he covered up in the corner to figure it out," Micah would recall. Micah cocked his right arm for a haymaker, but got a better idea. "I kicked him in the face so hard, I broke my toe," Micah says. "And his nose."

Dingdingding.

Micah's arm was jerked into the air, while a doctor began probing Shepherd's eyes to make sure his retinas were still attached. Another KO for the Gypsy Cowboy. He couldn't wait to get back home to celebrate with Melinda. But Melinda, he discovered, had a knockout of her own to deliver. And long before that conversation was over—long before she'd finished telling him about the affair and her plans to leave him for another man and move back to Seattle—Micah's brain was buzzing with questions. Not for her; for him.

He'd just smashed a man's face on national TV, and why? To be great in someone else's eyes? To be a performer whose achievements were only measured by someone else's affection? He wasn't stupid; he could connect the dots between the nervous boy with the Great Santini dad and the lonely, love-hungry drifter he'd become. Was he a great fighter, in other words, or just a needy one?

Soon after, *Karate* magazine called. The year-end rankings were about to come out, the reporter said, and the Gypsy Cowboy's upset had made him the fifth-ranked light-heavyweight kickboxer in America. The Cowboy's career was about to skyrocket; once *Karate* hit the stands and the offers started pouring in, he'd have plenty of big-money opportunities to find out whether he truly loved fighting, or was fighting to be loved.

"Excuse me," Micah told the reporter. "But I just decided to retire."

Making the Gypsy Cowboy disappear was even simpler than dispensing with Mike Hickman. Everything Micah couldn't carry on his back was discarded. The phone was disconnected, the apartment abandoned. Home became a '69 Chevy pickup. By night, he slept in a sleeping bag in the back. By day, he hired himself out to mow lawns and move furniture. Every hour in between, he ran. If he couldn't have Melinda, he'd settle for exhaustion. "I'd get up at four-thirty in the morning, run twenty miles, and it would be a beautiful thing," Micah said. "Then I'd work all day and want to feel that way again. So I'd go home, drink a beer, eat some beans, and run some more."

He had no idea if he was fast or slow, talented or terrible, until one summer weekend in 1986 when he drove up to Laramie, Wyoming, to take a stab at the Rocky Mountain Double Marathon. He surprised even himself by winning in six hours and twelve minutes, knocking off back-to-back trail marathons in a scratch over three hours each. Racing ultras, he discovered, was even tougher than prizefighting. In the ring, the other fighter determines how hard you're hit, but on the trail, your punishment is in your own hands. For a guy looking to beat himself into numbness, extreme running could be an awfully attractive sport.

Maybe I could even go pro, if I could just get over these nagging injuries. . . . That thought was running through Micah's mind as he coasted on his bike down a steep Boulder street. Next thing he knew, he was blinking into bright lights in the emergency room of Boulder Community Hospital, his eyes caked with blood and his forehead full of stitches. Best he could recall, he'd hit a gravel slick and sailed over the handlebars.

"You're lucky you're alive," the doctor told him, which was one way of looking at it. Another was that death was still a problem hanging over his head. Micah had just turned forty-one, and despite his ultrarunning prowess, the view from that ER gurney was none too pretty. He had no health insurance, no home, no close family, and no steady work. He didn't have enough money to stay overnight for observation, and he didn't have a bed to recover on if he checked out.

Poor and free was the way he'd chosen to live, but was it the way he wanted to die? A friend let Micah mend on her sofa, and there, for the next few days, he pondered his future. Only lucky rebels go out in a blaze of glory, as Micah knew very well. Ever since second grade, he'd idolized Geronimo, the Apache brave who used to escape the U.S. cavalry by running through the Arizona badlands on foot. But how did Geronimo end up? As a prisoner, dying drunk in a ditch on a dusty reservation.

Once Micah recovered, he headed to Leadville. And there, during a magical night running through the woods with Martimano Cervantes, he found his answers. Geronimo couldn't run free forever, but maybe a "gringo Indio" could. A gringo Indio who owed nothing, needed no one, and wasn't afraid to disappear from the planet without a trace.

"So what do you live on?" I asked.

"Sweat," Caballo said. Every summer, he leaves his hut and rides buses back to Boulder, where his ancient pickup truck awaits him behind the house of a friendly farmer. For two or three months, he resumes the identity of Micah True and scrounges up freelance furniture-moving jobs. As soon as he has enough cash to last another year, he's gone, vanishing down to the bottom of the canyons and stepping back into the sandals of El Caballo Blanco.

"When I get too old to work, I'll do what Geronimo would've if they'd left him alone," Caballo said. "I'll walk off into the deep canyons and find a quiet place to lie down." There was no melo-drama or self-pity in the way Caballo said this, just the understanding that someday, the life he'd chosen would require one last disappear-ing act.

"So maybe I'll see you all again," Caballo concluded, as Tita was killing the lights and shooing us off to bed. "Or maybe I won't."

By sunup the next morning, the soldiers of Urique were waiting by the old minibus that was idling outside Tita's restaurant. When Jenn arrived, they snapped to attention.

"*Hasta luego*, Brujita," they called.

Jenn blew them screen-siren kisses with a big sweep of her arm, then climbed aboard. Barefoot Ted got on next, climbing up gin-gerly. His feet were so thickly swathed in cloth bandages, they barely fit inside his Japanese bathhouse flip-flops. "They're not bad, really," he insisted. "Just a little tender." He squeezed in next to Scott, who willingly slid over to make room.

The rest of us filed in and made our sore bodies as comfortable as possible for the jouncing trip ahead. The village tortilla-maker (who's also the village barber, shoemaker, and bus driver) slid behind the wheel and revved the rattling engine. Outside, Caballo and Bob Francis walked the length of the bus, pressing their hands against each of our windows.

Manuel Luna, Arnulfo, and Silvino stood next to them as the bus pulled out. The rest of the Tarahumara had set off already on the long hike home, but even though these three had the greatest distance to travel, they'd waited around to see us off. For a long time afterward, I could see them standing in the road, waving, until the entire town of Urique disappeared behind us in a cloud of dust.

Table of Contents

•

The book you are about to read is true. Some of the names and places have been changed to protect the innocent, my clients, and—most of all—me.

CHAPTER I

•

Death Wish

"The shadow of Babylon had fallen over Hollywood, a serpent spell in code cuneiform; scandal was waiting just out of camera range."
—Kenneth Anger, *Hollywood Babylon*

Here in Hollywood, drugs are no big deal. In some circles, a little coke is a normal part of the daily routine. Uppers and downers are about as hard to score as vitamin C and aspirin. So what else is new? At one time, I had a fairly casual attitude about drug use. No more.

Early in my career, I worked for Judy Garland—a legendary performer whose drug problem kicked in when she first started working in films. In those early days, the little pills they gave Judy to put her to sleep and keep her functioning on the set were thought to be relatively harmless mood enhancers. At least that's what the studio moguls and doctors claimed after drugs had destroyed her life.

Judy lasted into her forties—a ripe old age for a show biz druggie. Hell, poor River Phoenix never made it out of his twenties. Neither did Charles Bronson's stepson Jason—a kid I felt close to. His death still haunts me.

I remember the first time I met Charles Bronson and his wife, actress Jill Ireland. The Bronsons' attorney, Guy Ward, had called to explain that Jill's adopted son from her first marriage to the English actor David McCallum was in some kind of trouble. Guy routinely turned to me when his celebrity clients or their children got in over their heads.

I've worked for some strange characters, but I've never come across a client as difficult as Charlie. From the first, he seemed determined to take me on at every turn—even if it destroyed our chances of success.

I didn't have much information when I walked into the Bronsons' beautiful Bel Air home. What I knew was that seventeen-year-old

Jason was deeply involved with drugs. He was also in the midst of an affair with a friend of Jill's—an older married woman whose rock-star husband was reputed to have ties to organized crime. The parents wanted me to find out exactly what Jason was up to and clean up the mess.

I was led into a spacious den. The instant Charles Bronson and I were introduced, he began shouting:

"Are you going to take a deposition?

"What the hell are you going to do for me?

"God damn it, you better show some results—and fast. I'm not about to waste my money."

The Hollywood tough guy's face was a twisted mask of rage and pain. Bronson looked a lot smaller in person than he did on the big screen. I'd seen him blow away dozens of bad guys in the movies. Now he'd apparently decided that I was the enemy. Yet I was the one guy who could help his family deal with some very serious problems. I had two choices: walk out, or try to take control of the situation.

"Sit down," I said firmly. "This ain't *Death Wish*. It's real life, and people who make stupid mistakes can wind up getting hurt."

Bronson's eyes flashed even more intensely, as if my words were a personal affront. I thought he might take a punch at me right there in his den.

I've handled some tough customers during my three decades in this business, and I wasn't about to be intimidated by this celluloid vigilante. But rough stuff isn't my preferred style—especially when it comes to clients. So I decided to try a little reason, hoping that might defuse the situation.

"Let me spell it out," I said firmly, but without venom. "Guy Ward tells me that Jason is having an affair with a married woman whose husband has mob connections. If he finds out about this affair, he could have Jason's legs broken—or worse. That's why we have to keep it out of the tabloids."

"Fuck the tabloids!" Charlie shouted. "I don't care what they write."

I pointed out that, if the story became public knowledge, the girl's husband was going to feel humiliated and angry. "His friends are not the kind of people we want to deal with."

That snapped Charlie right back into his *Death Wish* routine:

"If anybody messes with me or my family, I'll get my gun and blow the bastard away."

Jill Ireland had heard enough at that point. "Charlie," she implored, "just sit down and lighten up." Then she turned to me. There was fear in her eyes. "Thank God you're here," she said, in a voice that had started to crack. "My husband and I really appreciate your help, Don. We'll do whatever you say."

As she spoke, I found myself beginning to feel protective toward Jill. Underneath all the wealth and glamour was a loving mother who feared for her child. I knew I would go to great lengths to remove the terror I saw in those eyes.

As Charlie dropped his tough-guy posturing, I could see he was a proud and defiant man who hated the idea of turning to someone else to solve his problems. Maybe he blamed himself for Jason's predicament. That didn't matter now. This family desperately needed help. Even with me on the case, it wasn't going to be easy.

Jason's routine was to wait for Jill and Charlie to go to bed. Then he jumped out his bedroom window for an evening of drugs and partying. Charlie's brother, who was living with the family at the time, had caught Jason sneaking in at six in the morning, and had immediately told the kid's parents. Jill had suspected the affair between Jason and the rock star's wife for two years—ever since the woman had gone with the family on a summer vacation.

Charlie and Jill didn't have a clue about how to solve this complicated puzzle, but I was ready to jump right in. "Before I can put a plan into place, I'm need more to go on," I told them. "The only way to get the information I need is to put a recorder on Jason's private phone line."

"We can't do that," Charlie protested. "It's not right. You've got to have a better idea than that."

But I didn't. Bugging the kid's phone was the only way to go.

"Do it," Jill said softly. "Put a tap on Jason's phone."

My electronics expert was John Hall, and I set him up with his own laboratory in my Beverly Hills office. Together, we've come up with a lot of useful innovations on the basic bug. These have included tracking devices so we could follow a subject's car, a business briefcase with a built-in tape recorder, and white-noise jamming devices to thwart the bugs planted by other PIs.

John came over to the Bronson home and proceeded to hook up a voice-activated bug on Jason's phone line. The tape recorder was planted in the basement inside an unused dumbwaiter. We could record six hours of conversation on one side of a cassette. This would give me the insight I needed into Jason's life, but there was a catch. Someone would have to change the tape every day.

"Not me," Charlie said. "No way."

"I'll do it," said Jill quietly.

I wanted to hate Jason for the pain he was causing his family. I wanted to hate him for his selfishness and indiscriminate drug abuse. But as I listened to his taped conversations over the next few weeks, I found myself warming to this young man.

Jason was a generous person, always ready to help out a friend. He was bright and had a great sense of humor. Unfortunately, the kid had boarded a bullet train bound for prison or the morgue.

The tapes confirmed my suspicion that Jason was sneaking out his bedroom window just about every night. Most evenings included some very serious drug ingestion. Jason's partner in this debauchery was Hugh O'Connor, son of *All in the Family* star Carroll O'Connor. The two of them were almost like brothers.

School was no longer a priority for Jason, and he wasn't getting much sleep. I had the unpleasant task of talking to Jill daily, debriefing her on the contents of those tapes. She listened stoically to the details of how her son was destroying his life.

Jill may have wanted to cry, but never did. Neither did she ask questions like, "Why is this happening to me?" Now that we had gotten rolling, she remained focused on a single question: "How do we get my son out of this mess?"

Before I could deal with Jason's drug problem, I first had to get him away from his thirty-three-year-old seductress. Since the woman's rock-star husband was on the road more than he was home, the woman could see Jason whenever she wanted. I didn't object to the kid having a good time, except this was one bad broad. Every time he linked up with her, she broke out a crystal bowl full of cocaine. After each rendezvous, Jason would leave with a baggie full of the stuff.

The tapes also led to another revelation: Jason had recently become involved in a second affair, this one a liaison with Jill's twenty-five-year-old personal secretary.

I was almost starting to envy this kid's success with women. He was handsome and personable—a real lady killer. But he was living in a fool's paradise.

Jill went ballistic when she learned of Jason's affair with her secretary. She began spewing profanities, and struggled mightily to contain her rage when I told her to hold off from taking any action.

I wanted both the secretary and the rock star's wife out of the boy's life. Both fed his drug habit, and the lure of sex and drugs was too much for this seventeen-year-old to resist. But I still wasn't quite ready to move.

The secretary worked in the Bronson house. During the day, she and Jason liked to smoke pot down in the basement. This girl was drop-dead gorgeous. Not only that, but she was completely infatuated with the kid. He wasn't going to give her up easily.

A couple of weeks later, I realized that Jason was running out of time. On one tape, I heard him tell Hugh O'Connor about an orgy of cocaine, Quaaludes, marijuana, and vodka at Jill's secretary's apartment. Afterwards, he vomited in her fireplace. That little barfing session may have saved his life.

The human body can take just so much, and people with drug problems have a way of pushing the envelope a little too far. The clock was definitely ticking for this kid, but I'd figured out what I wanted to do. Before I could move, though, I needed Jill and Charlie's permission. I set up a meeting in Guy Ward's Century City office, and proceeded to detail Jason's latest exploits.

"We've got to bring this to a head—right now," I concluded. "I want to put Jason under surveillance. If we put a tailing device on his car, we can follow him at all times."

Every top-flight private investigator has one specialty that sets him apart. For some it's electronics. For others it's disguises.

I made my mark in the early days as a "wheel man." I could follow anyone without being detected.

Subjects rarely outran me, and on the few occasions that they did, I went out the next day and got a faster car. I modified all my cars, wired them with toggle switches to turn off one headlight, then the other—an illusion that kept subjects from identifying my car and realizing they were being tailed.

I used tricks like pulling over, cutting the lights, and then resuming the chase, roaring down the dark, busy streets fueled by nerve and adrenaline. I followed cars on parallel roads studded with traffic signals. I could work those traffic lights better than anyone.

Even with the luxury of a tailing device planted on a subject's car, you had to stay close. If you made a wrong turn while following a car on the streets of Los Angeles, you'd lose it forever. Planting a device on a subject's car is a tricky proposition. As it happens, my wife, Theral, is one of the best at that job.

Theral is a top PI in her own right, and we've been working together for over twenty-five years. One of Theral's tricks is to take our dog for a walk and throw a ball under the subject's car. When the dog stops near the car, Theral climbs underneath to get the ball. In a split second, she plants the device in a wheel well, and we're in business. I knew we could put an electronic tail on Jason's car. No sweat.

I told Charlie and Jill that Jason's latest escapade was a red alert. I feared Jason could die of a drug overdose at almost any time. I suggested round-the-clock surveillance—figuring if we caught Jason red-handed, we might be able to scare him straight.

Suddenly, Charlie reverted back to his confrontational mode. "How do I know that the investigator who's supposed to be following Jason isn't just sitting in a bar having a drink?"

"You son of a bitch!" I exploded, bounding from my chair. "Theral or I will be following Jason at all times. You're not going to find two better investigators.

"I don't appreciate your implying that I'm a thief, but it really doesn't matter what you think of me. All I've got on my mind is your son. I'm afraid he's going to overdose and die. So go right ahead and be a tight ass if it makes you feel better, but that's not going to help Jason."

"All right, Don, you've made your point," he said, extending his hand. "I'm sorry. I shouldn't have said that."

I'd finally gotten through to Charlie.

From that time forward, he and I got along fine. He never tried to intimidate or undermine me again. He finally realized that I genuinely cared about Jason, and that I wasn't another LA con artist trying to separate a celebrity from his money. Charlie and Jill gave me the go-ahead, expressing complete confidence in my judgment. I started laying out my plan. Step one was getting both girlfriends out of the picture.

I drove with my electronics guy, John Hall, to the rock star's wife's house in Coto de Caza, a resort fifty miles south of Los Angeles. I didn't require John's technical talents on this occasion, but I wanted company on the long ride. Besides, it always pays to have a witness on this kind of job, just in case any wild accusations are leveled after the fact.

I identified myself as a private investigator through the condo door and told the woman I wanted to talk to her about Jason Bronson.

"I'm not dressed. Do you want to come in?"

"First get dressed and then I'll come in."

John was shaking with knowing laughter. In this business, there's no shortage of romantic opportunities. Some women try to seduce you, hoping to screw their way out of jams. Some are clients looking for a discount on their bills. Others are just plain lonely. I didn't know what this woman's game was, and I had no desire to find out. Once she put her clothes on and let us in, I got right to the point.

"You've been screwing around with Jason Bronson for two years now," I told her. "You've been supplying him with cocaine. That's contributing to the delinquency of a minor. I can have you put away for that."

Her eyes started to moisten.

"You've been having sex with him," I went on. "I can run off a long list of felonies you've committed. Plus, I don't think your husband is going to be too happy about any of this when he finds out."

She knew I had her.

"My God," she cried. "Don't tell my husband. If he finds out, it will be the end of me. He's crazy enough to have me killed."

I wasn't about to let up.

"Okay, here's the deal," I told her. "If you keep it up, you're going to jail. And you better hope you don't get bailed out, because if you do, your husband just might kill you. I'm sure he's going to be real happy when he finds out you've been balling a seventeen-year-old kid behind his back."

Now she was shaking and crying uncontrollably. She had definitely gotten the message.

"If you ever come near Jason again," I concluded, "or even have a conversation with him, I'll know about it. And I'll see to it that your ass is planted in a prison cell. This is the end of the line for you and Jason. Don't even take his calls anymore."

I didn't feel the least bit sorry for this woman. She had originally been a friend of Jill's, ingratiated herself with the Bronsons, then seduced Jason. All things considered, she was lucky to be facing my wrath, not Jill's.

By the time I left, Jason's lover was thanking me profusely for not arresting her. She may not have fully understood who I was, but she believed I had the power to destroy her life. I drove back to LA, secure in the knowledge that this part of the problem had been solved. It was time to go to work on Jill's secretary, whom I'll call Mary.

I asked Jill and Charlie to set up a meeting in their house that very day. I had them sit on a love seat in the same den where I'd first met them. When Mary walked in, I showed her my I.D. and told her to sit in a hard, straight-back chair on the other side of the room. I stood, facing her.

Mary had no way of knowing that I'd listened to countless hours of her and Jason on tape, and that I was aware of some of their most intimate activities. But she definitely knew that something heavy was going down. I decided to hit her with the punch line right away.

"I could put you in jail right now," I began. "Jason is only seventeen years old and you are contributing to the delinquency of a minor."

"Oh, my God," she said softly, tears welling in her eyes.

Suddenly, Jill stood up behind me and began shouting: "You fucking bitch, how dare you do this after I brought you into my home!"

Turning around, I glimpsed the murderous look on Jill's face. I thought she might attack Mary, and I certainly didn't want that. I had come too far to let an out-of-control client blow the case.

"Jill, calm down right now!" I snapped. "Let me handle this." I needed a signed statement from Mary at the end of this session, and hysterics weren't going to further my cause. Jill had returned to her seat next to Charlie, so I just kept on with the script.

"You're twenty-five-years old and you've supplied drugs to a minor. You've also had sex with a minor. Those are both felonies."

In reality, I knew the cops would have no interest in pursuing this case, but Mary didn't know that. From the look on her face, I knew she was already a believer. As I leaned in closer, I could almost smell the fear on her breath.

"Now, here's how it's going to be," I continued. "You're never going to see Jason again. You're going to write him a note, that says the relationship's over. Then, you're never to talk with him again.

"Your job here is terminated as of now. As far as Jason is concerned, you've quit. You're out of his life. If I ever find out that you had any contact with Jason, I'll have you arrested in a heartbeat."

At that point, I had Mary write and sign a statement listing the times she'd been with Jason and the drugs they'd used. Here is part of that statement:

—Jan. 19th, Roxy w/Jason, marijuana and Quaaludes.

—Jan. 21st, Jason stayed the night and we had sex.

—On two occasions that I can recall we smoked marijuana in Jason's car.

Jill and I signed the paper as witnesses. I assured Mary that I'd use that document to get her thrown in jail if she ever came near Jason again.

The young woman was crying hysterically, but Jill still wanted to punch her lights out. I'd never seen Jill so mad—and I don't think Charlie had either, because he was shaking his head and muttering, "Oh God. This is really getting out of hand."

Bronson may have been flustered, but he didn't try to interfere. By the time I left the house that day, I had stripped Jason of the two women who were perpetuating his drug habit.

I decided to let a few days elapse before implementing the final phase of my plan. I asked Charlie to bring Jason to my office on a Saturday, when the place would be empty. I didn't want distractions when I went one on one with Jason. Charlie shook his head when I insisted that he not tell Jason who I was.

"What should I tell him? he asked. "How am I going to get him there?"

"It really doesn't matter to me. Tell him you're meeting with a producer who may want him for a television commercial."

"I can't do that, Don. It would be lying. If I lie to the boy he'll never trust me again."

"If you don't lie to him, Charlie, you won't have to worry about him trusting you, because he probably won't be alive much longer."

Finally Charlie agreed. But he still couldn't figure out how to get Jason to my office.

"You're an actor, Charlie," I said. "You've made people believe things a lot more preposterous than this. I know you'll figure something out."

Charlie and Jason showed up at my office on schedule. The boy looked relaxed and confident as he strode through the doorway, apparently thinking he really was meeting a TV producer.

I'd heard Jason and his friend Hugh O'Connor talk about "pulling a Murph" during one of their taped conversations. That was their slang for driving into the hills of Malibu and raiding a marijuana field. Pulling a Murph was also a good way to get killed, because those marijuana growers have been known to set deadly booby traps to protect their crops.

When Charlie introduced Jason to me, I put my arm around the boy's shoulders and said, "Hey, Jason and I are good friends. We went on a Murph together the other night."

As soon as I said the word *Murph*, I could feel Jason's body tense under my arm. His confident smile dissolved into a look of sheer terror. I noticed Jason eying the CII logo on my door—which stands for Crutchfield Investigators Incorporated. Later, the boy told Charlie he thought the logo said CIA. Even without knowing that, I could see the kid was good and scared.

"I am so damn angry at you," Charlie told a stunned and mute Jason. "You're seventeen years old and taking all these drugs. It's bad enough that you've completely screwed up your life. Your mother's more upset than you can imagine. I'm so mad, I can't even sit here and listen to this shit."

"What's going to happen to me?" Jason stammered.

"Well, Don and I are old friends. I'm going to leave that decision totally up to him."

As Charlie stormed out of the room, Jason began to shake. I motioned for him to sit.

"Jason, whether you walk out or get carried out of here today depends on what you tell me. And whatever you tell me, it had better be the truth."

There was no way Jason could get away with lying. After listening to his personal calls for a month, I knew all of his secrets. It was my hope to turn this invasion of privacy into a tool for fixing a troubled kid's life.

Jason offered up a full confession—and every word of it was true. This was the key to the whole plan. Now that Jason had passed my truth test, I held out some hope that the kid could be rehabilitated. In any case, he looked relieved to get all that deception off his chest.

"Here's what I'm going to do, Jason," I told him. "I'm going to put you on probation. Charlie is going to be your probation officer. If you break probation, we're going to put you in jail—for your own good.

"The first thing I want from you is a promise that you won't associate with anyone who does drugs."

"You're telling me I can't go to school then," Jason answered. "Almost all the kids are using."

"No, Jason. I'm telling you that you're not going to parties where drugs are used. You're not going to sneak out of your bedroom window at night after your parents go to sleep. I know all about you and Hugh running around at night partying. I know everything."

Jason had no reason to doubt me now, but something was on his mind. Finally, he spoke up in a small voice.

"I don't mean any disrespect, but I just want to know one thing: How did you follow me on that Murph?"

I laughed slowly and looked right through him. Truth is, it would have been nearly impossible to follow him on that Murph without a helicopter, and I was damn glad I never had to do it.

"Hey kid," I answered. "You think you're hard to follow? You're a piece of cake. The bottom line is I'm a pro, and you're a rank amateur."

"Yes sir, yes sir," Jason mumbled. I laughed, thinking to myself that Charles Bronson wasn't the only actor on the premises that day.

I asked Charlie to step into the room and informed him that Jason had confessed to everything. "I'm putting him on probation to you," I told Charlie, who was prepared to play along. "You must give me your word that if he breaks probation, you will inform me immediately so the authorities can take the proper steps."

"Yes, I swear I'll do it," said Charlie, jumping right into character.

"Okay. I am hereby releasing Jason on formal probation to you as of now."

I pulled Jason aside one last time and told him, "I know you probably hate my guts, and you've got good reason to. I blew your whole game apart. But, believe me, you got off easy this time.

"One of these days, you're going to thank me for saving your life. I want you to know that I think you're a great kid. You can be anything in this world that you want. But you've got to stay off drugs."

Charlie put his arm around Jason and led him toward the door. When they walked out of my office, I closed the case file, convinced that I had made a difference in these people's lives. It was a rare, gratifying moment. But before I could sit back and enjoy that feeling, the case took a bizarre twist.

A few days after my meeting with Jason, I received a phone call from Mary, Jill's former assistant. She was crying. "I've got to tell you something, Mr. Crutchfield. I'm in love with Jason, and I want to see him again."

"I don't want to hear this," I told her. "You're twenty-five and he's a seventeen-year-old kid."

She cried harder. "I don't do drugs!" she insisted. "I only did drugs because Jason wanted to. I haven't violated any of your rules. But Jason called me. He wants to see me, but I'm terrified you'll have me thrown in jail."

"Hey, you know what the agreement says."

"Yes, but you don't understand. I could be good for Jason. If you let me see him I'll keep him off drugs," Mary said. "I'll make sure he does his homework, and I'll make sure he gets home on time too."

I didn't answer right away, because her proposal did make a kind of cockeyed sense.

"What you're asking is completely off the wall," I told her. "You know how Jill feels about you. In any case, it's not my decision to make. I'll propose it—but if I go to bat for you and find out later that you let Jason get screwed up with drugs again, you won't have to worry about the police or anybody else. I will personally deal out the justice."

Only in La La Land would anyone make such a ludicrous request. Still, the more I thought about Mary's plan, the more sense it made. We had taken everything away from Jason. The kid needed some fun in his life. Judging by his past, he wasn't going to stay away from the ladies for long. Here was an opportunity to let him have a good time while making sure he stayed away from drugs. I believed that Mary was too scared to double-cross me. Maybe seeing her would prove to be good therapy for Jason. At the very least, we'd be able to monitor the situation.

When I phoned Jill, Charlie answered. I told him about this latest twist, as Jill listened quietly on another phone.

"If we set this up right, it will help us monitor Jason," I said. "We can let her come over and see him. She can help with his homework. No more drugs, no more sneaking out at night. We can use her to control him for the next few months until you go to Canada to start your next film. You were planning to take Jason with you anyway. Maybe at that point, the relationship will die a natural death."

The more we talked about it, the more Charlie seemed to like the idea. Suddenly Jill spoke up.

"This has got to be the most insane thing I've ever heard," she said, her voice shaking. "My son was screwing a girl that I hired—

screwing her in my own house. Now you're asking me to turn her loose on him again." In strictly logical terms Jill had a good argument, but this wasn't about logic.

"It's better than drugs," I argued. "It's better than the rock star's wife. Think of it as a diversion to keep him happy while he beats drugs."

Charlie and I finally did convince Jill. I told them I wanted   Jason and Mary to come into my office and sign a contract, spelling out the terms of their relationship. Up to this point, my ploys had worked. I saw no reason to go conventional at this late stage. I had my secretary draw up an official-looking document detailing what was expected of Jason. Here is a portion of the statement he signed:

> I, Jason Bronson, do hereby agree to the following terms:
> It is my understanding that if the terms set forth are met I
> will be allowed to see Mary Jones [sic].
> 1. Stay home four nights per week.
> 2. Be home by 11:00 PM on the nights that I go out.
> 3. Maintain a B average in school, as well as a 97%
>   attendance record.
> 4. Not associate with anyone who takes drugs.
> 5. Refrain from the use of drugs and alcohol.
> 6. Stay away from places frequented by users of drugs.

I had Mary sign a similar contract, spelling out that she would not use drugs or alcohol in Jason's presence, would stay away from places where these substances were available and would use her best efforts to keep Jason drug-free and on track in school.

"Can Jason and I have sex?" Mary asked.

"I won't tell if you won't," I answered.

Mary paused for a moment and said, "Yeah, but you're going to know about it, aren't you?"

After I finished laughing, I reminded Mary of the confession she had signed for me. Jason and Mary signed their interlocking contracts. Moments after they left my office, I called Jill and told her what had happened.

"Don, I still think this is the craziest plan I've ever been part of," she said, almost laughing. I took that as a compliment.

I ended my official association with the Bronsons, feeling good about myself and what I'd accomplished. I enjoy using my imagination and thinking fast on my feet. This case had tested my mettle on both counts. More importantly, I'd helped a kid get off drugs and cleaned up a little corner of the world.

One day, about a year later, the phone rang. It was Jason. "Mr. Crutchfield, you told me that some day I'd call to thank you. I'm doing that right now. I've been clean and free of drugs since our meeting. My life is great, and it's because of you. I just wanted to let you know I'm appreciative."

There's no drug in the world that could possibly duplicate the high I felt after that phone call. I later asked Charlie if he'd put Jason up to it, but he hadn't known about it. "Good for Jason," Charlie said. "He's becoming a man."

I went through the next nine years cherishing this case as a milestone—one that gave me a real sense of accomplishment. I had contributed to changing the course of a troubled kid's life. What more gratification can any man get out of his job?

Unfortunately, the story didn't end there. In November 1989, Jason Bronson died after a lengthy battle with heroin addiction. Six months later, Jill Ireland succumbed to breast cancer following a long and heroic fight. Another Hollywood family had been destroyed.

For all my creativity and investigative muscle, I was ultimately powerless to change anything. Sure, I'm great when it comes to fixing people's short-term problems. But if this is, the final result, what's the use?

When Jason died, a little piece of me died along with him. It's easy to become depressed and cynical about human nature— especially when you live and work in a perverse place like Hollywood. But Theral and I agreed that you can't ever stop trying to salvage troubled young lives when the opportunity presents itself.

It doesn't happen often. But every now and then, I find myself in a position to help. I've always given it my best shot, and I intend to keep doing so. I owe that much to myself and to all the babes so vulnerable to the temptations of Babylon.

Autographed photograph given to author by Jill Ireland, showing
the actress on a stroll in Moscow with husband Charles Bronson.

Jill Ireland and son Jason at a book signing for her bestselling autobiography, *Life Lines*. (Photo credit: Kambad/Michelson)

Hills police, but kept them in the dark as to the full details of what was in the briefcase.

I was standing there with a brown paper bag containing $25,000 in make-believe cash. The subject pulled up in a taxi, holding the briefcase. He opened the back door and reached over to make the exchange—obviously hoping not to get out of the cab. Frank wasn't too happy when I pulled him out of the back seat, but his eyes bulged when I showed him the bag of shredded paper he assumed was cash.

Two Beverly Hills police detectives were hiding in the bushes. The moment Frank and I made our exchange, they darted out and placed him under arrest. The cops put Frank in their unmarked car and took him to the station. I called Brian Epstein and asked him to meet me at the Beverly Hills police station.

Brian, Frank, and I looked on as one of the detectives placed the briefcase on the counter. Brian confirmed that it was indeed his property. The detective then opened the briefcase so that he could inspect the contents.

"My money's gone," Brian said. "But these appear to be my papers." When he came to the large plastic bag filled with marijuana, Brian acted surprised.

"What's this?" he asked.

"It looks like a bag of grass to me," the police detective answered. Then he turned to Frank.

"What do you know? he said to his partner. "We got ourselves a drug dealer—as well as an extortionist."

"Come on, guys," Frank pleaded with me and Brian. "You know this shit ain't mine. Please don't burn me."

As a uniformed officer dragged Frank to a cell, the little thief tried to spit at me. Then he screamed: "You know damned well it ain't my drugs."

I just looked at the police detective and said, "It sure as hell isn't ours."

Talk about being outsmarted. This unscrupulous hustler wound up doing hard time for getting busted with someone else's drugs. Meanwhile, Brian Epstein had retrieved his contracts, and nobody ever found out who the marijuana really belonged to.

The Beverly Hills cops never managed to unravel the situation, though I think they tended to believe Frank's story about the marijuana being Brian's. Still, they had nailed a scumbag extortionist. They probably didn't mind using the drug charges to put another nail in his coffin. In any case, they would have had a difficult time proving anything against a powerful man like Brian Epstein, so they chose to accept things at face value.

I was very happy with the way things turned out. Possession of even small amounts of grass was still a fairly serious matter in California, but I never could get too worked up over it. Extortion, on the other hand, always rouses my anger, so I was well pleased when our subject took the rap.

I interviewed Frank while he was in custody, and he jumped at the opportunity to curse me again. "You son of a bitch," he said without an ounce of humor. "I didn't care that you were following me, but I hated it when you flattened my tires."

I didn't want to laugh in his face, but I was chuckling inside. Frank was a little punk who'd received his just desserts. I found it amusing that he seemed less concerned with going to prison than with being blackballed from the entertainment industry.

"That's how it goes, man," I told him. "You start stealing from a guy like Brian Epstein when he's at the height of his power, and you're gonna get blackballed."

As for the Beatles, their image remained squeaky clean until *they* decided to turn on the world a few short months later. Once they went public, they did it in a big way.

On July 24, 1967 *The London Times* ran a full-page ad that was headlined: "The Law Against Marijuana Is Immoral in Principle and Unworkable in Practice." Sixty-four prominent citizens called for the government to encourage research into all aspects of cannabis use, including its medical applications. They asked that marijuana smoking on private premises no longer be an offense; that it should be taken off the dangerous-drugs list and be controlled rather than prohibited; that possession of cannabis be legally permitted or at most be considered a misdemeanor; and that all persons "now imprisoned for possession of cannabis . . . should have their sentences commuted."

Brian Epstein and all four Beatles were among the sixty-four prominent signatories to the ad. "I believe that marijuana . . . is less harmful than alcohol," Epstein told the English music magazine *Melody Maker* shortly after the ad appeared. "I think there is a terrific misunderstanding about marijuana and its effects. So many people have said it must be bad that this verdict is accepted without question. And, of course, there is a malicious association between drugs and pop music. I think society's whole attitude to soft drugs must eventually change."

Unfortunately, I still see a lot of hypocrisy concerning drug use. And the false spin surrounding young rock stars has become more dishonest. It turned out that the Beatles were all pretty good human beings, even if they had their vices. At least they were real people who eventually spoke their minds. Too bad the same can't be said about some members of the rock groups who succeeded them.

In April 1990, I got a call from one of my media contacts. Let's call him Steve. "I'm working on a story about New Kids on the Block for a weekly magazine," Steve told me. "And there are some facts I'd like you to verify."

Steve had been contacted by a twenty-nine-year-old woman named Lisa, who related a rather sleazy story about the New Kids—America's most popular young rockers at the time. It seems that Lisa was approached at the Tampa Airport by a guy who said he was the New Kids' stage manager. He brought her took to the Embassy Suites, a hotel where the group was staying.

It wasn't long before Lisa went into a room with Donnie and Jordan—the group's two big heartthrobs. She took off her blouse and bra, and commenced to have oral sex with both of them. While all this was going on, one of the New Kids' roadies managed to videotape it. Lisa found out that the tape was being shown around—and she was concerned.

Lisa wasn't your typical groupie, nor was she a hooker. This was a woman who sold real estate and had a seven-year-old son. Maybe she had been stoned at the time and looking for a one-time thrill. In any case, she was now having second thoughts. My media source was all set to run the story, but he wanted to be sure the videotape actually existed. That's where I came in.

At that time, the New Kids were scheduled to perform in Los Angeles. They were staying at the Belage Hotel in Beverly Hills, and I had the room number of the guy in charge of their security. His name was Al. I called him up and introduced myself as Lisa's representative. I told Al up front that I knew what had gone down in Tampa, and that I had no problem with consenting adults doing whatever they wanted—however kinky that might be. But I was concerned that the sexual encounter had been taped, and was calling to find out whether such a tape actually existed. Al was very evasive, so I tried to get him to lower his guard. "Hey man," I said. "Nobody is looking to extort anybody or to make money off this. Lisa just wants the tape back, because she's worried about her young son and her reputation in the community."

Al sort of grunted, so I said, "Listen, I know she should have thought about that at the time. But what the hell. Who knows what goes on in a person's mind?"

Al seemed a little more responsive, so I continued to make my pitch. "Now here's the problem," I went on. "When Lisa called to express her concerns, she was told in so many words to fuck off. If you tell *me* that, the situation is going to be out of my hands, and I won't be able to help your guys."

Al told me that there was nothing he could do, but he promised that I would get a call back from someone who could deal with the situation. A few hours later, I did get a call on my answering machine from a guy who said he could be reached in room 206 at the Belage Hotel. His message said, "You called Al regarding a tape. Could you call me at this number? I'll be waiting for your call. Ask for me under my code name: Chip Chocolate."

You get to hear a lot of jive in this line of work. But a black guy using the code name Chip Chocolate? Give me a break. This guy represented himself as the New Kids' road manager. I knew he was the one who set the whole thing up.

I called Chip Chocolate back as soon as I got his message, and we shot the breeze for a few minutes. When I finally told him that I needed to get that tape back, he played right into my hands. "I've got to tell you that the tape no longer exists," he said. "Donnie's brother burned it."

"He burned it?" I asked.

"That's right," Chip Chocolate answered. "He melted the thing down, because he was afraid his brother might get into trouble if someone got hold of that tape by accident."

Chip Chocolate continued to assure me that the tape was gone—which it probably was. No matter. He admitted that there was a tape, and that was all my reporter friend needed to run his story. But I kept on talking to this character anyhow.

"This whole thing wasn't a very bright move all the way around," I told him. "It was dumb on all their parts. And showing that tape around was really stupid. Now my client is despondent about it, and threatening to go to the tabloids."

"Just tell her that I can't afford the bad press, and neither can she," Chip Chocolate responded. "Look, I don't want anything to happen here. The tape is gone, and I'd be glad to talk to Lisa and put her mind at ease."

"That would be great," I said. "I know your guys have a squeaky, clean reputation, and they're well loved by everybody. There's no reason we can't keep it that way. But there's one thing I would appreciate," I added. "Send me an autographed picture of the Kids for my wife's nephew."

"Hey man, I'll be happy to do that," Chip Chocolate said. "You can count on it."

Guess what? That creep never did send me an autographed picture—which was a pretty stupid move on his part. Little slights like that can piss people off and end up causing trouble. But I'm not a petty person. Besides, why would I ever take the word of someone who calls himself Chip Chocolate?

As it turned out, the story never did run. Apparently some kind of deal was made to give Steve's magazine some exclusive interviews with the group. So another major scandal was averted. Steve also mentioned that his editor feared that running the story could eventually hurt the weekly magazine as much as the rock group. Here's how the editor expressed his concerns:

"Just imagine some ten-year-old girl reading that article about the New Kids and asking her mother: 'Mommy, what's a blow job?' That would be the last time that mother ever bought our magazine."

Today, The New Kids on the Block are about as hot as an orange popsicle, their fifteen minutes of fame long since past. But for a while they were the most happening group in the world.

I recall having lunch with my reporter friend shortly after everything had been settled. I mentioned that it would have been quite a coup if I had gotten my hands on that incriminating tape.

"Just think," Steve said. "If you had done that, you would now be the manager of the New Kids on the Block."

"Thanks anyway," I answered, "but I've got more than enough problems to deal with already."

The Beatles on The Ed Sullivan Show (February 24, 1964): The beginning of Beatlemania. (Photo credit: AP Wide World)

Brian Epstein, the man who guided the Beatles' rise to world stardom.

The Fab Four. (Photo credit: The Gene Busnar Collection)

The Beatles on holiday. (Photo credit: The Gene Busnar Collection)

The Beatles in a serious pose. (Photo credit: The Gene Busnar Collection)

A pre-hippie promo shot of the Beatles. (Photo credit: The Gene Busnar Collection)

Donnie Wahlberg, Jordon Knight, and girls in Miami Beach having one of those real good times. (Photo credit: Manny Hernandez/Ron Galella Ltd.)

New Kids on the Block, performing before an auditorium of screaming fans. (Photo credit: Anthony Savignano/Galella Ltd.)

CHAPTER 4

•

Wheel Men

*"Down these mean streets a man must go who is not himself mean.
. . . He has a sense of character, or he would not know his job. . . . He
is a lonely man and . . . you will treat him as a proud man or be very
sorry you ever saw him. . . . He might seduce a duchess and . . .he
would not spoil a virgin. . . . If there were enough like him, the world
would be a very safe place to live in, without becoming too dull to be
worth living in."*

—Raymond Chandler, *The Simple Art of Murder*

Broken marriages can be painful, and we get more than our share in this Babylon they call Hollywood. For years, divorce paid many a private investigator's rent. That all changed with the arrival of no-fault divorce in the 1970s. But when I first got into this business, there was an entire subculture of freelance PIs who lived off divorce cases. They were known as *wheel men.*

A lot of these guys lived along a sleazy part of Santa Monica Boulevard that ran from Fairfax up to Western, and they were almost Damon Runyonesque in character. Your average wheel man was the product of a broken marriage, living in a cheap, messy apartment, often shacking up with one of the many groupies and hangers-on who were attracted to his edgy, dangerous lifestyle.

The PI business is more regulated now than it was in those days, even though it still has its share of characters and screwballs. Back then, a licensed PI could hire almost anyone to work under his license. There was nothing stopping a licensed private detective from hiring ex-cons, drunks, and other seedy types, which is exactly what some of them did.

The police have always had mixed feelings about private detectives. On occasion, we've been able to solve cases and hand them the perps on a silver platter. The cops appreciate that, but they are also wary because PIs tend to play by their own rules. To my knowledge, very few wheel men were involved in committing serious crimes. Still, the cops always thought they might know something.

It was like the police captain said in the film *Casablanca:* "Round up the usual suspects." Which is exactly what happened whenever an unsolved crime became an embarrassment. A half dozen of the more shabby wheel men would be rounded up and sweated for a day or so. Eventually, they would all be released, at which point they'd head straight for the Shell gas station on Santa Monica and Fairfax. That Shell station was home base, because you needed your car to be ready to roll at a moment's notice.

I was just a kid when I started working with these guys. My specialty was tailing subjects, hoping to catch them cheating on their spouses. In those days, evidence of wrongdoing could mean big bucks in a divorce settlement, and a wheel man would go to great lengths to get that evidence.

In order to be successful at this game, you had to follow your subjects without their knowing it. I had any number of surveillance tricks that I used, depending on the situation.

I always carried a cheap watch in my glove compartment, which I'd place under the subject's back tire. When he pulled out, the weight of the car would cause the watch to flatten and break—revealing the exact time the subject left that particular location.

Another one of my tricks involved the use of a a lit cigar. If I wanted to follow somebody, I'd use that cigar to burn a tiny hole in the red lens of the subject's tail light. This would create a narrow beam of white light that I could spot from a block away. Eventually, I found out where the subject and his lover were having their rendezvous, and our case was made.

When all else failed, I had to resort to electronic bugging devices. But no trick or device was as important as a surveillance man's stock in trade: the ability to stay on a subject's tail, come hell or high water.

People who ride with me today often remark on how courteous I am to other drivers. But back in the days when I worked surveillance, I drove like a mad man. I guess I'm trying to make amends, because it's a miracle that nobody got killed or seriously hurt when I was on a tail. And I was a relatively sane driver compared to the crowd I was running with.

The wheel men had hot-ass cars with souped-up engines. The most popular cars were Mustangs, Trans Ams, and GTOs. My main car was a silver-gray GTO with a black top, and I rarely lost a subject when I drove that baby.

Every surveillance artist also had backup cars in case the main car suddenly died—or if you were spotted and had to slip into another car in a hurry. That might mean borrowing a car from your friend, your sister, your grandmother, or whomever. A wheel man needed to have as many backup cars as possible, because time was money and you had to keep rolling no matter what.

One of the fastest things I ever drove was one of my backup cars. It happened to be a Chevy II, which was one of the first gas-efficient American compacts. This was one of those freaks that occasionally rolls off the assembly line. It had a four-barrel carburetor, and it could shut down a Corvette. When I drove that sucker, I felt as if I were in a rocket ship. Still, as hot as that Chevy II was, it was strictly a backup. The GTO was the machine that helped me make my bones in surveillance.

At times, I would literally leave my tires on the street. I'd be gone, but large chunks of tire rubber would still be there. That was another reason we all hung out at the gas station: You could get a new set of tires installed at any time, day or night. You could also put together a surveillance team at the drop of a hat.

The attorney you were working for would call and ask you to tail a cheating husband to a motel. You'd come screeching into that Shell station on two wheels and holler, "I need two guys for a surveillance right now." Before you could even hit the brakes, all sorts of freelance PIs would start kicking jacks out from under their vehicles and jump right into your car. Within seconds, you'd be burning rubber after your subject.

There was a great adrenaline rush in that kind of work. To most wheel men, the job was everything. These were people who cared nothing about where they lived or how they looked. There were only two things in which a wheel man took pride: his skill at the job and his car (also known as his *ride*).

Many of these guys spent more time in their rides than in their apartments. They may have lived in pig sties, but their cars were always immaculate and as finely tuned as a Stradivarius violin.

As a rule, the wheel men didn't have very stable relationships with women. Most of their girlfriends were groupies, whose main thrill in life was going on a surveillance. There was, however, an unwritten rule that you never took a groupie along on jobs. Many of these girls were loose cannons, and they could do a lot of damage if they felt you'd rejected them.

This one guy, Bobby, took a particularly young, attractive groupie with him on a surveillance job. A few weeks after Bobby dumped the groupie, she reported him for conducting an illegal wiretap—which may or may not have been true. In any case, Bobby wound up losing his PI license.

Another group of women who were part of that scene were called roller derby queens. Unlike the groupies, the roller derby queens actually worked with the wheel men. A lot of these gals were lesbians, even though many of them had been married at one time. Some even had kids.

Most of the roller derby queens were not all that great at surveillance. They tended to back off when things got dangerous—and that was probably the smart thing to do. The guys would just push on no matter how weird things got.

As a rule, the roller derby queens didn't hang out at the gas station or at the bars and coffee shops frequented by the wheel men. Most of these women were kind of gnarly looking, so they didn't generate a lot of interest on a romantic level. But at times they could be highly effective on stakeouts.

None of the roller derby queens looked anything like a private detective, which worked to their benefit. Sometimes they'd even use their kids as decoys. For example, a roller derby queen might open the hood of her car as if she'd broken down. The subject would see a lady in distress with her little brats running around, and he'd be completely thrown off.

There were lots of colorful players in the divorce surveillance game: First, there were the cheating husbands and wives. I guess you could think of them as the real villains, but it wasn't always so easy to make that judgment. In some cases, the spouses who claimed to be wronged were even worse adulterers, looking to get a better deal on the community property settlement.

Celebrity clients were among the weirdest and cheapest people to deal with. You'd think major stars would be glad to pay for services rendered, especially when you'd gathered evidence that would lead to a fat settlement. No, sir.

There were exceptions, but a lot of these household names didn't believe in paying bills. They would refer you to their business managers, who acted as if you should be grateful for the privilege of serving their clients. Eventually you'd have to go to court to collect.

Judges were also key players in this game. When a divorce case finally came to court, a cooperative judge was the best friend you could have.

If a judge came to you with a problem, you fixed it for him. No questions asked. If he needed an escort to rendezvous with his lover in such a way as to not arouse his wife's suspicion, you were glad to accommodate him. Then, when you appeared in that judge's court with your client, he'd only have one question: Which side are you representing? At that point, it all was over. You won the case hands down.

We had several judges in our pocket. The most powerful was this 350-pound guy who couldn't hold his liquor. During my early days in surveillance, I worked for a respected PI named Clyde Duber. Clyde often invited this judge over for parties. One night, the judge got drunk, took off all his clothes, and collapsed in the bathtub. We could have used a bulldozer to pry him out and get him home.

I was in on one case where this judge was listening to a proceeding. Suddenly he said, "Hold it a minute, sir. You're in a lot of trouble. What you need is a good PI. I'm going to give you Clyde Duber's phone number, and he's going to help you. I'm going to postpone this hearing for now. We'll resume after you've been advised by Mr. Duber."

Needless to say, the man hired Clyde, and the judge found in favor of Clyde's client. It's highly irregular for a PI to have a judge recommend him from the bench, and this was a clear case of one hand washing the other. By the same token, you were always subject to getting crossed up by a judge who was greased by the other side.

It was up to the wheel men to gather the adulterous evidence, and we did a lot of crazy things to get that evidence. The main thing you wanted was a photograph of your subject in the act. If he had a steady lover, you'd follow the couple to a motel or to one of their apartments. Then you'd make your move.

At the time, California law stated that a spouse had a legal right to be any place where the other spouse was. If your husband or wife was in a motel, you had every right to break in, no matter what it took to accomplish that. The wheel men interpreted that glitch in the law as license to kick down a door of a motel room and walk right in. In fact, there was a coordinated system in place to deal with these situations.

First, it was essential that the husband or the wife be present, since that's what gave you the authorization to break into the room where the other spouse was shacking up. There was a team of specialists to implement various phases of the operation. One guy specialized in nothing but breaking down doors. There was a photographer, who snapped the incriminating pictures, and two big monsters whose main job it was to protect that photographer. That was the key to the whole deal, because the sole object of the operation was getting the photographer and his photos out of harm's way.

Looking back, it's amazing that nobody got killed during one of these door-breaking deals. If I were in a motel room, and a bunch of goons started busting down my door, I'd grab my gun and start shooting. Under the circumstances, I'd probably be able to plead self-defense. How is anyone supposed to know that a bunch of strangers busting down the door aren't a gang of murderous Charles Manson copycats.

Fortunately, nothing like that ever happened. Still, it wasn't always pretty, and the wheel men sometimes stretched the letter of the law until it damn near cracked. PIs weren't allowed to carry badges. Nevertheless, everybody had a bogus badge, and they'd flash it whenever necessary. If a motel manager or parking lot attendant gave you a hard time, you might show him anything from an LAPD badge to an FBI badge. Every so often, a wheel man would flash a badge at an undercover cop and get popped for it. But you had to take chances in order to catch your subject in the act.

Here's how the routine went in those days: After the cheating couple was followed to their motel, the door specialist would do his thing. The room clerk got a fast $40 for the busted door. Since it cost him only $25 for a replacement, he wasn't about to call the cops. Once the incriminating evidence was captured on film, the rest of the team crossed in front of the photographer, who split as fast as he possibly could. Those pictures would be developed in a matter of hours. At that point, your side was home free and could call any shot.

By the time I got into the business, judges had started to frown on the practice of busting down doors. Mostly, we would just tail the subject to the motel or his girlfriend's house and photograph the cheating couple walking in and out.

There were instances where spouses were suspected of cheating with several lovers and could not be pinned down to any one place or time. The wheel men had ways to deal with those situations too, even if some of their techniques bordered on entrapment.

One way to nail a cheating husband was by pulling a *rope job*. A good-looking hooker would be hired to pick the subject up in a bar and take him back to her room. The guy would think he'd conquered the world. But while he was in the act, a team of wheel men would bust in and start taking pictures.

Every now and then, a wheel man would make the mistake of screwing a hooker himself. Such indiscretions could compromise the case and get you fired.

With this kind of rope job, it usually wasn't necessary to break down the door, since the hooker knew to leave the locks open. At times, the room would be wired in advance, and the surveillance team knew just the right moment to go in and start taking pictures.

Rope jobs were also used to nail cheating wives. In these cases, a male investigator would pick the female subject up in a pre-appointed place and try to get her into the sack. A motel room would be selected in advance and the door left unlocked, so that the team could walk right in at the appropriate time.

As far as anyone knew, the investigator who roped the subject was just some guy she happened to pick up for a one-night stand. The PI had to make sure his face was out of the picture, or some-body might get nailed for entrapment. On the other hand, it was essential to get the cheating wife's face in the picture. When those and deposited her at the Loving's farm. Meanwhile, Marlon and one of his drinking buddies drove to Chicago for a night on the town. This couldn't have done much to improve Christian's sense of security.

Christian's aunt found the boy to be testy and mean-spirited. "[Christian] has been subjected to a great deal of arbitrariness and whim," Fran Loving wrote to the judge, "probably an inevitable result of constantly changing hired help." He would sometimes physically attack his girl cousins and classmates for no apparent reason.

That was the Christian I knew all right. Evidently, all the progress he'd made with me was reversed by yet one more upheaval in his life. Still, by the end of his six-month stay on the farm, Christian was showing improvement. But that too was short-lived.

I had told attorneys Sussman and Gary that we'd better stay on top of Anna during the six-month period and not take anything for granted.

"We need to keep her under surveillance from time to time to find out if she's still using drugs and sleeping around," I said. "If that kind of thing is still going on, we'll be able to nail her in court." Unfortunately the attorneys didn't heed my advice. Meanwhile, Anna pulled off a major surprise.

Anna Kashfi had a knack for hiring incompetent lawyers. These guys would ask questions they didn't know the answers to, and they were invariably made to look stupid. This time around, she retained a former superior court judge. He immediately got the venue changed from Santa Monica to LA, where his buddy would be presiding over the case. The very scenario I'd feared most came to pass almost exactly as I had envisioned it.

The presiding judge essentially asked Anna, "Have you been a good girl for the past six months?"

"Yes, I have," she answered sweetly.

"Then the boy is yours, forthwith."

Our legal team started to go nuts, shouting: "Wait, Your Honor, please hear us out." But the judge essentially said, "Don't bother confusing me with facts. I have already made my decision."

A furious Marlon Brando called the ruling "barbarous," and it was. Still, even a fair-minded judge might have cast a skeptical glance at Marlon. During this cooling-off period, Marlon was still married to Movita, and living with his common-law wife, Tarita. Not exactly the kind of parental profile the court likes to see.

I felt that Christian's only chance was to remain on his aunt's farm. Had Marlon received custody, I'm pretty sure that's what he would have wanted. By giving the boy back to Anna, this judge had ensured Christian's ultimate destruction.

The whole scene had really gotten to me, but I had to bite my tongue at this judge's bogus decision. Many's the time that the fix was in for our side in court, so I was hardly in a position to complain.

Eventually, Marlon received joint custody of Christian, but that didn't improve the situation. The boy continued to be used as an emotional hostage. Anna was still as screwed up as ever—as was Marlon in his way. And Christian was a helpless pawn in their dirty little war.

Once, when Christian was thirteen years old, Marlon petitioned the court for permission to take him to Paris during summer vacation. When the judge approved the request, Anna went completely bananas and had Christian kidnapped. She proceeded to hand him over to a bunch of hippies, who hid him out in a primitive town near Mexicali.

Jim Briscoe was one of the detectives who retrieved Christian and drove him home from Mexico. The boy wasn't in very good shape when he was found. He had lost a lot of weight and was terrified. This wasn't the kind of kidnapping where a gun was held to his head. But how would you feel if your kid was forcibly placed in the hands of some longhaired dopers?

Christian has never found himself. He dropped out of school in the eleventh grade, and has worked as a tree-trimmer, a welder, and a construction worker. Christian was married for six years, but wound up in a bitter divorce battle. He was reputed to be a heavy drug user and gun collector.

Christian hated being Marlon Brando's son. His father's fame and fortune brought him only pain. Friends say that he was most comfortable in the woods, far from the harsh lights of Babylon.

◆

I was on a cruise when I heard about Christian shooting his half-sister's lover. I really couldn't imagine Christian intentionally murdering someone, but I certainly could picture him in a drunken rage, pointing a gun in someone's face and making threats. When that gun went off and killed a man, I'll bet Christian was in a state of shock. The kid always did have a dark side and a hot temper, but I don't believe he had it in him to kill.

I hadn't seen Marlon Brando for a number of years, and I wasn't asked to work on Christian's defense team. Marlon had retained Robert Shapiro, who had his own investigators. Still, I felt the need to let Marlon know I was there if he needed me, so I called him. Marlon sounded sedated over the phone—kind of like the Godfather after he'd been shot. We had a nice conversation, and Marlon thanked me for my kind words. A few days later, I wrote him a letter which read in part:

> . . . *When I worked for you, I was in my twenties and just starting out. You always treated me as a friend. I want you to know that in your time of need I am your friend and always will be. I've been fortunate enough to achieve success as a private investigator. In the process, I have established many valuable resources. These are now at your disposal. If I can be of any assistance now or in the future, please don't hesitate to call on me.*

I haven't heard from Marlon Brando, but I continue to keep tabs on him and his family. In January, 1996 Christian was released from prison. At last report, he was living in New Hampshire and working as a welder. Maybe Christian can get his life in order far from the glaring lights of Babylon, where he was forced to carry the burden of being Marlon Brando's son.

I'd heard that Christian really got himself together during his prison stay. I certainly hope so—but think of the irony! Here is a child of privilege—a son of one of the most renowned actors in the world—and he needs a stint of hard time to turn his life around.

The sad truth is, prison may have actually provided more of a reality check than Christian ever received from his parents—

however grim that reality might be. In a way, I'm amazed that Christian made it into his thirties. If ever there was a child programmed for an early suicide, it had to be him. Maybe now Christian can finally get a handle on his life.

And what of my old friend Anna Kashfi? I've been on a number of TV programs, talking about my experiences with the Brando family. On one show, they had Anna listening to me talk about some of her sordid escapades. Her responses were predictable. "Drugs? No, never! Carrying a gun? The man is making up stories. Running around with strange men in the presence of a young son? Absurd!" Oh well, what else can you expect?

Anna and I weren't in the same studio when that TV show was being taped, though I have run into her a few times over the years. On one occasion in the late 1960s, when she was straight and sober, I spotted Kashfi walking toward me. Naturally, I clenched my fist and was prepared to take a fighting stance. But she just offered her hand and said, "Hi, my name is Anna Kashfi. I don't believe we've ever met."

I stepped back, looked at her and said, "You're right. You and I never have met before. I may have once met somebody that looks like you, but I've never met you before."

We then proceeded to make small talk. But I was on my guard every second. Who can tell when a psycho like that is going to turn into Ms. Hyde?

Anna Kashfi received lots of publicity when she was awarded one of the largest divorce settlements in California history. She must have had one hell of a drug habit, because she apparently spent all her money.

I recently found the former Mrs. Marlon Brando working as a chambermaid in a Chula Vista trailer park. I didn't want to laugh at her misfortune and could only shake my head in dismay. Here was a woman who spent years fighting to gain custody of the son she professed to love, yet she never once showed up at Christian's trial or visited him in prison.

Maybe Christian Brando is better off without his mother's pathological attention. He sure could have done with less of it while   he was growing up.

Marlon Brando and Anna Kashfi on the eve of their wedding (October 11, 1957). (Photo credit: AP Wirephoto)

Anna Kashfi slaps Brando in Santa Monica court after a bitter
child-custody hearing. (Photo credit: AP Wirephoto)

Christian Brando doing the shackles strut.
(Photo credit: Ramey Photo Agency)

Miko, Christian, and Marlon Brando arrive for pretrial motion, Santa Monica court: Don't worry kid, I'm going to make 'em an offer they can't refuse." (Photo credit: AP Wide World)

CHAPTER 6

•

The Marriage of
Show to Business

"[Michael Jackson] is the perfect picture of a child molester. He has the perfect circumstances. . . . But you know what? People don't know anything, so these stupid . . . [jerks] go, 'Well, we let our kids sleep with him and share his bed, 'cause he took 'em to Toys R Us. He's a nice, nice boy. . . . Yeah: He's Peter Pan, so we can let our little boys sleep with him."

—Roseanne Barr in a 1994 *Vanity Fair* interview

I f you're rich and famous, getting away with a crime is easier than ever. Today, a megastar standing accused of child molestation—or even a grisly double murder—can count on being judged, not by the nature of his illegal acts, but by the spin placed on those acts.

Some have tried to turn the child molestation allegations against Michael Jackson into a racial issue, but I'm not buying it. Nobody is out to get this man just because he is black. In fact, the outcome of his case had a lot more to do with money and power.

Most people—whatever their color—don't have a team of publicists, high-powered attorneys, and PIs working for them. Your typical child abuser can't afford to pay millions in hush money for the parents' silence. Then too, most pedophiles don't have parents delivering children to their bedroom doors. But when you're a   superstar in this business they call show, the rules are different.

The so-called royal wedding between Michael Jackson and Lisa Marie Presley turned out to be the ultimate marriage of *show* to *business*. Coming on the heels of the child-molestation allegations against Michael, it produced one of the biggest media circuses in recent years. Which would be all well and good if the welfare of children hadn't been compromised.

I've been privy to the details of Michael's now-defunct marriage to Lisa Marie, as well as other controversial aspects of his life. I was also the first to uncover the facts behind Michael's twisted relationship with Jordan Chandler, the thirteen-year-old boy whose family was paid tens of millions of dollars to drop the child-molestation charges. But by that time, many of the gory details in legal depositions and documents from the California Bureau of Child Services had been leaked to the press.

On September 14, 1993, case #SCO26226 was filed in Los Angeles Superior Court. That was the day plaintiff Jordan Chandler's criminal case against defendant Michael Jackson officially became a matter of public record.

Defendant Michael Jackson repeatedly committed battery upon plaintiff by engaging in harmful sexual contact with the plaintiff. These harmful contacts include but are not limited to defendant Michael Jackson orally copulating plaintiff, defendant Michael Jackson masturbating plaintiff, defendant Michael Jackson eating the semen of plaintiff, and defendant Michael Jackson having the plaintiff fondle and manipulate the breasts and nipples of defendant Michael Jackson while defendant Michael Jackson would masturbate.

Despite these allegations and a mound of incriminating evidence, Michael managed to buy his way out of civil and criminal trials. But his image suffered a major blow. A number of lucrative commercial endorsements were terminated, and Michael's singing career was in jeopardy. He had to do something spectacular to convince the world that he was a normal man—not some perverted freak.

When Michael and Lisa Marie took their vows in the Dominican Republic, my operatives were close to the scene. I found it hard to accept their lame attempts to make the world believe they were lovers.

We had to wade through all sorts of smoke screens and double-talk as Michael's well-oiled publicity machine tried to put a positive spin on anything that threatened to bring him down.

I've been on national TV dozens of times over the past few years, trying to share some of what I've learned. Typically I spend maybe an hour talking to a reporter, only to see the interview cut down to a couple of catchy sound bites. Now I get to paint the whole picture.

On the surface, Michael Jackson and Lisa Marie Presley seem very different. Yet, at the core, the two have a great deal in common. For one thing, they are both products of sick family backgrounds.

Michael was sold into an unreal show business neverland at age eight. Lisa Marie's mother, Priscilla Beaulieu, was essentially sold to Elvis Presley at the age of fourteen.

That down-home country boy–turned-soldier promised Priscilla's daddy he would care for her like a daughter, send her to a good Catholic school, and not have sex with her until she was eighteen. Daddy put his reservations aside and proceeded to turn his little girl over to Elvis. Just what he received for this arrangement is not clear. But one thing seems certain: Joseph Paul Beaulieu, an Air Force captain, would never have agreed to such an arrangement had the suitor not been the King.

Sources reveal that Elvis kept his promise. Apparently he and Priscilla didn't consummate their relationship until the day she turned eighteen. Before and after that waiting period, Elvis was reportedly screwing lots of other women, downing a wide variety of pills, and generally leading the self-indulgent life of a superstar. Everything and everyone Elvis wanted, Elvis bought—with his fame and his money.

In 1968, when Priscilla Presley was twenty-three years old, Lisa Marie was born. One year later, eleven-year-old Michael Jackson had his first top-ten hit with the Jackson 5—a group consisting of Michael and four of his brothers. The Jacksons came from Gary, Indiana, some 500 miles from Graceland. They were more than a decade behind the Presleys in the stardom game. Still, Joe Jackson, the family's abusive, whip-cracking patriarch, was determined that his brood would catch up in time. And they did.

The price Michael paid for spending his childhood in rehearsal studios and on performing stages can never be calculated. But it seems that he has never grown up.

The 2,700-acre ranch Michael has dubbed Neverland is about ninety miles north of Los Angeles. Neverland features a private zoo of exotic animals, a choo-choo train, a merry-go-round that plays Madonna's "Like a Virgin," a lake, and a theater where young guests can play video games or watch any film their little hearts desire.

Does such an environment reflect the whims of a rich and famous man-child who sees himself as Peter Pan? Or is it the perfect setting to seduce young boys?

Even if he's innocent of pedophilia, as some loyal sycophants continue to insist, Michael Jackson is clearly a very disturbed individual who seems incapable of anything resembling a normal relationship with women—or with children. That's why his marriage to Lisa Marie was so ludicrous.

I learned the true details of the couple's wedding ceremony in the Dominican Republic through my international sources. The marrying judge described Lisa Marie as one of the unhappiest brides he'd ever seen. The judge also expressed shock when bride and groom refused to kiss at the conclusion of the ceremony.

Many of the wedding guests were members of the Church of Scientology, a pseudoreligious organization that lists Priscilla and Lisa Marie Presley as two of their most devoted celebrity parishioners. It appeared that the Presley-Jackson wedding was staged under the auspices of the Scientologists. I remember thinking that it was too bad Tina Turner wasn't at that ceremony. She could have sung "What's Love Got to Do with It?"

Questions about the legal standing of the marriage in the United States were raised almost immediately. As for the romantic status of the Jackson-Presley relationship, it's hardly surprising that rumors of a pending breakup began surfacing right after the nuptials.

The couple ostensibly planned to go on a well-publicized honeymoon a few weeks after the wedding—at least that's what the press reported. During the time they were supposed to be honeymooning in Europe, several of my operatives followed Lisa Marie to a plastic surgery clinic in Agoura, California. We were not aware of any health problems, so what could she have been doing there?

I told my people to stake out the clinic as long as Lisa Marie was a patient. A source in the clinic revealed that the newlywed bride had checked in to have breast augmentation and liposuction performed on her thighs. These procedures, which normally prevent a patient from having sexual relations for some time, reveal the kind of honeymoon the happy couple planned. Why would a passionate wife, so early in a marriage, undergo elective surgery that precludes sex?

Michael had successfully passed himself off as an innocent waif who identified with and cared for children. To some extent, his concern seemed sincere. Michael gave a good deal of money to children's charities and developed close relations with several terminally ill kids. But these and other acts of kindness do not preclude a person's being a pedophile. Michael's child-like veneer—coupled with his extraordinary wealth and power—made it all too easy for him to lure young boys into his bed.

Just as Priscilla Beaulieu's father could not resist Elvis's clout, star-struck stage moms could hardly say no when Michael Jackson expressed a desire to get close up and personal with their sons. Occasionally a parent would be hesitant, but Michael overcame their reservations. His strategy was simple: Pay them off—with expensive gifts, with elaborate vacation trips, with the implicit promise that he'd provide their children access to show business fame.

In some cases, Michael's young paramours were stars in their own right. One of his constant companions was the young actor Macauley Culkin. Before that, he had an intense relationship with Emmanuel Lewis, a tiny twelve-year-old TV actor whom Michael carried around like a baby. After the two checked into a Beverly Hills hotel as father and son, Lewis's real parents put an end to the relationship.

Michael met Jordan Chandler when the boy was twelve years old. During the months that followed, they were constantly together—accompanied on most occasions by Jordan's mother, June.

At one point Michael flew Jordan Chandler, June, and Jordan's half sister to Las Vegas in a private jet. Michael and Jordan reportedly slept together, while the boy's sister and mother spent the night in an adjoining room. But the next night, Jordan's mother reportedly protested when Michael invited the boy to share his bed. Michael became highly emotional.

"We have a special friendship," Michael cried, "and you're spoiling it. This is not a sexual thing. It's about being a family. Why don't you trust me?"

When Michael said that Jordan could sleep wherever he wanted, the mother relented—as many others had done in the past.

Were these parents aware of what was going on? Or did they really believe the line about Michael's fondness for innocent sleepovers with little boys? We may never know the answer, but think about it: If you were the parent of a young boy, would you let him sleep in the same bed as a thirty-five-year old man who looks and sounds like Diana Ross?

Jordan Chandler's mother now admits that she was incredibly stupid, naive, and scared.

June Chandler's fear was understandable. She didn't want to cross a powerful person like Michael Jackson. Despite his soft, high-pitched voice and gentle manner, everyone in Hollywood knew that Michael was capable of playing hardball—both in business and on a personal level. In most cases, the superstar didn't need to get tough. Paying families off with exciting trips, expensive gifts, and hefty sums of cash was usually all it took to buy their silence.

I located a number of boys who'd been close with Michael. Like Jordan Chandler, they'd often slept over at Neverland and traveled with Michael. None of these kids—or their parents—would say a bad word about Michael. I found it interesting that many of these families had been the recipients of generous trust funds set up by Michael Jackson for his "special friends."

When I looked into the terms of these trusts, I learned that the proceeds were paid out over a period of many years. Also, it appeared that the trusts could be revoked at any time. So if any of these boys or their folks ever accused Michael of wrong-doing, they would never see another dime.

Michael Jackson and his advisors evidently relied on such cynical largesse to ensure that none of these families would blow the whistle. But they would soon learn that revenge can sometimes supersede greed.

Although Jordan Chandler's parents had been divorced for years, their relationship was amicable. Both parents had mixed feelings about their son's relationship with Michael Jackson. Eventually this became a central issue in a contentious custody battle. That's when Michael began to lose control of the situation.

Before I'd even heard the name Jordan Chandler, I received a call from a reporter friend of mine. He happened to spot Michael Jackson with the boy in question at a restaurant hotel before it was open for business.

"You should have seen them, Don," he began. "They were sitting at a back table—and it looked more like a date than anything else. Michael was hugging and kissing the boy, thinking nobody was watching."

Since I'd already pegged Michael as a pedophile, I was hardly surprised. Shortly thereafter, I was hired to investigate the relationship between Michael Jackson and the Chandler boy. This was before any allegations of child molestation had become public. I soon learned that custody of the child had been transferred from the mother to the father. That told me something heavy had gone down. The agreement stated that the mother could see the boy with the following stipulation:

> *Petitioner [Evan Chandler] shall have sole physical custody and control of the minor child until the minor child marries, dies, reaches the age of majority, or becomes emancipated.*
>
> *Respondent [June Chandler] shall not allow the minor child to have any contact or communication in any form, directly or indirectly, including, but not limited to, telephone communication, with a third party adult male known as Michael Jackson. In the event it is discovered Respondent has violated this condition of reasonable visitation, she hereby agrees any subsequent visitation with the minor child shall be limited to situations in which a third person monitor, approved by Petitioner or approved by the Court, is present. Respondent agrees to bear all cost and expense for the presence of said third person monitor, if required.*

This stipulation made me suspect that the father believed Michael was molesting his son with the tacit approval of the boy's mother. This change in the terms of custody should have put an end to that relationship, but Michael couldn't let it rest. A few weeks later, he had his attorney intervene to get custody returned to the mother. This would have the effect of allowing Michael to continue seeing the boy. I wondered what the attorney was trying to accomplish here: Procuring prey for a predator?

Criminal charges still hadn't been filed. Once that happened, the media would treat this story as if World War III had broken out. But Michael Jackson's tight little world was already starting to fall apart, and he was in need of serious help.

Michael hired a private investigator named Anthony Pellicano to be his spokesperson. Pellicano had a well-earned reputation for using fear and intimidation to get results for his clients.

Private investigators often deal in gray areas. But Pellicano has crossed the line so many times that I'm amazed that he hasn't lost his California PI license. Among other things, he has allegedly tried to pass himself off as an attorney. He has also bragged about using bribery and extortion to make sure things go his way.

Pellicano likes to let people know how tough he is. "I'm an expert with a knife," he boasted to one inquisitive reporter. "I can shred your face like a head of lettuce." Pellicano claims to be an expert in martial arts, but when a Chicago PI who has known Pellicano for years was told that he was bragging about his expertise in Kung Fu, the man said: "Kung Fu? Hell, Pellicano is even afraid of Chinese food."

Hard Copy reporter Diane Dimond, who was responsible for breaking a number of important developments in the Jackson–Chandler case, told me that she received threatening messages from Pellicano that were delivered by third parties:

"Tell Diane Dimond I'm watching her."

"Tell her I hope she stays healthy."

People like Pellicano have no qualms about threatening women, but they will rarely go head to head with somebody they can't intimidate.

John Connolly, an ex-cop who is now an investigative reporter for *New York* magazine, wrote an article in which he revealed Pellicano's mob connections. Before the article went to press, Connolly offered Pellicano an opportunity to refute the charges. Pellicano never replied, but Connolly's apartment was ransacked and members of his family received threatening phone calls.

Connolly was so enraged he called Pellicano up and said: "Hey Anthony, you've got a problem. I'm flying to Los Angeles on Monday. I'll be staying at the Belage Hotel. You and I are going to have a heart-to-heart, so you'd better bring your Louisville Slugger."

During his visit to LA, Connolly went to a book signing in Beverly Hills, knowing in advance that Pellicano would be present.

"Hey Anthony," Connolly said with a sardonic smile. "How are you doing?"

"I'm okay," Pellicano answered. Then he slithered to the other side of the room and pulled an acquaintance aside. "Who the hell is that guy?" he asked.

"That's John Connolly."

Pellicano suddenly discovered that he had someplace else to go and made a quick exit.

Michael's use of Anthony Pellicano as his frontman spoke volumes. Innocent people generally don't have to resort to hard-fisted tactics to defend themselves, nor do they hire intimidators to do their dirty work for them. Considering all the evidence was pointing to Michael's guilt, it's hardly surprising that his people would resort to threats and bribery. At the same time, it's clear that Jordan's father came to see Michael as a meal ticket and was looking to cash in.

Pellicano claimed that Evan Chandler was trying to extort money from Michael Jackson. In a meeting at which Jackson was present, Evan Chandler allegedly asked for $20 million for a deal to write four screenplays.

Evan Chandler was a Beverly Hills dentist by trade, though he also had a screenwriting credit for the Mel Brooks film, *Robin Hood: Men in Tights*. Supposedly, Evan's son Jordan had come up with the concept. Now Chandler wanted to give up his dental practice and work full-time on new screenplays with his son.

When Pellicano told Chandler there was no way he would receive $20 million, Chandler allegedly pointed at Jackson and said: "You're going to be sorry, Michael. This is not the last you're going to hear from me. If I don't get what I want, I'm going to go to the press! I'm going to ruin you!"

Pellicano insisted that he didn't tape that meeting or other conversations during which Chandler and his attorney were allegedly demanding money. Under the circumstances, I can't imagine an experienced investigator not setting up a tape. Pellicano claimed that it would have been illegal to have done so without informing the police in advance. That's not the case.

Under California law, it's legal to secretly record a person without his knowledge if there is reasonable fear of extortion. Pellicano claims to be an expert at taping people without their knowledge, and has done so on many occasions. Why wouldn't he have recorded Evan Chandler's threats if he suspected they would support the allegations of extortion?

It would appear that the Jackson camp tried to bribe Evan Chandler not to go to the authorities by offering him money to develop screenplays, but the price was apparently higher than Jackson was willing to pay.

Evan Chandler subsequently brought the child molestation allegations to the attention of the authorities. But he waited far too long. Any parent who really loved his kid would have taken decisive action sooner. It sickens me to think that he tried to negotiate a payoff, because he preferred writing screenplays to drilling teeth.

Evan Chandler revealed some of his true priorities in a series of phone conversations that were covertly recorded by Jordan's stepfather. The stepfather's motives were unclear, but he turned over the crudely edited tapes to Pellicano, who distributed them to   the media.

Chandler is heard threatening to bring Michael down and destroy his career. "When the facts are put together," he tells the stepfather, "it's going to be bigger than all of us put together, and the whole thing is going to crash down....and destroy everybody in sight. . . . Michael is an evil guy. He's worse than that, and I have the evidence to prove it. . . . I will get everything I want, and . . . Michael's career will be over."

When the stepfather asks how those tactics would help Jordan, the father replies: "That's irrelevant to me[!] The bottom line to me is . . . his mother is harming him, and Michael is harming him. I can prove that. . . . If they force me to go to court . . . I will be granted custody, and she will have no rights whatsoever."

When Evan Chandler made those taped statements, he still hadn't figured out what he was going to do. But when he was

informed that his ex-wife's attorney was about to file papers ordering him to return custody of the boy to her that very day, he took
Jordan to a psychiatrist.

During a three-hour session in the psychiatrist's office, Jordan
proceeded to reveal the details of his relationship with Michael Jackson. The psychiatrist was legally obligated to turn the matter over
to the California Bureau of Child Services, at which point the sexual-
molestation allegations became a matter of public record.

This effectively put an end to all negotiations between Evan
Chandler and the Jackson camp—at least for the moment. Children's
Services concluded that both parents appeared unworthy of caring
for their son, and they had a point. Jordan's mother had continually
exposed him to an alleged child molester, while the father seemed
most concerned with profiting from the affair.

Authorities considered placing Jordan in a foster home, but the
boy was ultimately allowed to remain with his father. As for Michael
Jackson, his worst nightmare was about to be realized as authorities and the media began a full-court press in their attempt to prove
the child molestation allegations against him.

Michael was out of the country at the time, but the police searched
Neverland for incriminating evidence. I'm sure they must have
wondered why Michael so often shared his bed with young male
visitors. It certainly wasn't for lack of space.

When Michael returned from abroad, he was ordered to strip so
that police could check the birthmarks on his genitals with Jordan
Chandler's description. Despite Michael's vehement denials, Jordan had reportedly given authorities a near-perfect rendition.

Michael was in a state of panic. He'd been found out and was
potentially looking at a nice chunk of prison time.

If anything is certain, it's that Michael Jackson could never survive prison. Prisons are tough places, designed to take control of
your life—and Michael could never handle that. Also, convicted
pedophiles—"short eyes" in prison language—are at the bottom of
the food chain in these walled jungles.

Michael would never have made it through a week in a
prison environment. But so what? As they say: If you do the crime,

be ready to do the time. Michael Jackson may well have done some serious time had the Los Angeles district attorney not blown the criminal case.

Most of the time, the police will make an arrest if they have a victim and an alleged perpetrator. Yet Michael Jackson was never arrested—and I think I know why.

Civil suits had been filed by Jordan Chandler and both his parents. District Attorney Gil Garcetti apparently decided to wait and see how those civil suits turned out. This would spare his office the embarrassment of arresting a megastar for a crime the justice system still hasn't learned to cope with. Meanwhile, the Chandlers' attorneys would be doing all the leg work and absorbing the cost of developing incriminating evidence, which they'd agreed to turn over to the DA's office.

Had Michael been found guilty in the civil suits, District Attorney Garcetti could have stepped in and used the same evidence to prosecute the criminal case. But once the family allowed Jackson to buy their silence, there was no longer a victim who would testify.

To me, this outcome was a major disappointment. I've had experience with cases of this kind, and I'm convinced that Jordan Chandler was telling the truth. This was a thirteen-year-old boy who was grilled by everyone from the police, to the Bureau of Child Services, to attorneys taking depositions. Through it all, the boy's story remained consistent in every nauseating detail. I would have had a hard time coaching Marlon Brando to fake a performance like that.

Truth is, Michael wasn't all that discreet about his sexual preferences. Many of the people around him knew what was going on, though most have been afraid to talk. But five of Michael's former employees who claim to have seen their boss cavorting with young boys filed a lawsuit against Jackson, his lawyers, and members of the OSS—Michael's heavy duty private security force. The former employees alleged that they were abused and physically threatened after they refused to cooperate with attorneys who were preparing Michael's child-molestation defense.

I recently interviewed Jerome Johnson, a former member of Michael's OSS squad. JJ, as he is called, worked for Michael for eight years, and often saw him with "as many as four . . . little boys who would sleep in his room all night."

JJ has testified on behalf of the five employees he once helped intimidate. JJ has also filed his own lawsuit, alleging that Michael Jackson and one of his attorneys tried to induce him to sign a false pro-Jackson affidavit. In his lawsuit, Jerome Johnson states:

> One day, Bill Bray [Executive Director of the OSS] and Marcus Johnson (another OSS man) got in a fight in a recording studio in Sherman Oaks. Marcus Johnson told Mr. Bray to "fuck off." Mr. Bray wanted Mr. [Michael] Jackson to fire Marcus Johnson; but Mr. Jackson wouldn't fire him. Mr. Bray took his pistol and said he was going to shoot Mr. [Marcus] Johnson. I had to stop Mr. Bray from leaving and took his gun from him. I had Ms. [Bettye] Bailey [Executive Administrator of the OSS] talk to Mr. Bray and calm him down. When Mr. Bray returned, Mr. Jackson called to speak to him. I had taken the call and I put it through to Mr. Bray. I was standing in the doorway and could overhear Mr. Bray's part of the conversation. Mr. Bray was upset with Mr. Jackson and he was telling Mr. Jackson how Mr. Bray had lied to the Grand Jury about Mr. Jackson molesting boys to protect Mr. Jackson. After the conversation, Mr. Bray told me directly that he had lied to the Grand Jury regarding Michael Jackson molesting little boys.
>
> Bettye Bailey also told me that she knew that Mr. Jackson had been molesting boys.

If it ever can be established that Michael Jackson's employees perjured themselves to protect their boss, the molestation investigation could be reopened. But by paying off the Chandlers, Michael had avoided prison—at least for the time being. Still, his career and reputation had suffered irreparable damage. The child-molestation charges had become the number-one news story, and Michael could not face his public. He claimed he was sick, that his voice was shot, and that he was in a London rehab facility for addiction to prescription drugs.

Concerts were canceled, and promoters were left holding the

bag for millions of dollars. Pepsi no longer wanted Michael to endorse their products—nor did any other corporate sponsor. Sony, Michael's record company, canceled plans to issue a greatest hits album. Despite their public denials, executives there were clearly worried about his commercial appeal.

Money was the driving force for everyone in this drama, and the Jackson family was no exception. Family members called the tabloids, eager to clear their wronged brother's name. Most demanded hefty amounts of cash for their stories.

The family also tried to launch a self-produced $6 million TV special, *The Jackson Family Honors*. As usual, they counted on Michael's participation to make the show a success. He did make a token appearance, but the show lost a bundle, and the family never paid off the debts they incurred putting the extravaganza together.

Michael was having his own problems. He sorely needed something or someone to resurrect his tainted image. Staging a marriage was the perfect strategy. Not just any marriage, but a sanctioned union with the daughter of the King.

As for Lisa Marie, her stated reasons for going through with this marriage never did wash. She continues to insist that she married for love, but I'll never believe that. And as heir to the King's $100 million estate, she certainly didn't need any of Michael's money.

It has been suggested that Lisa Marie was using Michael to forge a show business career of her own. If so, Michael apparently didn't deliver fast enough. I guess he was too consumed with resurrecting himself to help his wife, but so what?

It seems to me that if Lisa Marie had any singing or acting talent, being Elvis Presley's daughter should have given her biz a nice jump start. True, her marriage to Michael has made Elvis's only child one of the most talked-about women in the world. Still, if all this was a publicity stunt to get her name in the headlines, Lisa Marie must be an even sicker puppy than Michael.

What the former Mrs. Michael Jackson did to her two young children was, in some ways, worse than what Priscilla's parents did to her. Even if the sexual molestation allegations against Michael were never proved in a court of law, would you have allowed your children to live in close quarters with someone who authorities were on the verge of arresting for pedophilia?

Another theory concerning Lisa Marie's motivation for marrying Michael centers around her involvement with the Church of Scientology. This makes a certain amount of sense to me, and may also partially explain why Lisa dumped Michael.

Scientologists tend to stick together. You rarely find a marriage between a committed scientologist and a nonbeliever. Danny Keough, Lisa Marie's first husband and the father to her two children, is a practicing scientologist, as is Lisa's mother. Lisa reportedly did try to recruit Michael into the fold. Although a number of scientologists argue that the organization would not have recruited someone with Michael's baggage, I'm not buying it.

First of all, Michael is capable of bringing a tremendous influx of cash into an organization. Second, the Church of Scientology has long been in a blood feud with the psychiatric community. Imagine what a feather in their cap it would have been had they been able to take an allegedly pedophilic homosexual and convert him into a normal heterosexual male.

My sources reveal that Michael did submit to some initial Scientology auditing. But if Lisa Marie was hoping to lure him into the Church, her chances were never very good. This guy is a control freak who is not about to put his faith in anything or anyone else.

Michael has his own security force at his Neverland ranch, as well as his own fire department and his own water supply. He even maintains his own landfill for garbage disposal, which prevents tabloid reporters and curiosity seekers from going through his trash.

Michael owns the high ground that surrounds Neverland. This prevents people from getting anywhere near his property. He's also got his own airspace—and the local sheriff strongly recommends that unauthorized planes refrain from flying over it.

As it happens, I had an opportunity to fly a reconnaissance flight over Neverland in 1991. I had been retained by one of my media clients to cover Elizabeth Taylor's wedding to a construction worker named Larry Fortensky. This heavily secured event would turn into a circus—complete with a skydiver who descended onto the grounds only a few feet from the wedding ceremony. The press was so desperate to get the inside track that someone paid off a Neverland employee to hide a camera on the underside of a llama.

Two days before the actual wedding, I was in a plane, circling above the rolling hills and stately oaks that surround Neverland. I remember thinking to myself: This place makes Disneyland look like a strip mall.

The connection between Michael Jackson and Elizabeth Taylor is well known. Elizabeth has been like a mother to Michael, and she was a rock of loyalty during his ordeal. The aging actress literally got out of a sickbed to fly to Singapore when Michael was first accused of molestation. She was his only true friend when every-one else either ran for cover or tried to capitalize on the scandal.

I was dazzled by the media air force that turned out to cover the wedding. The night before the nuptials, one of my investigators and I had a few bourbons at Millie's Tavern—an old stagecoach stop in Los Olivos, just a few miles north of Neverland.

This was horse and cattle country, and the place was full of real-live cowboys. There was also a crowd of media types who stood out from the townies. With our Levis and plaid shirts, my associate and I fit right in with the locals. Nobody ever suspected we were investigators.

I recall buying no fewer than a dozen Bud longnecks for a lanky, sunburned cowboy named Hank who'd been living in the area for more than ten years. Hank was an honest-to-goodness cowpoke, not a Hollywood phony with lizard boots and a blocked Stetson. This guy actually broke horses and herded cattle. As he sat and downed one beer after another, I tried to get some information about Neverland from him.

"What's the deal with Michael Jackson's ranch?" I asked. "I hear it's a damn fortress."

"Shit, he's got all these fancy-assed security guys. He's so scared somebody'll get on that faggot Disneyland." Hank slapped the table hard. Then he spoke again: "That freak doesn't belong here in the valley!"

"What do you mean?"

"People around here like to hunt. But if you shoot somethin' along

Jackson's fence line and it goes onto his property, his goons will shoot you!" Hank belched. Then he continued. "Jackson put the word out that he don't want any of us riding our horses along his property line—especially on the day of the wedding. Screw him! I'll ride my horse anywhere I damn well please!"

Michael isn't the only superstar who is obsessed with privacy, but I've never seen it taken to such an extreme. One of Michael's former bodyguards told me that Neverland is "an absolute dictatorship where paranoia has replaced trust," and I have every reason to believe him. Sources reveal that:

—*Michael has wired the floor that surrounds his bedroom. As soon as anyone gets within five feet of this top-secret sanctuary, bells start to ring.*

—*Most people who enter Neverland are required to sign a confidentiality agreement, promising not to speak to the press about what goes on there.*

—*Newly hired staff are instructed never to converse with Michael or look him in the eye.*

—*Employees are expressly forbidden from taking a walk on the grounds.*

It seems to me that someone so hung up on control would be a hard nut for even an aggressive group like the Scientologists to crack. Why should such a self-centered icon subordinate himself to any organizational controls?

In a sense, Michael is running his own cult of personality, complete with a large staff of servants, bodyguards, spin merchants, astute advisors, and millions of adoring fans.

Michael had once been a Jehovah's Witness, but split with that group when they began telling him how to conduct his life. The fact is that Michael Jackson—who has a huge painting hanging on a wall at Neverland, in which his head is mingled with those of George Washington, Albert Einstein, and Isaac Newton—apparently believes he is some kind of deity.

"I think he thinks he's Jesus," a Hollywood producer who has known Michael since childhood told *Vanity Fair*'s Maureen Orth. "He feels he's going to save the world through children."

Michael Jackson might have led Lisa Marie on, but you can bet that he never intended to submit his mind—or commit his dollars—to an organization like Scientology.

The breakup of Michael Jackson and Lisa Marie proved to be the least surprising event in the entire sordid affair. It's been alleged that the couple lived mostly apart, and their public demonstrations of physical attraction were about as transparent as a piece of plastic wrap.

The end came shortly after Michael collapsed while rehearsing for an HBO concert at New York City's Beacon Theater—leaving yet another promoter holding the bag.

Michael was said to be suffering from low blood pressure and severe flu-related dehydration. Whatever his problem, he lay in a hospital bed, hooked up to a bunch of intravenous tubes, for five days.

At one point during his hospital stay, Lisa Marie paid a visit to her soon-to-be ex-husband. According to Jackson sources, that's when she broke the news that the show was over. From here on in, it would be all business. A few days later, all of Lisa's public statements were being handled by a team of divorce attorneys.

As for Michael, he hardly seemed broken up by the separation. Shortly after checking out of the hospital, he and several young friends boarded the Concorde and hightailed it to Euro-Disney, where Michael was seen waving to a throng of fans from the balcony of his favorite room at the Disneyland Hotel: the Sleeping Beauty Suite.

Yeah, right. Some fairy tale!

Michael Jackson and Tatum O'Neal on a date (June 1987): Tatum meets the Wolfman (Photo credit: Scott McKiernan/Zuma)

Dec. 22, 1993

Live from Neverland Valley

Michael Jackson as he appeared on television to denounce child-molestation charges.

The author with Hard Copy senior reporter Diana Dimond.

Aerial view of Michael Jackson's Neverland. (Photo credit: Crutchfield Collection)

Michael Jackson candy bar.

The author with Michael Jackson candy bar: "Hey, little boy, want a candy bar?" (Photo credit: Joel Acker)

Lisa Marie Presley on her fifth birthday with mom Priscilla and the King. (Photo credit: Ramey Photo Agency)

Lisa Marie's daddy. A very young Elvis on stage. (Photo credit: The Gene Busnar Collection)

Michael and Lisa: the kiss.

Lisa Marie (covered by blanket) leaving Agoura Hills Plastic Surgery Clinic. (Photo credit: Frank Griffin)

Lisa Marie departing clinic in back seat of Mercedes. (Photo credit: Frank Griffin)

Michael and Lisa Marie: the happy couple. (Photo credit: Ramey Photo Agency)

The author with Michael's father, Joe Jackson, at the MGM Grand, Las Vegas. After we shook hands, I checked to see if I still had my ring. (Photo credit: Crutchfield Collection)

CHAPTER 7

•

Yellow Brick Road Revisited

"The story of Judy Garland's life would strain credibility to the breaking point were it the product of a writer's imagination. So rife is it with the harsh realities behind the American dream, with hidden sexual secrets, abortion, suicide, drugs, alcohol, power, emotional pain, and ultimate tragedy that only the truth separates it from the most sensationalistic 'Hollywood novel.'"

—James Spada, *Judy and Liza*

The Michael Jackson and O.J. Simpson cases may be the most notorious to come out of Hollywood in recent years. But, to my mind, the embodiment of Babylonian excess and tragedy is still Judy Garland. There have been very few performers who could hold an audience like Judy could when she was on. Unfortunately, she was a victim of everything that's bad about Hollywood.

My involvement with Judy Garland stemmed from my association with her estranged third husband, Sid Luft. I first met Sid in the early 1960s through my mentor, Clyde Duber, and we became fast friends. Sid had a reputation for being a hustler—a tough guy who carried a revolver. Maybe so, but as far as I could tell, he did everything in his power to keep Judy clean. Sid watched her like a hawk, but Judy was always able to get drugs.

I recall one occasion when Judy was opening in Las Vegas, shortly after doing a stint in the hospital for a drug overdose. She had sworn up and down that this time she would stay clean. But one way or another, Judy always managed to score. On this night, somebody had sent her a bunch of pills concealed in a large bouquet of flowers.

It was ten minutes before showtime, and Judy Garland was lying unconscious on the floor of her dressing room. The performance had to be canceled, and the paying customers given their money back.

Judy pulled this kind of thing so many times that she eventually got herself blackballed in Vegas. Promoters were hesitant to hire her, because dealing with Judy was like playing a game of Russian roulette. One night, she could give a mind-blowing performance, and the next night she might slit her wrists. You didn't need to be a psychiatrist to figure out what made Judy such an emotional wreck.

Ethel Gumm, Judy's mother, epitomized the sick stage parent who forced her talented but vulnerable child into show business. Judy's resentment of her mother has been well documented.

"My mother was no good for anything except to create chaos and fear," Judy once said. "She didn't like me because of my talent. She resented it. . . . I enjoyed it because I didn't get any affection from my family. Instead, I got applause from strangers."

By the time she was a teenager, Judy was being pushed through the Hollywood star system. *The Wizard of Oz* had catapulted her to the top, and the people who were guiding Judy's career saw her as a money-making machine.

Drugs came into the picture early. Judy often felt too tired to work, but the uppers they gave her provided boundless energy and kept her weight under control. By the end of the day, Judy was usually too wound up to sleep. So barbiturates were provided to take her in the other direction.

These pills were not street drugs; they were pharmaceuticals duly prescribed by physicians. There was nothing wrong with dispensing them, even to a child; at least that's what Judy's handlers claimed. At that time, there was no scientific proof that uppers or downers were harmful or habit forming. Still, as far as I'm concerned, somebody should have known that putting a child on a daily regimen of heavy-duty pills was bound to screw her up. Which they did.

Ultimately, those drugs and the deep-seated emotional vacuums they filled created a life-destroying poison that Judy would inevitably feed to her own children. As one of her biographers, James Spada, has noted:

> *Judy may have been Hollywood's most tragic victim; she in turn could terribly victimize those around her—most painfully her first born, Liza. Judy considered herself a victim of her mother, then took on many of that woman's worst qualities. Liza was put through a Grand Guignol of horrors in her life with Judy, only to emulate, as an adult, her mother's disturbed personality and lifestyle.*

♦

By the time I crossed paths with Judy, Liza Minelli had already launched her own show biz career. Sid Luft and Judy had recently finalized their divorce, and Sid was having problems seeing their two young children. When Sid asked me to serve Judy with some legal papers, I was glad to help him out. By then, he had told me the story of his tortuous relationship with Judy Garland many times.

Sid Luft had met Judy during a trip to New York while she was still married to film director Vincent Minelli. There was an instant electricity between the fragile star and this New York Jewish tough guy. Sid was very different from most of the other men Judy knew in Hollywood, and he soon took control of her life and career.

Sid didn't have much of a show business track record when he became Judy's manager. Still, he worked hard to resurrect Judy's faltering career and helped her achieve some of her greatest triumphs as a performer. Judy's drug escapades had pretty much destroyed her as a movie actress, so Sid talked her into launching a singing tour of Europe. Judy was terrified of performing live, but Sid refused to take no for an answer.

Judy kicked off the tour with a legendary performance at the London Palladium. This was followed by engagements in Glasgow, Manchester, Liverpool, Dublin, and Birmingham. Everywhere she went, Judy played to standing-room crowds that showered her with affection.

Judy was happier than she'd been for a long time. She had the two things she craved most—an adoring audience and a new man in her life. Sid loved Judy but was nervous about marrying her. At the time, he was still in the process of divorcing his second wife, Lynn Bari—a woman known around Hollywood as "queen of the B movies." Nevertheless, Sid promised Judy that once their respective divorces were finalized they would tie the knot. That's exactly what happened. Shortly after they both divorced, Judy announced that she was pregnant. She and Sid were married almost immediately thereafter.

By the 1960s, Judy had become so great a liability that few people in show business would take a chance on her. But Sid wasn't easily discouraged. One way or another, he always managed to talk someone into giving this extraordinary talent another shot.

Sid's handling of Judy Garland's career and finances was a mixed bag at best. Judy was often broke, even though she had made a lot of money over the years. Sid probably wasn't the greatest manager, but it's doubtful that anyone could have done much to counter the kinds of problems Judy brought upon herself. By the time the two of them broke up, Sid's main concern was getting his kids as far away from Judy as possible. I suppose Judy loved her kids, however screwed up that love may have been. In any case, she fought Sid every step of the way, both in and out of court.

Sid Luft and Judy Garland had two children, Joey and Lorna. During the time they were married, Judy attempted suicide no fewer than seventeen times. Every one of those attempts was drug-related, and many of them took place in front of the kids. Judy was a complete disaster as a parent and she caused horrendous problems for Joey and Lorna.

Sid was frequently away on business, and someone had to take care of the kids. Liza, who was in her teens, was given the impossible task of watching over her suicidal maniac of a mother—as well as the Luft kids. When Judy's doctor warned Sid that Judy was taking too many pills, it became Liza's job to chuck them down the toilet and refill the bottles with placebos. On several occasions, Liza had to talk her crazed mom out of killing herself. All this was going on in front of Joey and Lorna, and Sid was extremely worried.

Sid never knew what kind of sick games to expect from Judy—but he had learned to be ready for anything. When Judy started hitting those pills, there was no telling what she might do to get Sid's attention. Once, after a particularly bitter custody battle, Judy called a friend and told him that she was going to kill herself. The friend had heard this before, but he became alarmed when Judy added, "I've got Joey here, and I just might take him with me."

Sid was at the race track when he received an emergency call to rush home. Sid broke down Judy's bedroom door and found her lying in bed with their young son. Judy was obviously wasted on pills, though Joey was unharmed. Judy's need for high drama was familiar to Sid, but threatening to include their young son in her suicide was too much. Sid would never again relax when Judy had the kids.

By the time I entered the picture, Judy and Sid's custody wars had turned ugly. Understandably, Lorna and Joey weren't handling these battles well. They were both seeing a psychiatrist three times a week to help them deal with their parents' problems.

It later came out that Judy tried to turn Joey and Lorna against their father by claiming, among other things, that he had tried to poison their dog. Aside from wanting to win them over emotionally, Judy hoped the kids would testify against Sid at the upcoming permanent custody hearing.

The ink on the divorce papers was hardly dry before Judy was remarried to an aspiring actor named Mark Herron. Ricochet romance was her pattern when it came to men, and she followed it to the end of her life. Herron seemed to come out of nowhere. Press accounts described him as a gigolo, a dancer, a nurse, an adventurer, and a homosexual.

This last allegation was ironic. Judy's father was thought to have been homosexual, and she claimed to despise people of that persuasion. As it happens, Judy Garland had a huge following among gay men, and continues to be a favorite of that audience more than a quarter century after her death.

Whatever his sexual preferences, Judy's fourth husband was a struggling actor who'd appeared briefly in the Fellini film *8½*. Personally, I think Herron married Judy to further his career. Obviously that strategy didn't work, because nobody has ever heard his name since their divorce.

Sid had a brief phone conversation with Herron a few weeks before his divorce from Judy was finalized. He had called to speak to the kids, and Judy asked if he would say hello to her future husband. Sid agreed. After a few quick niceties, Herron cut to the punch line: "Mr. Luft," he began, "I just want to tell you that I'm very much in love with your wife, and I'm going be the greatest father to your children."

Sid was outraged. "Imagine the balls on this Herron character," he said. "That SOB is going to be a father to *my* children?" Sid was more determined than ever to get his kids away from Judy, but he wanted to do it in a way that would stick. Sid had been through some tough custody battles with his former wife, Lynn Bari, so he knew the ropes.

At one point in his fight with Bari, Sid decided he wanted to go back to court to increase his visitation rights. Lynn was a responsible mother, and Sid had no firm grounds on which to make such a request. That he was married to Judy at the time didn't do much to help his case.

There was a superior court judge Sid had met at a party at Clyde Duber's house. As it happened, this particular judge was an alcoholic whose favors could be bought. Not only that, the guy was a huge Judy Garland fan. When Sid arrived at the party, he found a drunken Judy sitting on the judge's lap. She was laughing hysterically at the judge's lame jokes.

As the night went on, Sid got friendly with the judge, and began talking about how he wanted to get better visitation privileges.

"No problem," the judge said. "All you need to do is get this matter transferred to my court, and everything will be taken care of."

Now, Sid had a very good attorney, which he obviously didn't need since the fix was in. When the matter went to court, Sid showed up with the most inexperienced associate that law office could send. This junior attorney had no idea that the result of the hearing was a foregone conclusion, so he just began going through the usual legal paces.

"Your Honor," the young attorney began. "I would like to make a motion granting custody of the two minor children to Mr. Luft."

"Custody is hereby granted forthwith," the judge replied.

Lynn Bari's attorney couldn't believe his ears. What kind of judge would order a reversal of custody without hearing a single shred of evidence?

"B-but Your Honor," he stammered.

"That's it," the judge shouted. "I said forthwith. This matter is over, finished!"

Sid's attorney was ecstatic. He couldn't figure out how he'd pulled off this coup, but he decided that he must be some sort of legal genius. Sid thanked the guy profusely, and I don't think anyone ever bothered to tell him that the fix was in.

Meanwhile, Sid got custody of his and Lynn Bari's children, when all he was after was more visitation. Lynn's attorney eventually got a change of venue and appealed this bogus decision. It took less than a month for Lynn to get her kids back, and Sid never did receive any better visitation privileges.

In his custody battles with Judy, Sid was committed to handling things by the book. He felt confident that Judy's erratic behavior would tilt the odds in his favor.

Sid and I were eating lunch when he mentioned that he had some papers he wanted served on Judy and Mark Herron. The idea was to get them into court to improve his visitation rights with Joey and Lorna. Sid hoped this would eventually lead to his obtaining full custody of the two children.

Sid told me that Judy had recently gotten mad at her new husband and had set his entire wardrobe on fire right in front of the terrified kids. Sid also had proof that Judy often removed the kids from the house during his assigned visitation times. We both knew, of course, that these were far from the worst examples of Judy's dark side, but Sid hoped these recent events might persuade a judge to be sympathetic to his cause.

Judy lived on Rockingham Drive—only a few doors down from the house O.J. Simpson later made infamous. At the time, I was living on Barrington, just five minutes away. All I had to do was drive down Barrington, hang a right on Sunset, and it was a quick shot to Rockingham. When I told Sid I'd be glad to serve the papers, he pulled out a handful of hundred-dollar bills.

"Put your money away," I said. "This one's on the house. Anyhow, serving them ought to be a piece of cake." Sid reminded me that you could never tell how Judy might respond. "Just be careful," he warned.

Around five o'clock that evening, I drove over to Rockingham and rang Judy's doorbell. A butler answered the door and saw that I was carrying some sort of official papers. I sensed that he was about to slam the door in my face, so I immediately said: "Do me a favor. Don't shut the door in my face. I've got subpoenas here for Miss Garland and Mr. Herron. If you shut this door on me, here's what I'm going to do.

"I happen to know that Liza Minelli is opening at the Coconut

Grove tonight, and that Judy and Mark are planning to be in the first row. When they sit down, I'll serve the papers right in front of every gossip columnist in Hollywood. Now, I'm not looking to cause any trouble, so please help me."

"Okay," the butler began. "I'm not going to shut the door. I'm just going to close it a little bit. Please wait here; don't go anyplace, all right? Don't think that I'm shutting the door in your face, because I'm not doing that."

"No problem," I said, "I'll be waiting right here."

A few minutes later, a man came to the door. "I'm Mark Herron," he said.

"I know who you are, and I have your subpoena. It's all wrapped up for you," I said. Then I handed the subpoena to him. Herron gazed at me and said, "I'll take Miss Garland's as well."

In most cases, I would have let a husband accept his wife's subpoena, but I'd pegged Herron as a snake. "No, you will not take Miss Garland's," I replied. "I have to serve that to her in person. You've got yours, but I need to give this one to her."

"Well, she's getting dressed right now," he muttered. Suddenly he smiled and turned on his phony show-biz charm. "Would you please come in and have a seat?"

"Sure, I'd be happy to," I answered in my thickest saccharined voice. While I was waiting in the den, Joey and Lorna came in, and I started playing with them.

A few minutes later, Judy Garland entered, looking great. She was dressed in a beautiful beige gown. A Japanese girl was at her side, applying gargantuan amounts of facial makeup. Judy had a chronic weight problem, see-sawing between obese and anorexically slim. At this particular moment, her weight was just about right, as were her manners.

"I want to thank you for being a gentleman and not embarrassing my family," she said, extending her hand.

"Well, Judy, I think the world of you—just as I think the world of Sid. I would never do anything to embarrass you."

Judy thanked me again, accepted the papers, and we parted company.

The whole deal had taken less than a half hour, including drive time. My job was done the minute I served her and Herron with those papers, but I was pleased that the interaction ended on a cordial note.

In his gossip column the next day, Harrison Carroll shared the following piece of information, which he had received from an unnamed source: *A private investigator had threatened Judy Garland that if she didn't accept a subpoena at her house, he would serve her at the Coconut Grove and create a public spectacle.*

This struck me as strange. I hadn't discussed this incident with anyone other than Sid Luft. At first, I thought it might have been the butler or Mark Herron who leaked the story. I later concluded that it was probably Judy Garland herself. This wouldn't be the first or last time Judy served as the source of her own negative press.

It would be months before I crossed paths with Judy Garland again, but I continued to see a good deal of Sid Luft. Judy and Sid were in constant financial trouble, a circumstance which each blamed on the other. Even after Judy died, Sid was still trying to pay off their long-standing debts. At one point, he decided to auction off some of Judy's memorabilia and other possessions. He rented the ballroom at the Beverly Wilshire Hotel and asked me and a couple of other guys to act as shills.

Over the years, Sid had auctioned off an undetermined number of red shoes that Dorothy supposedly wore in *The Wizard of Oz*. On that particular Saturday, he was auctioning off a bunch of Judy's crystal and jewelry, as well as an autographed picture to Judy from President John F. Kennedy, which she had treasured. Once the auction began, we all started calling out bids to jack up the price.

Sid was a loyal friend, and I was trying to do him a favor. Still, the man could be ruthless, and he'd screwed a lot of people over the years. I don't count that Saturday at the Beverly Wilshire as one of my proudest. It felt strange to see Judy's things being sold off that way, and it angered the kids. Liza never forgave Sid for that stunt.

I believe in the long run Sid did Judy more good than harm. In her case, the die was cast during childhood, and I doubt that anyone could have saved her from a drug-induced early death. Everyone in Hollywood believed that Judy would one day succeed in committing suicide. That's why I was surprised when I was asked to rescue her from a stranger who had threatened to take her life.

It had been a little over six months since the evening I served those papers on Judy and Mark Herron. I was sitting around my apartment when the phone rang. It was Judy's male secretary, begging me to come over immediately.

"We have a very serious problem," the secretary said. "Somebody has threatened Judy's life, and we're terribly frightened."

I rushed right over. By this time Mark Herron was long since gone, and the kids were nowhere in sight. I was shocked to find an emaciated and withered Judy Garland standing in the doorway. Before I could even absorb the radical change in her appearance, the actress put her arms around me and cried: "Oh Don, I'm so afraid. I'm so glad you're here."

Judy wouldn't let go of me. She was trembling and cuddled up to me like a child. I was still holding her when we moved to the couch. As Judy planted herself on my lap, I recalled a time when I'd sat on her lap.

As a youngster, I grew up in Culver City, where many of the Hollywood studios were located. One of my closest boyhood friends was Don Duber, whose father Clyde gave me my start as a PI. Clyde was a good friend of Judy's and Sid's, and they were regulars at his parties.

Once, when I was eleven, I was at a Christmas party at the Duber home. I'll never forget how Judy sat me on her lap and sang "Somewhere over the Rainbow." It was the thrill of my young life. Who could have guessed that years later our roles would be reversed under such strange circumstances?

"My God Judy, what's the matter?" I asked, as this terrified shell of a person buried her head on my shoulder and cried uncontrollably.

"This guy really is going to kill me," she said. "My life is over."

Because of her history of drugs and unstable behavior I was more than a little skeptical about Judy's claim. However, within a matter of hours I verified that we were dealing with an emotionally disturbed fan who lived in New York.

Over the years, I've worked hundreds of threats to life and limb. I myself have been threatened many times. People have called me up and said: "When you come home, I'll be waiting to blow your brains out."

Generally the creeps who make these threats are cowards who are trying only to scare you, or psychos looking for a cheap thrill. Rarely do any of these guys follow through. Nevertheless, I have a professional obligation to take any such threats seriously when a client's safety is involved.

In the case of Judy Garland, I was concerned because the threat had come from a fan. For the most part, Judy's fans loved her and would never think of harming her. But there are always a few wackos out there who will twist that love into something sick.

I went into Judy's office and called the head of her fan club. After an hour on the phone, I had all my facts together. The guy threatening Judy still hadn't left New York, though that could easily be changed by a cross-country plane ride.

Our subject was an obsessed person who had no life. "I love Judy more than anything in the world," he told several members of her fan club. "If I murder her, my name will forever be linked with Judy Garland's, and I will become immortal."

After I got off the phone, I tried to make Judy feel a little more at ease. "This guy doesn't pose an immediate danger, in the sense that he's not hiding in the bushes right now," I said. "We've got to be prepared, but I don't want you to worry.

"I know who this guy is and I've got people in New York tracing his every movement. If the SOB shows up, I'm ready to deal with him. I'm going to stay with you until this thing is resolved. So please don't be frightened."

Looking at Judy, I could tell that she'd dropped some pills in the short time I'd been on the phone. She didn't even look like the same person. Still, I was unprepared for what was coming next.

"Don, I'm terrified," she rasped.

"Judy, I've taken every precaution. Believe me, nobody's going to harm you in any way. I just won't let that happen."

Suddenly, Judy's face turned beet red, and she began hitting me with a barrage of curses every bit as vile as those you'd hear in the worst barroom brawl. After she finished calling me every filthy name under the sun, she shouted:

"How dare you tell me I don't have anything to worry about. What the hell do you know about what it's like to be Judy Garland for forty-five years?"

I knew all about Judy's tirades. But I was not about to take that kind of abuse from anyone—no matter how much I liked her singing.

"Listen, bitch," I snarled. "I came here to help you, and this is how you thank me. I don't need that. Maybe your little faggot of a secretary can handle this crazy son of a bitch when he shows up, because I seriously doubt that the LAPD will set up surveillance here." Then I stomped out of the house, never to return.

That was one of the few times in my career that I walked out on a client, and it's haunted me ever since. Given the circumstances, however, I had little choice. Judy Garland died of a drug overdose two years later, at age forty-seven—though she looked a lot older. What a shame to see such a brilliant light snuffed out. I've always felt bad about the way things were left between us.

Judy Garland was my first celebrity client to succumb to drugs. Considering my chosen business was that of a private detective in the land of Babylon, I figured she wouldn't be the last.

Late breakfast for Judy, then-husband Sid Luft, and kids Joey and Lorna.
(Photo credit: AP Wide World)

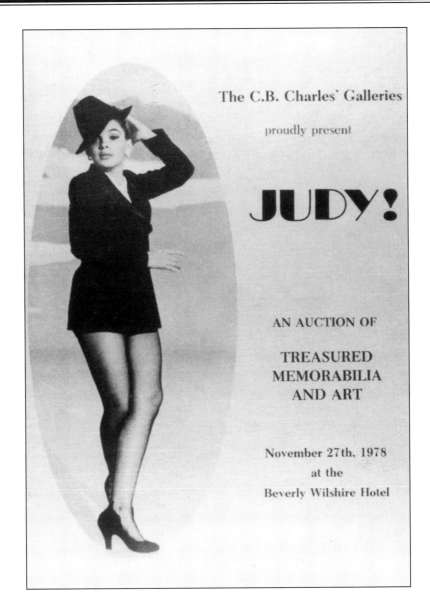

The C.B. Charles' Galleries

proudly present

JUDY!

AN AUCTION OF

**TREASURED
MEMORABILIA
AND ART**

November 27th, 1978
at the
Beverly Wilshire Hotel

Front cover of catalog for auction of Judy Garland's possessions, held by Sid Luft.

O.J. enrolled the boy in a strict military academy, and Jason managed to graduate. But his troubled relationship with O.J. still haunted him.

I recently viewed some intimate footage of O.J.'s wedding to Nicole. At that time, Jason appeared to be a nice, well-mannered boy. He and A.C. Cowlings were O.J.'s best men. There was a great deal of high-spirited banter going on between O.J. and his many friends, but Jason looked like an outsider.

All this rejection took a heavy toll as Jason moved from adolescence to young manhood. He experienced several drug overdoses which resulted in hospital stays.

Nicole tried to take a tough-love approach after an apparent drug-related suicide attempt. While visiting Jason in the hospital, she reproached him for attempting to end his life. "Your father would never do anything like that," she told him. "He would never quit, much less try to take his own life. You're a disgrace to the family. Pull yourself together."

Jason was still very close to Marguerite, and he never did approve of O.J.'s new wife. Nicole's well-intentioned lecture was not appreciated, and caused Jason to despise her.

Jason's troubles continued to deepen. After the suicide attempt, O.J. acknowledged that Jason was hurt by the divorce and by his own lack of attention. But instead of reaching out and trying to help, O.J. became more disapproving.

Jason's younger sister, Arnelle, was attractive, bright and upbeat—much more the image O.J. Simpson wanted for his children. He liked to show Arnelle off, but continued to ignore Jason.

One night, Jason and a group of teenage friends were hanging out at the Rockingham house. O.J. and Nicole were off vacationing, and the other kids were not around. Suddenly, O.J.'s handyman heard loud banging noises coming from the backyard and ran down to see what was going on.

There was Jason, apparently stoned, bashing a life-sized statue of his father with a baseball bat. The handyman watched in horror as O.J.'s treasured shrine was about to be smashed to smithereens. The handyman tried to calm Jason, but the boy just kept swinging away and shouting: "I hate my father! I hate my father!"

The handyman called Ron Shipp, the former LA cop who was to testify at the 1995 trial that O.J. admitted dreaming of killing Nicole. In 1986, Shipp was still close to the Simpson family and had taken a special interest in Jason. So when the frightened handyman told him what was happening, he rushed right over.

According to a member of the household staff, Shipp was able to talk to the boy and calm him down.

"My father pays no attention to me," Jason complained. "He's hardly ever around. And when he does see me, all he does is put me down."

Shipp encouraged the boy to talk things out with his dad, but Jason was afraid. "If he ever finds out I busted up his statue, he'll beat the hell out of me."

"Hey man," Shipp reassured him, "I'll explain things to your father, and he won't beat on you. I promise."

Ron Shipp got the handyman to repair the damaged statue while O.J. was still out of town. Shortly after he returned, Shipp just told O.J. that he and Jason had a man-to-man talk about the boy's problems. But O.J. realized that something was up and insisted on hearing the whole story. Shipp agreed to tell what he knew, but only if O.J. promised not to punish Jason. O.J. agreed to those terms.

A few weeks later, Nicole informed Ron Shipp that O.J. had "kicked the living shit out of Jason." The boy now felt doubly betrayed. Not only was he more alienated from his father, Jason had also lost the one grown man he could confide in.

From that time, things went from bad to worse for Jason. O.J. had used his connections to get the boy into USC, but it was painfully clear that Jason would never come close to replicating his father's success—either on or off the football field. His feelings of failure fueled Jason's worsening substance-abuse problems and caused him to become violent.

In the years that followed, Jason was busted several times for drunk driving and assault. In December 1992, he was arrested for attacking a restaurant owner with a knife after being fired from his job as a cook. In a plea-bargain agreement, Jason pleaded guilty to one count of disturbing the peace. He received two years' probation and ten hours of community service.

Jason had also been in trouble for a number of traffic violations. At one point, he rear-ended a car and injured the female driver after partying at Johnny Depp's Viper Club. Instead of stopping to see if the woman was okay, Jason split. To make matters worse, he was driving with an expired license.

Just two months before his father was charged with murder, Jason Simpson reportedly stalked and beat his longtime girlfriend to the point that she told a friend, "I thought I was going to die."

Following the attack, the girlfriend talked to Nicole Brown Simpson about her problems with Jason. After hearing her story, Nicole allegedly remarked: "Don't blame Jason. He's just like his father."

You don't have to be a shrink to recognize the tragic legacy of violence and jealousy this son has reaped from his notorious dad. Shortly after O.J. was locked up in the Los Angeles County jail, one of my sources overheard a conversation Jason had with his father: "You're the man of the house now," O.J. reminded his firstborn son. "I expect you to take on a whole new load of responsibilities."

At the time, I would have predicted that Jason would continue to follow in his father's troubled footsteps. But apparently I was wrong. The boy seems to have learned a lesson that may turn his life around for good.

At this writing, Jason is working as a chef in a West Hollywood restaurant frequented by celebrities. I am told he is doing well at his job, and is not being ostracized for the sins of his father. In fact, Jason has been rebuffing what he feels are O.J.'s false attempts to repair their relationship.

"Jason feels that his father is trying to use him and Arnelle to present a pretty family picture to the world," a source told me. "Right now, Jason thinks that O.J. is a phony, and really doesn't want to have much to do with him."

O.J. Simpson may have been acquitted of the double-murder charges, but he is still perceived by much of the public to be guilty. O.J. is no longer welcome at most of the better restaurants or at the golf courses he used to frequent. Most of his show biz friends have deserted him, and his neighbors want him to move.

In January 1996, I was asked to look into allegations that Nicole Brown-Simpson and Ronald Goldman were murdered by a serial killer named Glen Rogers. It turns out that Rogers, who had worked as a house painter in Nicole's neighborhood, bragged to a friend that he dated Nicole and subsequently killed her with a knife.

As I suspected, these allegations were dreamed up by someone trying to cash in on the million dollar reward O.J. has offered for information leading to the arrest and conviction of the "real killers." Somehow I think that money will never be paid out.

Could it be that Jason Simpson has also grown skeptical about his father's innocence? That's hard to say. But it appears that O.J.'s fall from grace may at last free Jason from his futile and destructive attempts to live in his father's shadow.

I certainly hope so, because until recently, it appeared to me that Jason was a ticking time bomb, destined to follow in his father's troubled footsteps.

Jason, Nicole, and O.J. Simpson in a more tranquil time.
(Photo credit: Abruscato/Michelson)

The author reveals
his findings on
The Danny Show.

Don Crutchfield
INVESTIGATED NICOLE'S MURDER

Has anyone seen my glove? It's about this size.
(Photo credit: A. Savignano/Galella Ltd.)

Keep on truckin'. Jason Simpson and girlfriend.
(Photo credit: Ramey Photo Agency)

The author at the fights with Robert Shapiro: MGM Grand,
Las Vegas. (Photo credit: Don Duber)

"The Juice is loose."
(Photo credit: Lisa Peterson)

CHAPTER 11

•

One Mother's Twisted Legacy

"We may boast of our accomplishments, but underneath the trappings lies a dungeon where we secretly and incessantly torture ourselves."

—Melody Beattie, *Codependent No More*

There are times when a parent is clearly responsible for a child's problems, like when a mother foists her drug habit upon her kids. What chance does any child have to grow up whole under such circumstances? I got to see some of the tragic results of this situation when I worked on a case involving the actress Joanna Moore and her children, Tatum and Griffin O'Neal.

When I entered the scene, Tatum O'Neal and her then-husband, tennis star John McEnroe, had returned from Wimbledon to LAX and were met at the airport by Joanna Moore. Tatum loaded most of the luggage into her limousine, but inadvertently put a couple of bags containing valuables into her mother's Mazda, a car that had been purchased by Tatum. The next morning, Tatum realized her mistake and phoned her mother, who had a very unusual story to tell.

Joanna Moore claimed that the car had been stolen overnight and that she didn't know anything about her daughter's valuables. Tatum knew this story was a fabrication, so she called me in to investigate.

Tatum told me right off that her mother had a serious drug problem, and expressed no doubt that Joanna had stolen the bags. Tatum was missing a piece of Louis Vuitton luggage that held a smaller Cartier bag containing passports, $160,000 worth of jewelry and $15,000 in cash.

Tatum's skepticism about her mother's story turned out to be well founded. Joanna Moore lived in a Sherman Oaks apartment building with a security garage. She claimed to have parked the Mazda on the street that night because the garage gate wasn't working. I contacted several of Joanna's neighbors, all of whom stated that there was absolutely nothing wrong with that garage gate.

"How do you want this handled?" I asked Tatum.

"I want my mother to admit she did it," my client instructed. "I want her to go into rehab and get some help for her drug problem. If she doesn't go for that, then I don't give a damn if you put her in jail. I've just about had it with her taking advantage of me."

I immediately placed surveillance on Joanna Moore and applied myself to retrieving Tatum's belongings. I wanted to meet with Joanna, but knew that would have to wait.

Joanna had already reported the Mazda stolen to the police. She was going to be hard to nail, but I had an idea. Maybe I could get to Joanna through her son, Griffin O'Neal. In 1986, I had worked on the defense team for Griffin when he'd been accused of manslaughter in a Maryland boating accident that took the life of Gio Coppola, the twenty-three-year-old son of director Francis Ford Coppola.

Griffin, who was twenty-one at the time, was indicted on six counts, including boat manslaughter. Griffin told police that Gio was piloting the fourteen-foot boat when it ran into a tow line connecting two power boats. But eyewitnesses swore under oath that Griffin was at the helm when the collision occurred. To make matters worse, Griffin's blood-alcohol count was far beyond the legal limit. Apparently, the two-year drug rehab program he completed in 1985 didn't work.

Griffin may have been guilty of negligence, but the manslaughter charges were the product of an eager-beaver district attorney who wanted to make a name for himself by nailing the son of a major Hollywood star like Ryan O'Neal.

Before the trial, we took Griffin to Hawaii to get him cleaned up. He was supposed to spend two weeks at one of those rehab places where they shave your head and put you through a kind of boot camp. We hoped the judge would be favorably impressed that Griffin was trying to turn his life around. Naturally, Griffin wouldn't cooperate.

I had assigned a PI named Cliff Stewart to put Griffin on a plane to Hawaii, accompanied by an attending psychiatrist. When Griffin tried to bolt, I had Cliff fly to Hawaii with him and deliver Griffin to the rehab center personally.

Shortly after he returned from rehab, Griffin faced a court trial with no jury. Fortunately, the judge threw out the manslaughter charges. Griffin was found guilty of negligent boating and sentenced to thirty days of community service.

Griffin was lucky. The Maryland judge even consented to allow him to do his community service in Los Angeles. Instead of thanking his lucky stars that he was let off easy, Griffin ignored the sentence. That was his pattern. Griffin had been busted numerous times for driving under the influence. Eventually his license was taken away, but he kept right on driving. However, this was a far more serious matter. A young man was dead because of his negligence.

The Los Angeles authorities grabbed Griffin and extradited him to Maryland, where he did thirty days of hard time. That should have taught him a lesson—but it didn't.

Griffin is the kind of guy who doesn't learn from his mistakes. Furthermore, he can't be trusted. Tatum confided that she once invited Griffin over for dinner. John McEnroe and the kids were there, and they were all having a nice meal. Suddenly Griffin excused himself to go to the bathroom. When her brother didn't return, Tatum went to look for him—only to find Griffin in the bedroom rifling through her dresser.

Griffin is a kid who has never answered to anyone. Whenever the chips are down, Griffin's dad always bails him out. After Griffin sold a tell-all story about his father to the *National Enquirer,* Ryan cut off his funds. But he eventually allowed the boy to get back on the gravy train. Maybe if this kid had been forced to sink or swim just once, he'd grow up. Meanwhile, I needed this flake to help me retrieve my client's valuables.

When I found Griffin, he assured me he had cleaned up his act, was off drugs, and was about to marry his girlfriend, Rima. He also informed me that he didn't want to have anything to do with his mother and therefore couldn't help me.

"I can't be around her," he said, "because she turns me on to cocaine. She's always been a bad influence on me."

When I first started dealing with Hollywood celebrities, a mother's pushing drugs to her son would have seemed as heinous a crime as incest. But in this modern-day Babylon, there aren't many taboos left. I still thought it important to enlist Griffin's cooperation—even though I had a feeling he would repeat my every word to his mother.

"Tatum and I are convinced that your mom stole those bags," I told the son. "On top of that, she has filed a false police report, which means that she's in pretty deep. But I'm on the case now, and I'm pulling all the strings. I can make the police go away, but I need to have those bags back, with everything that was in them.

"The worst thing that can happen is if I leave this case, because then the insurance company will get involved, and they'll hound your mother forever before they pay out all that insurance money. Or I can call the dogs off now. Then everyone will write the whole incident off as a big mistake. Tatum just wants her stuff back. And she wants her mother to deal with her drug problem."

As I spoke, Griffin O'Neal just nodded his head in agreement. I didn't trust him—not for a second. In fact, I strongly suspected that Griffin might have been in on the heist. I left Griffin's house without anything solid. But hopefully I'd given him enough motivation to try to convince his mother to talk to me. In the meantime, I continued my surveillance.

At one point I spotted Joanna trying to ride a bicycle while walking her dog. Unfortunately the dog pulled so hard that Joanna fell off the bicycle. She proceeded to get back up and ride a few more feet. Then the dog pulled on the leash again, and Joanna came crashing down off her bike.

I felt as if I were watching a Charlie Chaplin film, observing this crazed subject continue her bizarre cycle of riding, getting up, and falling down again. I was getting some good laughs on the job. Unfortunately the situation was no closer to being resolved.

I grew more nervous with each passing day. As time slipped by, the probability increased that Tatum's jewelry was being fenced for pennies on the dollar. My best hope was to keep pressuring Griffin to set up a meeting with his mother. Eventually that's what happened. A meeting was finally arranged to take place in his apartment on a steamy Tuesday afternoon.

Griffin and his girlfriend, Rima, lived in a dive in a decrepit North Hollywood neighborhood. The instant I walked through the doorway, the overpowering odor of dog crap nearly knocked me off my feet. The couple had a Doberman pinscher and a pit bull. It was painfully obvious that those dogs went to the bathroom whenever and wherever they pleased. I thought I was going to pass out.

Rima was embarrassed and started to mop up some of the excrement. But it was going to take more than a mop to get that place in shape for anyone other than a couple of whacked-out drug freaks.

Joanna arrived a few minutes later, and I asked her to sit in a low, straight-back chair. I then proceeded to drop onto the sofa. I mean that literally, because the sofa didn't have any springs. All of a sudden, my butt hit the floor. Just what I needed, a Griffin O'Neal trick couch. Now Joanna was sitting about two feet higher than I was. Not the greatest configuration for interrogating a subject.

I finally managed to hoist myself up, when I noticed Griffin fidgeting in the kitchen. I observed him as he walked over to a tape recorder and casually flipped it on. I raced into the kitchen, turned the recorder off, grabbed Griffin by the shirt, and threw him onto his springless couch.

"Sit down, stop fidgeting, and don't move until I tell you," I said. Griffin seemed shocked that I had lain hands on him. But for once he obeyed. I was finally ready to begin my interrogation.

I hammered Joanna with questions for nearly an hour, warning her of dire consequences if she continued her deceit. Joanna was nervous, but she held fast to her story, as I had expected.

"I wish I could help," she said again and again.

"You will help," I told her. "I'm not here to hurt or embarrass you. But I've been hired to get your daughter's things back, and I intend to do just that. Lady, you've got a real foe on your hands now."

I didn't expect Joanna to confess, but I could tell I had gotten to her. When she walked out of Griffin's house that day, Joanna knew I wasn't bluffing about hounding her until I got what I was after. The only remaining question was what she would do about it. I didn't have to wait long for my answer.

The day after my meeting with Joanna, a mysterious call came into the Screen Actors Guild. A woman claimed that her son had stolen Tatum O'Neal's car. She wasn't willing to give her name, but wanted to help Tatum get back the car. SAG called Tatum's business manager, and someone from his office contacted me.

It wasn't hard to figure that Joanna was behind this little scheme. The mystery caller referred to the missing vehicle as Tatum O'Neal's car—even though the car was registered in Joanna Moore's name.

I found the Mazda unlocked, exactly where the mystery caller had said it would be. The rear seat was folded down, providing access to the trunk. There I found the Cartier bag, full of jewelry. A few hundred-dollar bills were scattered around the trunk. The Louis Vuitton bag wasn't there. Neither were the $15 thousand or the passports.

As I drove away from the scene, a dark thought crossed my mind. Joanna had left the car unlocked. Anybody could have come along and stolen those jewels. If that had happened, I would have been the prime suspect. Now I was fuming. This drug-crazed thief had tried to set me up, and she nearly succeeded. I'd worked too long and hard to have my reputation ruined by a stunt like that.

It took me almost half an hour to cool off. Finally I felt composed enough to call Tatum on the car phone.

"Any progress?" she asked.

"Absolutely," I answered. "I'll be at your place in about ten minutes with some of your goods."

Tatum was glad to recover the jewelry, even though most of the cash was still missing. I stepped out of the room for a minute. When I returned, Tatum was sniffing one of the crumpled hundred-dollar bills I'd found in the Mazda. "That's my mother's scent," she announced.

Tatum's investigative technique was a little weird, but she was convinced. "These bills have been in my mother's possession," she repeated. I couldn't very well dispute my client's conclusion, especially since I believed she was right.

At this point Tatum seemed satisfied. She was ready to let the matter go, but I wasn't. After all, she was still missing her Louis Vuiton bag, the passports, and most of the cash.

"Just tell your mother I want to talk to her again," I advised.

"Though I seriously doubt that she'll be willing to go through another encounter with me."

Tatum heeded my advice, and Joanna made it clear that the last thing she wanted was to face me again. Eventually, Joanna confessed to Tatum and returned $12,000, and of the money plus the missing passports. She also agreed to get help with her drug problem. At that point, my involvement in the case was officially over—although the family's problems have apparently not abated.

Griffin O'Neal's continuing propensity for violence was evidenced by a 1992 arrest for assaulting his ex-girlfriend and firing a .44 magnum into her parked car. He also violated my commitment to Tatum to keep the story of her mother's thievery out of the tabloids.

Although the headline story in the *Enquirer* did not specify Griffin as the source, my investigation proved that he was indeed the "source close to the family" who had sold the story, probably to obtain money to support his ongoing drug habit.

Griffin's treachery came as no surprise. I've been around too many druggies and dopers to expect anything else. A guy like Griffin cares only about getting that next fix—even it means dropping a dime on his own mother. Still, if that mother is the person who turned you on to drugs, she doesn't have a right to expect better.

◆

Shortly after Griffin sold his family out to the tabloids, Tatum and John McEnroe ended their six-year marriage. Although Tatum had won an Oscar for *Paper Moon* as a youngster, her movie career had been stalled for years. With her marriage on the rocks, she fell into a deep depression. Before long, Tatum was spotted partying in New York, and rumors of cocaine use abounded.

Tatum had always impressed me as a stable person, so those rumors were troubling. Still, I was hardly surprised. If I've learned anything, it's that drugs are part and parcel to the Babylon lifestyle. If you add to the mix a child growing up with an addicted parent, it's hard to avert disaster.

In September 1995, Tatum checked into an exclusive drug rehab center in Connecticut for a twenty-eight day cleanout. Shortly after her release, she was again spotted hanging out with a high-rolling, coke-snorting crowd. A few weeks later, reports had her checking into New York's Columbia-Presbyterian Medical Center for another round of drug treatment.

By now, John McEnroe had seen enough to convince him that his ex-wife was an unfit mother with a drug problem that wasn't likely to go away. When they first split, the couple shared custody of the kids. It eventually became clear that Tatum was unable or unwilling to perform her parental duties.

"Mac has been assuming almost all the parental responsibilities for the past several months," a close friend of his told a reporter. "He takes the kids for haircuts, to the doctor, to school, and out for fun. He's maintaining a family life for them."

"I'm fighting to protect my children from a sick woman," McEnroe told the friend. "Kids need a full-time mom they can count on twenty-four hours a day. A nanny can only do so much. Tatum can't be trusted to take care of the kids. When they're with her, I sometimes wake up in the middle of the night in a cold sweat worrying about them."

At this writing, John McEnroe has filed for sole custody of his and Tatum's three children. He seems serious about doing whatever is necessary to realize that goal.

"Get me all the evidence you can," the tennis star told the private detectives he hired to follow his wife. "I'm taking those kids away from her—even if I have to spend years in court."

Given Tatum's behavior and family history, one can hardly argue with the man's concerns. If I were in John McEnroe's position, I would probably do the same thing. Like many other unstable parents, Tatum seems determined to hang onto her children, however much it might hurt them.

At one point, Tatum enlisted her father, Ryan O'Neal, to intercede on her behalf.

"What do you want to do, kill her?" Ryan reportedly screamed at his former son-in-law during a heated phone conversation. "Those kids are all she's got to keep her sane. You take them away, and nobody's going to be able to put back the pieces again."

Excuse me, but I always thought that parents were supposed to be there to support their young children, not the other way around. Once a parent is under the sway of drugs, she may desperately want and need her kids. Unfortunately, she is probably the last person who should be given the responsibility for raising them.

Tatum O'Neal and her father Ryan in New York (June 1979).
(Photo credit: AP Wide World)

Tatum O'Neal and her mother, Joanna Moore, on the town (June 1981). (Photo credit: Betty Burke Galella)

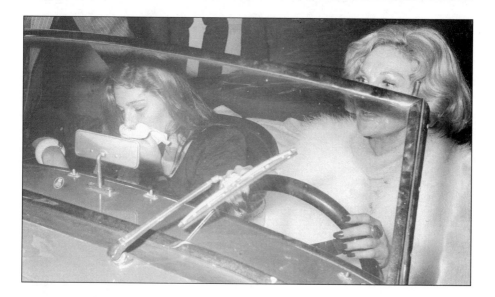

Tatum O'Neal, sick and vomiting, is driven home from Rod Stewart's birthday party by her mother, Joanna Moore.
(Photo credit: Betty Burke Galella)

John MacEnroe and Tatum O'Neal in New York City. (September 1992).
(Photo credit: Ron Galella)

Griffin O'Neal just after father Ryan knocked out his front teeth.
(Photo credit: Ramey Photo Agency)

minutes, it smelled more like horse shit. He got a good laugh seeing everybody run out of the room.

Aside from being a successful movie director, Hedley came from a wealthy family. He inherited $8 million and immediately turned it into $3 million. By the time I met Bruce Hedley, he was pretty much washed up in films. But between his royalties and the money his father had left in trust, it was almost impossible for him to blow all his dough.

My client lived in a beautiful home on Moraga Drive. He was rich, famous, and belonged to Hollywood's most exclusive country club, where he played golf and tennis with some of the most powerful people in town. Hedley's wife was very active in charities and volunteer organizations. The couple had often been seen at fancy balls and dinner parties, but that ended after Hedley threw up in one too many punch bowls.

This was the guy I was being paid to babysit. The first time he and I arrived to pick up the kids, Hedley's wife gave me a nasty look. I had a feeling she knew I was the one who wrapped her up with her lover down in La Jolla. God, who could blame this gal for looking elsewhere for love and affection? Still, no-fault divorce hadn't yet come in, and my screwy client had a hell of a lawyer in Guy Ward.

That Hedley was actually sitting in a good legal position was some kind of miracle, and Guy did not want him to blow it. My job was to keep Hedley clean. So, in addition to supervising visits with his kids, I became his keeper. I remember Guy calling me into his office and running the situation down.

"Okay, Don," he said. "I'm leaving it to you. Don't let this nut screw up. The wife may have him followed, so don't let him compromise the case. Stay on him and make sure he doesn't do anything crazy. I'll need access to him, and I want you to be able to deliver the SOB clean and sober."

Back then I was cash-poor, and I looked at a twenty-four hour-a-day bodyguard job as a real jackpot. If I could stay with a client for an entire week, I could bill for 168 hours of time. That was the equivalent of an entire month's worth of work.

Not only that, I got to sleep eight hours a night, and actually got paid for it. Everywhere the client went, I went. If he went to a fancy restaurant, I could eat anything I wanted—steak, lobster, whatever. It was all on the expense account. As it turned out, no perks were worth what I had to go through. I would have been out of there after the first night if I hadn't needed the money so badly.

The Bel Air Sands is where I usually like to hide people. In this case, there was nothing to hide. The sole objective was to stash this loose cannon and keep him out of trouble. The Bel Air Sands was centrally located, and you could get a nice suite, with two bedrooms and round-the-clock room service.

I could take Hedley for only twenty-four hours at a time, so I hired various people to relieve me. I had to get away from him, or I would lose my temper. Hedley did things calculated to make me mad. I'd be sitting there watching television, and he'd start drinking. After a few minutes he'd look at the TV, then he'd look at me. If he saw that I was absorbed in the program, he'd walk over and turn the TV off. Then he'd just sit there and try to stare me down.

Hedley was always staging these weird little power trips—but I could handle those slights. It was his bizarre public behavior that got to me. We'd go to a fine restaurant, but instead of eating, Hedley would drink. He'd order an expensive dish, then take one bite and push it aside. He'd rationalize his behavior by saying things like, "I'm getting all the vitamins I need. I'm drinking screwdrivers and they've got a day's worth of nutrition."

At first, I tried to dispute this reasoning, but I soon gave up. If the moron wanted to drink himself to death, fine. It was no skin off my back.

When we finished a meal, Hedley liked to get up and run out on the bill, as if he were screwing the restaurant. I'd be left there, supposedly holding the bag.

I'd pay the check and leave the waiter a generous tip. A few minutes later, I'd catch up to Hedley and say, "What'd you do that for?"

"Hell, I really nailed them, didn't I?" he'd laugh.

"You nailed nobody," I'd answer. "I paid the bill, but it's eventually going to come out of your pocket. So who's fooling who?"

"Why didn't you run out too?" he would ask in a serious tone.

"No," I answered, shaking my head. "I just don't do things like that."

Then Hedley would change the subject, which let me know that he intended to pull the same stunt the next time we went out to eat. What could he have been thinking? The man was loaded with money, but he was perversely cheap. On those rare occasions when he paid a restaurant check, he enjoyed pissing off waiters by calling them over and saying: "Excellent service. Please add a six-and-a-half-percent tip for yourself."

The first time Hedley pulled that, I nearly fell out of my seat. It's bad enough to give a waiter a lousy tip—much less ask him to stand there and figure out the math. But Hedley loved cheating people and sticking their nose in it. After I got wise to his tricks, I'd always ask for the bill and add on a twenty percent tip.

Bruce Hedley believed that everybody was trying to cheat him—and I was no exception. He was going to make damn sure I earned every cent of my money. If he could create a situation in which I had to punch someone out or get my shirt torn, that would make his night. Especially because he knew that I took every precaution to avoid confrontations.

One night we went to a club on Wilshire and Santa Monica. We were sitting at the piano bar, having a drink. After a few minutes, a nice-looking married couple came over and sat down next to us. They were both blond and in their early twenties.

My client looked up from his drink, and undressed the young woman with his eyes.

"Tell you what," he told her. "I'll give you a hundred bucks for the whole night."

When the husband heard Hedley's remark, his face turned beet red. "You son of a bitch," he snarled. "I'm gonna kick your ass."

Since I was there to protect Hedley, it was up to me to smooth the situation over. So I stepped between Hedley and the irate husband and started my verbal tap dance.

"Sir, I want to apologize for my friend," I said politely. "I know he's an asshole and he's drunk. I'm really sorry. Please let me buy you and your wife a drink."

The husband wasn't going for that. "I don't want to hear no lame excuses," he screamed. "I'm gonna teach this asshole a lesson!"

"Unfortunately, I can't let you do that," I said. "I know he's in the wrong, but I'm here to protect him. If you try to hit him, you'll have to go through me."

I was a lot bigger than the husband, and I'm sure that helped convince him to back off. But I was almost as angry at Hedley as he was. If someone had said that to my wife, I'd want a piece of him too.

I could never figure out Hedley's trip with women. All I know is that he ogled anything in a skirt, and never failed to blow his chance when it came along.

One evening we were having dinner and drinks at the Century Plaza Hotel. Hedley was relatively sober. A pretty brunette was sitting alone at the next table, and he started talking with her. They were actually having a nice conversation. I found myself thinking: "Gee, I'm proud of him. Maybe he's finally growing up."

Hedley eventually asked her to join us, and there seemed to be a nice chemistry between them. For the first time since I'd started this job, I was feeling hopeful. Maybe if this character could find a girlfriend he'd mellow out a bit. That would be the best thing for him, and it would take the pressure off me.

I emerged from my little daydream to find things progressing better than I could have hoped. Hedley and his new friend were holding hands and having a good time.

I'm thinking: God, this is wonderful. I don't even have to talk to him. Plus I'm getting paid for my time.

I should have offered this girl part of my pay, because she was doing my job for me.

With this guy, it was always risky to leave well enough alone. So I decided to join in the conversation and add to the positive energy. Before long, we had a friendly three-way vibe going. Another half hour went by, and I figured that it might be a good time to go back to the Bel Air Sands. That would make it easy for Hedley and his lady friend to pursue any romantic urges that might come up.

"Tell you what," I began. "Let's head back to the lounge at our hotel and continue the party there."

"That sounds great," the brunette said.

"All right, let's get the check," I said, and signaled for the waiter.

When the check arrived, Hedley picked it up and pointed to me. I should have anticipated what was coming next, but it was too late.

"Figure his bill and mine on one check," Hedley told the waiter. "And give the lady a separate check for what she had."

I felt my mouth opening, but no words came out. Just then, I heard Hedley deliver the coup de grace.

"Oh yes," he said to the waiter. "I appreciate the fine service. Add a six-and-a-half-percent tip for yourself."

At this point, the young lady stood up and walked away from the table in a huff.

"Hey," Hedley called after her. "Are you gonna meet us back at the Bel Air Sands?"

"Screw you," she said. Then she paid her bill at the cash register and stormed out.

"What's wrong with her?" Hedley asked, as if he were totally unaware of what he had done.

"Hey, man," I answered. "You're forty years old. You shouldn't need me to tell you that things don't work that way."

Hedley just shrugged his shoulders. I actually think he got his rocks off antagonizing the poor woman and watching her go through the indignity of paying her own check.

I felt bad for the brunette, but much worse for myself. I still had to play nursemaid to this cheap, paranoid turkey, and it was getting harder with each passing day. The agents who relieved me weren't finding it any easier to put up with him.

"That shithead isn't only crazy," a detective named George told me. "He's as mean as they come. One of these days I'm going to punch his lights out."

George was a good friend of mine, and my primary relief on this case. He handled Hedley with a calmness I admired, but even he was losing patience.

One night Hedley insisted that George accompany him to the Horn, a nightclub in Santa Monica. All the waiters and bartenders at the club were entertainers picking up extra money between gigs. On any given night, name acts like Joan Rivers would stop by to try out new material.

The Horn's management was very strict about customers being quiet during the entertainment, and you never knew when one of the waiters was going to break into a Broadway number. If another waiter happened to catch you not paying attention, he might snap you in the butt with his towel. This only added to the festivities of a club that had been a personal favorite of mine for years.

On this particular night, Hedley and George walked into the Horn and sat down at the bar. Our boy appeared sober at the time, and George was hoping against hope that there would be no trouble.

Hedley started talking to a lady seated on his right. The lady's husband, who was sitting close by, was talking sports with the bartender. This husband was a big old boy from Texas who sported an enormous ten-gallon hat.

Hedley and the Texan's wife were drinking and carrying on what seemed to be an amiable conversation about how nice the entertainment was. But at some point the booze caught up to Hedley. All of a sudden, he started whispering obscenities to this lady.

The husband was pretty bombed himself, but he'd picked up on some of what was transpiring. This Texan, who must have been about six foot six and weighed 275 pounds, got off his stool and gave Hedley a menacing stare.

George handled the situation about as well as anyone could. He leaped from his seat and grabbed Hedley by his shirt collar. Then he turned to the Texan and said: "Don't worry, I'm a bouncer, and I'll take care of this bastard myself."

George rushed Hedley through the front door, out of harm's way. George had to go out of town the next morning, so we didn't get a chance to speak. The following evening, Hedley and I were sitting around the hotel.

"Hey Don," he said. "I'm bored, Let's go hang out at the Horn."

When we got to the club, the manager stopped us at the door.

"No way," he said. "You're welcome here any time, Mr. Crutchfield, but your friend here is banned for life. I don't ever want to see his sorry face again!"

I later learned that the Texan had taken out his anger on Hedley the previous night by rearranging the Horn. Since Hedley had left the club before the damage was done, they couldn't make him pay for all the broken furniture. But they certainly would never allow him through the doors again.

It had become clear that going anywhere with this guy was hazardous duty. Aside from being a hopeless alcoholic, he was paranoid about people following him. About a week after the fiasco at the Horn, Hedley wanted to see a strip show. We were sitting at the bar next to a guy with his hand in a cast. Before I could turn around, Hedley ran over, grabbed this guy's bandaged hand, and started banging it hard on the bar.

"You've got a tape recorder hidden in there," my client shouted. "I know you're recording my conversations."

"Yeow-w-w!" the man with the cast cried out in pain. "What's going on here?"

There wasn't much I could do except pull my client off the poor guy and apologize profusely, while hustling Hedley out the door.

After five weeks of babysitting, I had about as much as I could take of Mr. Bruce Hedley, but Guy Ward pleaded with me to stay close to him, promising he'd make it up to me in the future, which he did. In the meantime, my dream job was turning into an endless nightmare. I think Hedley would have been pleased to know I felt that way, but I wasn't about to give him the satisfaction.

"Now, Bruce, no drinking tonight," I would say to him. "There are things we have to do in the morning, so I need you to keep a clear head. We're gonna watch a little television and go to bed early."

"Okay," he'd answer. Then he would pour himself a glass of tomato juice right in front of me. A few minutes later, he'd start sneaking vodka into the glass. In half an hour, he would be drunk on his ass.

One afternoon, Guy Ward had some papers that needed Hedley's signature. I was shaving in the bathroom when Guy called. By the time I got out, Hedley had headed over to Guy's office, drunk out of his mind. As soon as Guy saw Hedley he said, "You've been drinking, haven't you?"

"Oh, yeah!" Hedley answered. "I have been drinking all day. You know what I'm gonna do, Guy? I'm gonna lie down right here on your couch and sleep it off."

Before Guy could respond, Bruce had passed out on his reception room couch. I was still at the Bel Air Sands when the phone rang. It was Guy Ward, and he was steamed.

"Don, you get that SOB out of here right now," he shouted. "I don't care if you have to throw him in the middle of Wilshire Boulevard. Just get him out of my office!"

Naturally, I accommodated Guy. But in a way, I was glad that he got a chance to see firsthand what I had been up against for more than a month.

Hedley's two daughters were the real unfortunate figures in this scenario. They were both sweet little girls, and it was a shame Bruce couldn't behave for the few hours a week he was allowed to spend with them.

On custody day, he'd ask me to pick different places to go with the girls. One Sunday we took them an amusement park called the Long Beach Pike. In its day, "the Pike" was one of the great amusement parks in the world.

As usual, Hedley had been drinking the night before, and he had a giant hangover. The kids badly needed some attention from their father, but he was too strung out. At one point the girls wanted to play the game where you throw balls at lead milk bottles. If you knock them all down, you win a prize.

The two girls were throwing balls at the bottles and having a great time. Suddenly Hedley walked over and said, "Hey, let me try."

The pathetic drunk grabbed a ball, wound up, and started to throw; then he collapsed in a heap over the counter. The ball bounced right in his face, and Hedley began to spew vomit on to the counter.

"You crazy bastard," the woman running the concession shouted. "Get the hell out of here."

"Haven't you heard?" Hedley muttered, as he staggered away. "Life is one big barf-off."

Hedley managed to stumble onto a basketball shoot in the next booth. He grabbed a basketball and started to shoot baskets. Then he fell down on the sidewalk.

The poor little girls were in tears. They went home knowing full well that their next custody visit wasn't likely to go much better. As it turned out, that disastrous trip to Long Beach would be the last time they would see their dad for a while.

One night, about two weeks before the court date set for his divorce, Hedley threw up right in the middle of the Bel Air Sands lounge. This was the last straw, and we were asked to find lodging elsewhere. I now felt it imperative to get my client out of town. His erratic behavior threatened to bolster his wife's case in the divorce proceedings and weaken his position. Millions of dollars were at stake.

"What would you think about moving him to Acapulco until the trial?" I asked Guy Ward. "I've been going down there since high school, and I've got good relations with the authorities. We would have a lot easier time maintaining control. And if he did screw up, nobody would be the wiser."

"Fine," Guy said. "Go wherever you have to go, but just keep him out of town until all of this is settled."

I had booked a reservation at the Ritz Hotel in Acapulco for Hedley, myself, and another detective named Dub. But as the plane left the ground at 7 A.M., I realized that could turn out to be as bad as the situation at the Bel Air Sands. What we needed was a house with a maid—which I lined up within an hour after we landed.

We wound up renting a blue two-story house right off the beach. The house also happened to be around the corner from the Normandy Restaurant, one of my favorite spots in town. I had rented that house before, and knew it was exactly what we needed. The grounds were surrounded by a twelve-foot fence, and there was a security gate in the front. Now if we could only install a padded cell for my client, Dub and I could relax and enjoy this tropical paradise.

I had no reason to believe that Hedley would straighten up his act in Mexico, and he was quick to prove me right. Once we dropped our things off at the house, we headed down to the main beach. All the waiters and bartenders knew me. We were all saying, "Como esta, amigo?" and giving each other hugs.

And there was Hedley, frantically waving his hands at everybody and shouting "Hi, hi, hi," like he was an old friend. My Mexican buddies were looking at me like, "Who is this strange guy?" Still, everybody was smiling.

In Mexico, they serve great big glasses of fresh-squeezed orange juice, chilled in a cloud of ice cubes. The thought of that ice-cold juice reminded me how hot the sun was. I called a waiter over.

"Tell you what, amigo," I said. "Bring me two of those big orange juices."

The waiter turned to Hedley, who said: "I'm gonna have a zombie, okay?"

The waiter gave him a funny look, because it was still morning, and the drinks they serve down there have enough booze to lay you out at any hour. Hedley consumed three zombies in a matter of minutes. Not only was he still conscious, he decided he wanted a coco loco.

This drink is made by cutting off the top of a coconut with a machete. Half of the coconut liquid is poured out and replaced with gin. At this particular establishment, they put nearly a half pint of gin in those coconuts, then topped it off with crushed ice and a couple of straws.

After Hedley drank three coco locos, two beggars came up to our table. That part of Mexico is swarming with beggars of all ages and configurations, and they'll stare at you with their hands out until you give them money.

I've never seen anybody who could out-stare an Acapulco beggar, except for Bruce Hedley. He stared at them with such an other-worldly look in his eyes that the beggars must have thought they were facing the devil himself. I have never seen two people take off so fast in my life.

Those beggars weren't the only ones who were freaked out. It was time to move Hedley to a part of town where I wasn't so well known. It was still only two in the afternoon, and my boy hadn't even begun to drink. So we took a taxi down to Condesa Beach. I selected a restaurant that had a cement slab fronting the water. They had a dance floor and a band that played in the afternoon. That was fine. I was stone cold sober and badly needed some entertainment.

Between all the alcohol he had consumed and the tropical sun,

Hedley had become mellow. To be more accurate, he was nodding out. Every so often, I'd give him a little nudge and he'd wake up. When it got to be five o'clock, I suggested we order some dinner. Hedley agreed, but all he ordered were more of those potent trick drinks.

I finally decided I couldn't handle any more of this totally sober, so I ordered a pitcher of beer and a large platter of shrimp. In Mexico they often cook shrimp in the shell, so they've got to be peeled before you eat them. There was a bowl of coarse salt on the table, which you put on a spoon and spread over the shrimp.

"Care for a shrimp?" I asked Hedley, as the waiter set the platter on the table.

"By god, I believe I will," he replied. He grabbed two of those jumbo shrimp and ate them, shell and all. This extraordinary sight stopped the waiter in his tracks.

In a matter of seconds, Hedley was coughing and sweating like a pig. You could see he was having a hell of a time getting this stuff down his throat. Suddenly, he reached over and swallowed a spoonful of the thick salt.

Hedley managed to get about half the funky concoction down his throat. He spit the rest out on the floor. Then he looked at me and said: "Damn, that rice sure is salty!"

Maybe it was the beer, but I started laughing so hard I could barely catch my breath. The restaurant manager, who had been watching warily, suddenly reached his limit.

"I want you to leave right now," he told me. "Get this crazy man out of my restaurant. Take your shrimp with you and don't ever come back!"

"Let's go," I said to Hedley. "We've got to split."

"I need something to drink," he said.

"Yeah, I know you do, but we're going back to the house."

The cab ride home took about half an hour. By then, Hedley had straightened up just enough to start busting my chops about money.

"I know you've been cheating me all along. You've been stealing my money and I want it back."

"Wait a minute," I snarled. "Don't you start on me. I'm the only thing that's kept you alive, and I've never taken a dime from you.

I'm here to protect you and your money. I've done a damn good job of it too.

"I'm gonna tell you something. If you ever say anything like that again while we're down here, you're going to have to get back to LA on your own. I've put up with enough."

That was the only time I ever lost my temper with Hedley, but I was steaming. And he wasn't through.

"I'll tell you what you're gonna do," he said as he staggered up the stairs. "You're going make me a Bloody Mary right now."

I was about to tell him what he could do with his Bloody Mary, but I had a better idea.

"You're right, I am going make you a Bloody Mary. That's exactly what I'm gonna do."

I got the biggest glass I could find, poured about half a fifth in it, and added just enough tomato juice to give it color. I took it up to him, and he downed the entire drink in three swallows. Then, he held up the glass to show me he wanted another one, though all he could way was, "blub, blub, blub, blub."

I proceeded to fix him a second drink, just about as potent. He took a hit off that and passed out cold. I knew my boy was gone for the night, so I went out and hit the town. When he woke up the next morning, Hedley looked at me and said, "You know, that drinking can kill you."

"Really? You don't say."

The next night, I took him out again. I had decided to try a new strategy. In spite of all the crap he pulled on me, I wanted to make sure he had a good time. I felt sorry for him. I couldn't imagine what dark forces had made him so self-destructive.

We wound up in a bar, and Hedley spotted a hooker he liked. At least he thought he liked her. So I went over to the girl and said, "You see that guy over there? I want you to make him very happy."

"Well, that's going to cost," she said.

"Tell you what I'm gonna do. I'm gonna triple whatever your fee is. How does that sound? I want you to stay with him all night long. I've got the key to the gate, so you're going to need to come and see me before you go. I just want him happy, so do your best."

"This guy's gonna be the happiest guy in the world," she assured me.

"That's all I ask."

I locked the gate and dozed off in the front room. The next thing I knew, it was daylight and Hedley's hooker was limping down the stairs. She looked as if she'd spent a month in a concentration camp.

I yawned. "What happened to you?"

"Hombre, I never do that again for no money. Your friend, he climb on top of me and stay there all night. He never even move. It so hot, I think I going to die."

The girl had probably shed twenty pounds overnight. I felt bad for her, but at least she got paid. More important, I had gotten some much-needed rest.

About an hour later, Hedley came down. "Hey Don, I think my girlfriend is kind of sore about last night."

"Nah," I winked. "She told me she loved it. You did all sorts of dynamite things with her."

We stayed in Acapulco for ten days, after which we returned to get ready for the divorce hearing.

Custody was never at issue. The judge knew that Hedley could not be trusted to care for his children. Even though we proved the wife had committed adultery, she was able to establish that he had effectively driven her out of the marriage with his alcoholism and crazy antics. As a result, my client lost almost a million dollars.

My babysitting days ended after the hearing, but I still couldn't get Bruce Hedley out of my life. He'd get drunk and call me in the middle of the night, waking me up with some lame story.

Like so many other terrible Hollywood parents, Bruce desperately wanted to hold on to his children. Every so often, he would get it into his head that he could convince a judge to give him custody.

"I know that bitch is cheating on me," he'd say. "She's off skiing with her new lover and I want you to nail them."

"Who cares?" I yawned. "Your attorney doesn't care. I don't care. Why should you care? New information about her is not going to help us at this point. Besides, how do you know they went skiing?"

There was a restraining order that prohibited Hedley from

going to the house except during visitation days. However, he had kept a key and garage-door opener. One Friday he found his wife and daughters gone. Then he opened the garage and discovered the ski equipment wasn't there.

"They've got the ski equipment, but I don't know where the hell they went. You've got to find them."

I'd had more than my fill of this guy, but I decided to do this one last piece of work for him—at an exorbitant rate. Maybe then he'd stop calling me.

It turned out that Hedley was right. His wife was with a guy, and the girls had gone with them on a skiing trip.

I made some inquiries, and determined that they had gone to a skiing lodge called the Mammoth Mountain Inn.

I managed to get a room at the Inn and kept tabs on Hedley's family for the entire weekend. Since the wife and kids knew me, I had to walk around in a ski mask for a good part of the stay.

I didn't mind wearing the mask when I was out on the slopes, but sitting in the lounge with a ski mask on was another matter. There I was, looking like the Masked Marvel, trying to make small talk with people and remain incognito. I felt like a complete fool, plus the mask was hot and itchy. I guess the strategy worked, because Hedley's wife and kids never realized that weirdo walking around in a ski mask was me.

By the time I left Mammoth, I had it all: photographs of the wife and boyfriend skiing; photos of the two girls skiing without supervision; and copies of the registration and room-service receipts. I knew the girls slept in a separate room and that Hedley's wife and her lover had breakfast in bed on Sunday.

All that good surveillance work cost Bruce a pretty penny, but it didn't do him a bit of good. There was no judge on earth—not even in Hollywood—who would grant that psycho custody of two young children.

After the ski-lodge fiasco, Hedley started going downhill physically. He'd contracted bleeding ulcers and was throwing up blood.

"You're going to kill yourself if you keep going on like this," his doctor told him. "I want you to stop drinking and go on a bland diet."

Hedley called me one day to announce that he had actually quit drinking and was following doctor's orders. That didn't last long. Eventually he reverted back to his old ways, and even managed to find a doctor who told him that his self-destructive lifestyle was okay.

One night Bruce Hedley passed out in a drunken stupor with a cigarette in his hand. Within minutes, his whole apartment went up in flames, and Hedley along with it. He was forty-two years old.

I sometimes think about all the time and money that went into protecting this client and helping him maintain his legal position as the injured party. For what? In the end, his ex-wife wound up with most of his estate.

On some level, I see Bruce Hedley as Judy Garland's male counterpart. He had it all: talent, wealth, a thriving career, and a nice family. What were the incurable nightmares that made him want to self-destruct? I'm never going to know the answer, but for a time I felt kind of responsible. If I or one of my men had been there, I doubt he would have fallen asleep with a lit cigarette in his hand. We were good at preventing things like that.

Every cloud is said to have a silver lining, but I can't really find one for Bruce Hedley. At least the well-heeled members of swanky country clubs in Beverly Hills won't have to worry about his throwing up in their punch bowls any more. And waiters throughout the greater Los Angeles area will never again have to suffer the indignity of calculating a six-and-a-half-percent tip.

A few years before I met Bruce Hedley, I worked with a guy named Hank Cooper. Hank was in his early fifties. He'd been a career army man who had reached the rank of sergeant. Then he contracted heart problems and received a medical discharge. Hank was married to a schoolteacher. Between her salary and the small monthly pension   he received from the army, Hank lived a reasonably comfortable life.

Hank was about as far removed from Hollywood glitz as you could get. The man had very few material needs and desires. He worked only with us, two or three days a week to earn a little extra money. Hank was an alcoholic, and he could go through a case of beer on a good day. But, unlike Bruce Hedley, Hank never got obnoxious.

Professionally speaking, Hank was one of the least competent investigators I've ever come across. He was a nice gentle man, though, so we always tried to find something for him to do.

Working a surveillance job with Hank was a frustrating experience. He always got confused about his responsibilities. He was also a terrible driver who could never keep up in traffic. Having Hank drive the second car in a two-car surveillance was far less efficient than working the job solo. He'd usually get lost, and you'd have to waste time finding him after you had your subject wrapped up.

I got stuck working a couple of two-car surveillance jobs with Hank. We'd be covering two sides of the same street. I'd spot the subject driving in Hank's direction and call him on the two-way radio.

"Hank, they're leaving, they're leaving!"

There would be no response, so I'd take off after them. As I passed Hank's vehicle, I would get a glimpse of him sleeping on the front seat. Some partner!

When he could manage to stay awake, Hank tried to play at being a detective. He especially loved changing disguises. Hank would be following somebody, and he would put on a taxi driver's hat. Next, he'd take that off and put on a wig and a moustache. Then he'd change into a cowboy hat.

There was only one problem: Hank was still driving the same car, so the subject wasn't likely to be tricked by his pathetic dime store disguises.

Hank may not have been the world's brightest human, but he was a real sweet guy. He was also very distinguished looking. When you dressed him up in a suit and tie, Hank looked like a million bucks. He had gray hair, chiseled features and an athlete's physique. But the minute Hank opened his mouth, it was all over.

When he talked, Hank sounded just like Elmer Fudd. He'd say: "Don, I'm wooking wight at the subject's Pwymouth sedan. It's about to pull up on your weft-hand side."

After a while, we decided that Hank's presence on surveillance jobs was far more trouble than it was worth. So we started using him to run messages. We'd send him to attorneys to pick up legal documents, and we'd always tell him the same thing:

"Now Hank, don't say anything. Just pick up the papers, smile, and get the hell out of there."

At one point we had a female client who was worth over $20 million dollars. She was a gifted architect and a successful film producer. She was close friends with Lana Turner and other major Hollywood players. This gal was in her late thirties, and not especially good looking.

Despite her wealth, talent and superior intelligence, this client had a history of men exploiting her. At the time we got involved, she was married to a guy who was after her money. He had tried to kill her several times. Once he attempted to drown her in the bathtub. On another occasion he shoved her down a flight of stairs. Right before we were called in, she'd caught him trying to poison her food.

"I've tried everything," he told a friend. "But the bitch just won't die."

The client had obtained a restraining order against this murderous spouse, and we were hired to make sure the SOB stayed away from her. We had people bodyguarding her twenty-four hours a day. But there was a problem. She was always trying to get the bodyguards to sleep with her, but none of the guys were into it.

I finally came up with a solution. The client had an apartment over her garage, so we would install a man to live in that apartment and keep an eye on things. By now, the husband realized there were bodyguards around and was making himself scarce.

By coincidence, Hank had recently broken up with his wife and didn't have any place to stay. It seemed like the perfect setup for him. Hank moved into the apartment over the garage. His salary was to be $200 a week, in addition to an address in Beverly Hills and all the food he could eat. Hank didn't have to work very hard at all. What a great deal. Between his pension and the $200, he could buy all the beer he wanted.

Hank's new employer was on the rebound from a husband who had tried to murder her. It was obvious that he'd been using her all along. The poor woman desperately needed someone to provide a little tender loving care.

Hank had a buzzer in his apartment that the client could activate whenever she needed him. Whenever he heard that buzzer, Hank was to rush to the main house. The very first night Hank moved in, his buzzer rang and he responded.

"I'm afraid, Hank," the woman cried. "I heard some noises outside. Please don't leave me here alone."

Good old Hank. He stayed the night and never again went back to that apartment over the garage. After he'd lived in the main house for a couple of months, his wealthy new lover said: "Hank, I'm in love with you and I want to marry you." The two of them married and Hank became a gentleman millionaire.

I lost touch with Hank for a period of time. But I was glad about the way things turned out for him. I was happy for his new wife as well. Hank was a kind soul, and I knew he would never mistreat her.

One night, about two years later, I walked into the Luau Restaurant and there was Hank. He was sitting at the bar, having drinks with the actor Cesar Romero.

"Hank, how the hell are you? Where have you been?"

"Well," he answered. "Cesar and I have been over to Harry Cherry's getting fitted for some hand-tailored suits. We just stopped by to relax and hoist a few."

I remembered that Hank had a heart problem. Back when he was working with us, the doctors had told him that if he didn't quit drinking he would die.

"Hank, it's great to see you," I began. "But didn't the doctors tell you that the booze would kill you?"

"Hell," he chuckled. "Who cares? I can afford to die now."

I sat down with Hank and listened as he recited the many joys of married life.

"My wife is just wonderful—and so talented. Do you know that she's designing the house we're building in Tahiti all by herself?"

Hank went on to talk about their farm in Ohio and their house next to the golf course at the Desert Inn—not to speak of the mansion in Beverly Hills.

"She treating you okay?" I asked, pretty much knowing what his answer would be.

"Hey, let me tell you. We were sitting around the pool, having our lunch. Suddenly she says: 'Hank, you must be bored. doing the same thing every day. Why don't I give you fifty thousand dollars to start your own business?'

"I looked over at her and smiled. Then I said, 'Now honey, what am I going to do with a hot dog stand?'"

We both had a good laugh over that one. Hank never was a guy to overestimate his capabilities. He knew he had lucked out, and he had no delusions of grandeur.

Hank died about a year after I saw him, but I'm certain he left this earth a happy man. I attended his funeral in Las Vegas, and I couldn't resist smiling inside. Considering his love of alcohol and the doctor's prognosis, Hank lasted longer than anyone expected. And he went out with both guns blazing.

In its own bittersweet way, Hank's is a classic Hollywood story. A very simple man with nothing much going for him steps into the high life without even thinking about it. I guess Hank's twist of fate goes to show that the power of being able to soothe a broken heart can transcend all material considerations. And Hank sure did make his wife happy, even if their time together was short.

I think I'll fix myself a tall bourbon and soda and toast the two Hanks. First, I'll drink to the incompetent PI who talked like Elmer Fudd and couldn't stay awake on the job. Then I'll drink to that distinguished millionaire in handmade clothes—the guy who hung out with movie stars and talked about his mansions in Tahiti and Beverly Hills.

Hank, you'll always be there to remind me that all things are possible here in Babylon—this land where glorious fantasies and hideous nightmares converge in a smog-covered sea of glimmering lights.

Table of Contents

Introduction

Sales always comes down to a single one-time opportunity to close.

A true professional, a real champion in sales, is *constantly* closing. We don't say *always* closing. You can't close all the time, but you can make sure that when you *do* close, that time is the perfect time. Most salespeople, especially the folks in retail, have one and only one opportunity to serve the needs of any given customer. Others, those people in high-dollar markets for example, will invest a lot more time and energy to land a sale. Still, the entire process, no matter how brief or how drawn out, always comes down to a one-time opportunity to close.

That's what this book is all about—the art of one-call closing. We also refer to the process as one-time closing and both terms are used interchangeably throughout this book.

We have invested years, decades really, into studying, learning, practicing and perfecting one-call closing techniques. We have discovered a profoundly simple, yet profoundly effective process. It's not magic. It's not manipulation. It's just a very logical way to match your product or service to the specific needs of your customer in a one-time closing situation. In the following pages we will show you specifically and in detail how to combine your people skills and your basic sales techniques with this powerful new sales strategy.

It works. We have tried it, tested it, improved it and now, best of all, we're sharing it. Think of the one-close process as one of those ancient circular mazes where the traveler starts on the outside and eventually winds his or her way to the center. That's what you'll be doing. Every step in the process brings you closer to your ultimate goal—serving the needs of your customer. Every move helps you zero in closer and closer until you are finally "home" at the win/win situation of a successful close.

Creating The "Right Place At The Right Time"

We predict that in the pages of this book you will be amazed to discover a number of time-tested and proven ideas that have never been published. We have combined these powerful "new" ideas with other, more familiar techniques that we have taught over the years. The result is a dynamic, step-by-step manual for those people fortunate enough to be making a living in sales.

Sell It Today, Sell It Now, Mastering the Art of the One-Call Close will show the new-comer and the veteran alike how to develop champion sales presentations for any sales situation by using the correct sequence for every prospect.

You've no doubt heard the phrases, "timing is ninety percent of genius" and "he was in the right place at the right time." Using the techniques in this book will show you how to say the right words at the right time. In other words, you'll learn how to create the right "sequence" for maximum effect.

There are no new words in sales. We all draw from the same pool of words, phrases and expressions and the pool isn't any deeper for top closers than it is for those on the bottom rungs. Why, then is there such a disparity between top sales people and the also-rans? The difference is that the top closers presentation is in harmony with the mindset of their prospect. Their presentations are in the proper sequence.

In later pages, we will show you examples of how sequence can and does affect all aspects of our lives. For the moment, the proper sequence for you is to read this book and put into action the techniques and methods contained in these pages.

Speaking of later pages, throughout this book we use a number of examples and scenarios featuring a variety of products and services. Naturally we have chosen some of the most prominent so that the examples apply to the broadest possible audience. *But please remember, the principles, techniques, strategies and tactics you find here will apply across the board.* Whether you're offering insurance or interior design, financial services or fighter planes, home improvements or highways, real estate or real-time streaming video, this book is for *you.*

Your goal is to present your product or service in such a way that the only sensible choice is for your potential client to make a buying decision *and to make it right now.*

The Art Of One-Call Closing Is More Than A One-Time Read

An associate in the advertising profession told us about the absolute necessity of repetition in selling. He says that numerous studies dating back at least to the early 1960s prove that consumers don't even recognize that they've read/viewed/listened to an ad, TV commercial or radio spot (or whatever medium) until they've been exposed six times. And that's just recognition. The selling hasn't even begun at that point. We also remember an important lesson a speed reading instructor told us. The purpose of speed reading isn't to get through a book faster. The purpose is to be able to get through the book several times in the same time period. The more you read the same material, the more you retain and will be able to put to good use.

We don't want this book to be just a one-time read for the very same reason. The more you study this book the more you will get out of it, the more it will enrich your life and enhance your future. We recommend that you read it once straight through and then go back through it again. Keep it always nearby so you can refer to it often. It is our hope and our belief that you will find it a constant source of information, thought-provoking ideas and inspiration.

1

Timing is everything.
It is as important to know when as to know how.

Arnold Glasow

The One-Time Job Description

M ost retail sales are one-time closes, or should be. The customer walks in, you make an approach, a presentation and then an effective close. "Thank you so much, and please call again." But even when helping people get involved with high-dollar items requiring multiple consultations, there's a distant-but-inevitable moment when the planets are in alignment, the stars are in your favor, and it's time for a close. That's the moment for a one-time close, as well. It's a one-time opportunity.

Regardless of your sales experience, or the lack of it, you are about to embark on a brand new leg of your career focused on the art of the one-time close. No matter how many years you have in the business, no matter how much real-world experience you've racked up, and apart from those "Salesperson of the Month" plaques you've earned, when you adopt the principles in *Sell It Today, Sell It Now, Mastering the Art of the One-Call Close*, you are starting a new job.

The one-call close approach is so different from what you've likely already mastered that it requires different thinking about what your job as a salesperson is all about.

Why are people in sales? What is the job description of someone required to close sales on the first and only opportunity? We've asked this question in classes and seminars all around the country. Some of the more popular answers are:

- to sell a product
- to feed my family
- to serve the needs of others
- to identify the needs of another person
- to show a product to a prospect
- to explain the benefits of a product or service
- to make enough money to _____
- uh…'cause…you know?

Certainly these are valid reasons, but they're not very accurate. That's like describing your reason for taking a passenger jet is because you like the peanuts, the in-flight movie, or you just have a thing for clear-air turbulence. All of those reasons may be valid, but that's not why you bought your ticket. The real answer for why we do what we do somehow eludes most people, even those who have for years reaped the benefits of this most wonderful of professions.

What sets the one-call close salesperson apart from the rest? Most of the products, services, and ideas we offer provide genuine benefits to our customers just like the rest of the world's sales people. We all help people get where they want to go. For most salespeople, the presentation is centered around features, turning those features into benefits and then offering proof to back up their statements. That is well and good and certainly necessary. After all, we couldn't make it through that cross-country trip without those peanuts and in-flight movies. However, you don't have to be a rocket scientist to know that the focus of a one-time closer is not on the peanuts or the movie, but like a laser beam, it is on selling it today and selling it now. And believe us, this is an art form, but it is an art form that you can learn, apply and even improve your skills with by internalizing the techniques in this book.

The difference in the art of the one-time close is in the significant amount of planning, time, and energy the salesperson invests in the process of the close. *Therefore, the job description of the one-time closing salesperson is **sell it today, sell it now!***

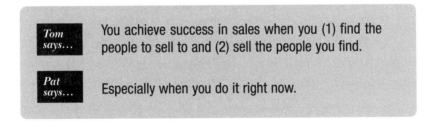

Tom says... You achieve success in sales when you (1) find the people to sell to and (2) sell the people you find.

Pat says... Especially when you do it right now.

Using Full-Court Pressure

We have created this book for two types of salespeople:

1. those whose jobs are defined by a need for the one-time close
2. those whose jobs evolve into a one-time closing situation.

In other words, this book is for everyone in sales. Despite our intense focus on closing, we do not advocate, nor do we recommend using high pressure sales techniques. Ever! And we haven't just served you up a big, heaping helping of contradiction either.

The age of the high pressure salesperson has gone the way of the dinosaur. It is as extinct and as frozen in the past as those T-Rex bones they keep digging up in Utah.* Our techniques focus on continual, gentle persuasion targeted to getting a one-time close *without using high pressure techniques.* We can help you overcome a customer's natural indecision and reluctance to autograph your paperwork. One of the worst experiences a salesperson can have is to make a heartfelt, enthusiastic, and sincere presentation only to hear:

- "I'd like to think about it some more."
- "Well, thanks. I'll have to get back to you."

---

*We understand from the Disney folks that the age of the dinosaur, at least the animated kind, has returned. That may be true, but salespeople today don't live in a cartoon world. No matter how "animated" the presentation, the high-pressure salesperson is likely to end up in some future museum with the other dinosaurs where incredulous people walk around thinking "I wonder how they ever managed to live like that."

- "You've given me a lot to think about."
- "That's certainly food for thought."
- "Could I have your card before I go?"
- "We don't jump in to something like this."

The "full court press" is a basketball term in which the defensive team doesn't run to their end of the court to get in to position and then wait for the team with the ball to show up. They start playing defense immediately at the other end of the court, forcing the team with the ball to fight for every inch of the floor. The one-time closing master works for that close every second of the presentation. From the first second of "Hello, what brings you folks out here today" to the "just authorize here to confirm our agreement" the salesperson is working—building toward the inevitable, successful close. It really is a full-court press designed to make sure your customer gets the goods or services she or he wants, needs and are truly good for them.

"I sold my heart out, but I just couldn't close him." How often have you heard that? How often have you said it! The one-call close puts the focus of the sales presentation where it belongs—on the close, which is the natural progression of selling. We do that by creating a genuine and honest sense of urgency throughout the presentation. It's a full-court press designed to help your prospect get the one, unique product or service (yours) that perfectly matches his or her unique need.

Some Day Selling

The problem a lot of salespeople have is what we call "someday selling." They aren't selling for a close now, they're working toward some ill-defined point in the future. That future "someday" may be only minutes down the road, but without the skills and techniques in this book that someday might remain "out there." Sometimes, someday never comes.

What makes this worse, is that the salesperson gets the picture too late to do anything about it. Feeling desperate, he or she will start using real high-pressure sales techniques (not one-time closing). The customer notices the abrupt change in tactics, feels his needs are being ignored, and ends up going across the street where the salespeople aren't so pushy.

Of course, we often hear that it takes pressure to create a diamond. Rarely do we hear the other side of that story. A diamond isn't created by abrupt pressure. It's created by continual, well-directed pressure over time. Do you see the difference? More important, your potential new client will feel the difference.

Use Outside Factors To Get The Inside Track

The one-call close shows you how to create a proper sense of urgency throughout your presentation which will lead directly to the win/win situation of a successful close today.

External factors can be used effectively to create the necessary urgency. Again, we're not for a second saying you should use or create a *false* sense of urgency. Not only is that dishonest, it's unnecessary.

There are always plenty of legitimate external factors at your finger tips. For example:

"This is the last SUV on the lot with this special, end-of-the-month investment."

"Our stock of winter coats goes on sale Saturday. By Sunday, I expect this entire rack to be empty."

"We're selling an average of three houses a week here. We only have three left, and only one in your desired investment range."

"There's obviously a reason we have so many satisfied customers enjoying this product."

"We need to clear out our inventory, so we're offering some really great special investments through the end of the month."

"The company is discontinuing the line next year. These are the last ones ever."

All of these examples are justifiable uses of urgency to legitimately serve a customer's need. In later chapters, we will describe in detail all the skills and knowledge you need to create this sense of urgency so you can close your sales in just one call.

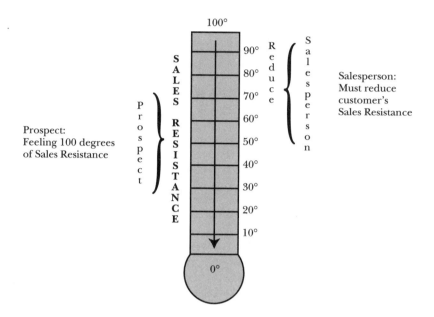

Decrease Sales Resistance Chart
"Before" Phase

One-Time Closing By Degrees

The above illustration uses a thermometer to show how a typical customer feels at the beginning of the sales process. This is a *before* sketch which will be followed by a *during* and an *after*. As if you didn't already know, the potential client usually meets you with a fairly high degree of Sales Resistance. In fact, he (or she) could be near the boiling point of resistance at 100 degrees.

Wait, you say. If the customer has logged on, made a call or walked in, that shows at least some level of acceptance. Doesn't it? Well, yes and no. Yes, the customer is interested in the product or service. That doesn't mean he's interested a bit in your specific brand, your company, or your sales presentation. The degree of resistance *you* face at that moment is right up there, pegging out at or near 100 degrees. Don't ever assume otherwise.

Any additional pressure applied to this customer will raise that level of resistance even higher. The situation could easily "bubble over" the top and you'll never get the opportunity to close. Your job is to begin rapidly lowering the temperature. If you give your prospect half a chance, he or she will help you do it. Remember, down inside they really want your product or service or they wouldn't have made or agreed to the contact. Again, if you apply undue, sudden pressure, your customers will seek relief in a cooler climate. They will bubble over, head out the nearest exit, cross the street and enter the comfort zone at your competitor's operation.

Customers don't visit your show room, 800 number, or web site to feel uncomfortable. See to it that they feel relaxed and comfortable and right at home immediately by lowering that temperature as quickly as possible. Our experience has proven that no one invests their money in anything unless they are relaxed and comfortable.

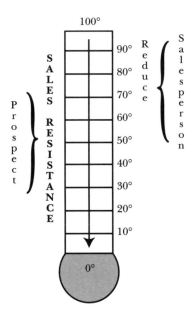

Decrease Sales Resistance Chart
"During" Phase

This chart illustrates what (ideally) should be happening during the various stages of your presentation. Slowly but surely, degree by degree, the customer's sales resistance is reduced. People buy from people they like and trust and the more you build rapport and trust, the more willing they will be to make that purchase. *You can't really start the sales process in earnest until you start reducing sales resistance.*

But, as they say on the television game shows, "Wait! There's more!"

Look back at the "during" chart and notice that as you reduce sales resistance, you are, in effect creating an empty space—a vacuum and nature won't allow a vacuum. Hypnotherapists recognize this factor and wisely incorporate it into their programs. For example, if a therapist cures an overeater by removing the craving for chocolate bonbons, a vacuum is created. Whatever motivated the client to overeat is gone, but there's a huge hole in the client's life. (Yes, and belly, too.) Something will rush in to fill that vacuum. One of those "somethings" could be the client's old bonbon habit or an ice cream habit. That's why the hypnotherapists fills the void with another, more positive behavior such as drinking water or chewing gum.

As salespeople, we have to do exactly the same thing. When we remove sales resistance, we have to fill that vacuum we've created with something positive. Otherwise resistance could easily slip back in.

You have to practice a little sales therapy and replace that negative with a positive. And that positive would be...sales acceptance.

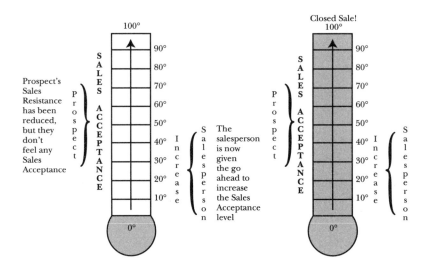

Increase Sales Acceptance Chart
"During" Phase

Increase Sales Acceptance Chart
"After" Phase

Replace Sales Resistance With Sales Acceptance

Notice the difference between the "before" and the "after" chart. You convert 100 degrees of negative into 100 degrees of positive. Sales resistance is completely replaced with sales acceptance as you zero in on the heart of that maze we mentioned earlier. Degree by degree you increase the sales acceptance temperature until you have a favorable climate for a win/win close. *And you don't have to use high pressure to do it.*

As we indicated earlier, nature will not tolerate a vacuum. The next time you see a news report about a drought somewhere on planet Earth, notice that there will be floods in another part of the globe. When it's unusually cold in one hemisphere, you will find that it is unusually hot in another. Nature balances things and sales is where you get to play Mother Nature. Keep your customer well-balanced by filling all that empty space you've created with positive motivation so they have a desire to say "yes" to the product now.

This slow-but-steady, soft approach may seem foreign to those of you used to a more "hard charger" approach, but this approach works phenomenally well. The authors and the thousands of people who have studied our principles, prove it year after year, decade after decade. *Sell It Today! Sell It Now!*

Your Customer Is His/Her Own Worst Enemy

Salesmanship is sometimes like a baseball game with the salesperson as the pitcher and the prospect swinging the bat at home plate. You keep pitching your best stuff, but he keeps hitting them out of the park. By the way, this analogy is where the term "pitch" came from in selling many years ago. It is a word we strongly recommend you remove from your vocabulary. While you're at it, remove the image of tossing anything at your potential client and move on to a smarter way of winning the game.

For example, let's suppose you're about to settle in for an evening with your family, a good book, or your classic CD "Flatt N' Scruggs Sing Countrified Duke Ellington." Suddenly, the phone rings and Mr. Hy Pressure starts his pre-planned, pre-programmed, pre-Industrial presentation on investing in mutual funds. Instead of listening to your favorite bluegrass version of Mood Indigo you're hearing a string of verbal nonsense about compound interest, steady returns, and modest investments. Naturally, you offer a polite thanks-but-no-thanks, hang up and get back to the pickin' n' singin.' It is safe to say that your sales resistance is at 100 degrees.

Later, however, you could be sitting before your computer "surfing the Net" and you venture across the web site of the company that Hy Pressure represents. You're about to click off when a sentence captures your attention. "Want To Earn Steady Returns With Modest Investment? Click Here." You click and are escorted immediately to a fact-filled page about the joys of mutual fund investing. Sounds interesting, you think. You notice another eye-catching phrase. "Want To Learn More About The Magic Of Compound Interest? Click Here." Again you click and again you're taken to another page where you learn how one dollar can become two and how two can become four, eight, sixteen and you can earn real wealth before you retire. Now, you're intrigued. You also notice that there's a free telephone consultation available. The site even offers a toll-free telephone number. You dial. You reach Mrs. O.T. Close. You ask questions, get answers and half an hour later you find your sales resistance has been lowered to almost zero.

But you still don't own those mutual funds. Why?

Your sales resistance has not yet been replaced with sales acceptance. The negative space needs to be filled with positive content.

Fortunately, Mrs. Close is a master salesperson and is about to bring you to the point where you whip out your credit card and start singing out your number and expiration date.

It's important to note that *building sales acceptance is a process*. It's something you do by degrees—step by step. We've heard the theory that there are no true opposites in the universe. For example, at what point does black become white? At what temperature does cold switch over to hot? At what decibel does quiet become loud? Instead of clearly defined lines, the universe is made up of degrees of change. Black and white are merely two ends of the same spectrum separated by degrees of change. Changing sales resistance to sales acceptance is the same. Degree by degree we help our customer make that transition. *No sale* soon becomes *sold*.

Let's return to that toll-free call with Mrs. O.T. Close. She says that since you are working directly with the company, there are no middle-men involved. She is in a position to offer the same mutual funds, stocks or bonds other companies offer, but at a discounted broker rate. Your interest is peaked. Tell me more, you say. And she does. She can also offer the company's Guide To Investing In The New Age absolutely free, but only while supplies last. Sold! A minute or so later you are the proud owner of a mutual fund account and are on your way to earning steady returns on your modest investment via the magic of compound interest.

We have taught people this sales process throughout the country. It's worked millions of times and will work millions of times more. By first reducing sales resistance and then gaining sales acceptance, master salespeople have helped millions of people acquire cars and houses, boats and planes, businesses, investments, educations, and safe and secure futures. And most of those satisfied customers began the process at or near 100 degrees of sales resistance.

Such is the "magic" of a well-trained salesperson.

It's Two Jobs, Two Jobs, Two Jobs In One!

Many years ago Certs breath mints ran a famous advertising campaign featuring pairs of twins as the friendly, smiling, fresh-breathed spokespersons. The angle of the ads was to increase market share by promoting a breath mint as a candy mint, too. One twin would claim "Certs is a breath mint." The other would say "Certs is a candy mint" and then the announcer would prove them both right with "it's two mints, two mints, two mints in one!"

The art of the one-time close is actually two jobs, two jobs, two jobs in one:

Job One is to reduce sales resistance.

Job Two is to gain sales acceptance.

You must complete Job One before you begin Job Two. You can't mix them up or you'll mess up your chances of success for a one-time close.

The process is quite simple. That doesn't mean it is easy. This is compounded by the fact that most salespeople are good at one job and not quite so proficient at the other. A person who is really good at making friends and disarming the prospect, may be nervous and tentative at closing and asking for the check or endorsement of the agreement. Conversely, the good closer can be overly eager in the initial stages of the process. "Hi, I'm Bob. Sign this." He or she risks losing the prospect and the sale before even getting a good start. That is where our turning Sales Resistance into Sales Acceptance system comes into play.

2

The Salesperson's Mind

Lord Chesterfield compared a weak mind to a microscope, always magnifying the tiniest things out of proportion while missing the big picture. There's a lot of truth there, especially for people building a life in sales. We salespeople must prepare our minds to be strong, flexible and always ready to accept the latest challenge. Now that we have covered your job description, let's get on with preparing you to handle that job to your best ability. Let's start preparing your mind to embrace the big picture.

If you don't already have an open mind, now is the time to bring out your mental can opener. Take a lesson from Chapter One. As we lower your resistance to learning a new system for closing the sale, we'll be increasing your acceptance of the one-time closing technique. We'll create a negative space by helping you wash your mind clear of a few outdated ideas and replace that empty space with exciting new ones.

Fear is one of the salesperson's greatest obstacles and showing you how to eliminate it is the chief goal of this chapter. A champion one-time closer recognizes fear for what it is, handles it and moves ahead with the task of serving the customer's needs. Let's take a closer look at fear. C'mon, what are you afraid of?

Fear. Son of Fear. Fear's Revenge. Fear vs. The Three Stooges

Even the most knowledgeable, most experienced of us faces fear on a regular basis, probably on a daily basis. Taking on the challenge of a sales career naturally puts you in situations which can bring up certain anxieties. Sometimes these fears are tiny little things gnawing at our confidence. Other times they're an army of Vandals stampeding over the gates and about to ransack and pillage the place where we live. How you handle those natural fears will to a great extent determine your success in sales.

So, what are our most common fears?
They are:

- Fear of loss
- Fear of the past
- Fear of the unknown
- Fear of failure

- Fear of the future
- Fear of making a mistake

That covers a lot of ground, doesn't it? We're pretty sure you'll find a bit of yourself somewhere in that list. And that's okay. Truth be told, a little bit of all of us is in there. Yes, even your authors get the jitters now and then.

Fear of loss often paralyzes salespeople, so much so that they actually create the thing they most fear—losing a sale. Champion salespeople realize that they will inevitably lose some sales. And that's okay. It's just part of the process. Accept it and move on. As they say in basketball, "you can't score if you don't shoot." In the long run, the misses don't matter because they're more than balanced by the shots that go through the hoops. In other words, don't let your fear of loss create loss.

Fear of the past isn't a reference to reincarnation and your unfortunate encounter with those hungry lions back when you were a rather clumsy Roman gladiator. We're talking about a more recent past, perhaps as recent as yesterday or even this morning. We all make mistakes that we are fearful of repeating. Have you ever gone into a presentation unprepared or lacking in commitment? You bombed, didn't you? The fear of repeating past mistakes is hard to bear because you've had actual experience with the pain it causes. And now, justifiably so, you're afraid of a repeat performance. Who wouldn't be? It hurts!

Fear of the unknown is just the opposite. In approaching a sale, you're scared of something of which you have no experience or point of reference.

In some ways, it's worse than some of the other fears because your mind can create all kinds of scenarios that are much, much scarier than whatever-the-heck the real thing may be. The salesperson thinks, "I don't know what I'm about to experience, therefore it scares me out of my mind." For top salespeople, the unknown isn't something to be feared, rather something to be embraced. It's a learning experience and after all, that's where you find success.

Fear of failure is a natural byproduct of wanting to take action. "Since I haven't a clue as to what is about to happen, I'm afraid I'm completely unprepared to handle it." Of course, nobody can be sure that he or she is 100% prepared for the next challenge. Even the most prepared salesperson faces the possibility that the prospect or customer will toss a fast curve ball. The unexpected is a constant threat to any sales presentation. The important thing is to remember that failure leads to success for those willing to learn from their presentation mistakes. Think of failure as a tool. It's not something to be avoided. In fact, you can't avoid it 100% of the time unless you never meet a new potential client, which would put you out of the sales business. So, study your mistakes. Learn from your failures and march on toward your inevitable success.

Fear of the future is the negative side of your mind (we all have one) saying, "Whoa! Slow down there, son." Even top salespeople who have achieved remarkable levels of success face this challenge. "Will I be able to do this again? Can I sustain my momentum? What if I drop the ball?" The future, by definition, is unknown and if we allow the negative side of our minds to take over, we can create a frighteningly bleak future. Like the country/western comedy song from the old television program, "Hee Haw," we see nothing but "doom, despair and agony on me, deep dark depression, excessive misery." Look at it this way, most people in the work force don't have near the opportunity for building a future as bright as we lucky folks in sales. Your future is an exciting event that you can shape with your own hands. Surely, that's something to create excitement rather than fear.

Fear of making a mistake often arises from past mistakes, earlier presentations that just didn't pan out as expected. When you discuss the exchange of their money for your product or service, there's this fear that it could happen again. As with fear of loss and failure, the fear of making a mistake is a misguided one. Of course, you're going to make a mistake. We all have. We all will. And, that's okay. Just learn from them. Perfect your presentation and keep your potential client's best interests at heart, and you'll be amazed at how many fewer mistakes you make than someone who doesn't do it this way. Part of your presentation has to reinforce the correctness and the intelligence of the purchase—that taking ownership of the product or service now, today, is a wise decision.

Face Facts And Freeze-Out Fear

Fear can be *de*structive or *con*structive. The outcome all depends upon how and how well you handle it. Or how you let it handle you! All of these fears can be controlled and, in some cases, even put to good use. Once you understand how fear affects you personally, you will begin to see how it creates obstacles between you and your goals. These obstacles, even when they're only perceived and not real, can be significant challenges. They can cause you to lose a sale, a job, a client and even a career. Does it really matter that there's not a hungry lion behind the door, if your *fear* of becoming tonight's supper keeps you from stepping in?

Once you use the information we are making available and learn to process it correctly, fear begins to fade. Sometimes it will fade away to nothingness. Even if it does stick around for awhile, you'll be able to control it. Some people actually use their fear to spur them on. As one salesperson said, "I am more afraid of not bringing home a paycheck to my wife and kids than I am of the prospect walking in the door, the voice on the other end of the line, or even the world-famous CEO behind the mahogany desk."

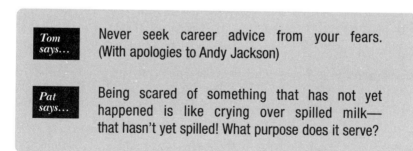

Tom says...   Never seek career advice from your fears. (With apologies to Andy Jackson)

Pat says...   Being scared of something that has not yet happened is like crying over spilled milk— that hasn't yet spilled! What purpose does it serve?

When Knowledge Comes In The Door, Fear Jumps Out The Window

The six fears just named are usually grounded in the salesperson's level of competency—in how well the individual thinks he or she performs at the job. As we increase our level of knowledge, we automatically see an increase in competence. This brings us back to our thermometer illustration from the previous chapter. As knowledge helps you drop your fear from the 100 degree level, that vacuum is replaced by a positive force known as competence.

We have studied the subject in-depth and understand that there are four basic levels of competence. These levels especially apply when you are learning anything new—such as tying your shoes, learning a computer, or mastering one-time closing. These are:

- Level #1—the unconscious incompetent
- Level #2—the conscious incompetent
- Level #3—the conscious competent
- Level #4—the unconscious competent

Different authors and lecturers may use different terminology, but the basis remains the same. Let's see how this relates to salespeople. Specifically, let's see how all this relates to *you.*

Level #1. The unconscious incompetent doesn't even know that he (or she) doesn't know what he's doing Like the kid trying to make his first bow in his tennis shoes, or the CEO learning her first computer, we experience Level #1 all our lives. Or, at least as long as we keep trying new things. In that sense, unconscious incompetence is a necessary, if not good, thing.

Generally, there's nothing to be embarrassed about. If you take up rollerblading to lose weight, you can count on being an unconscious incompetent before you can startle the neighbors with your whiz-zoom speed and agility. That's why sales of helmets and knee guards are so high. We can't get to full competency, much less step two in the printed instructions, until we master step one.

Challenges arrive when we take up residence at Level #1 and don't move on. Whatever, your level of experience in sales, with this book you are an unconscious incompetent in terms of one-call closing.

Let's compare this to something as simple and reflexive as driving. Assuming you do have a driver's license, you probably don't drive today as you did when you first had your learner's permit. You are at Level #4 when it comes to driving. It's become an unconscious move to turn on your blinker, your lights, and navigate your local area, right? So, you would say you're an unconscious competent driver.

Okay, let's say you're given a new driving experience. You are now sitting in the driver's seat at a Nascar race. Do you know how to drive? Yes. Do you know how to drive a stock car at 200 miles an hour around a circular track without hitting something or causing bodily harm to yourself in some way? Probably not. In that context, are you Level #4? No. You've just stepped back to Level #1.

The same applies to the strategies in this book.

Yesterday you may have been a master at the outdated techniques of high pressure sales and today you are as "lost as a goose" facing an entirely new way of doing business. Again, that's okay because you will move on to the next steps. Won't you?

Level #2, the conscious incompetent, is really a state of awareness. You vaguely know that there's a certain something out there. You also are aware that you really don't know very much about it. At this level you don't know everything you need to know about a subject. In other words, the conscious incompetent knows he or she doesn't know.

The people who are comfortable with Level #2 don't give it much thought. In fact, they avoid thinking about those nagging questions. People who want to move on and up with life, people like you, will be curious at this level. You want to learn more. If you're intimidated by the amount of information you must grasp, don't be. You will get where you are going. You will become a master of the one-time close because you have the drive and the discipline to achieve it.

And now you know that it's out there to be achieved. *The fact that you are reading this book means that you are already at Level #2!* Shoot, you're halfway there already.

Level #3, the conscious competent, is busy reading, studying, watching the experts, picking up new information and learning everything he or she can about the subject at hand. The person at Level #3 is even experimenting, trying new things, and learning what works and what doesn't work quite so well. It's an exciting level because things are happening. Progress is being made. And you don't find yourself paralyzed by fear so often. In fact, long stretches of time pass without you even thinking about some of the many things that filled you with apprehension in the recent past.

Level #4, the unconscious competent, is the level of the master closer, the closing specialist. If you stick with this program, you will get there and probably a lot faster than you now believe. This is the ultimate experience. You are so knowledgeable and experienced that one-time closing is a natural process. You barely have to think about it before you flawlessly execute your presentation. Your sales reflexes are so finely honed that the process has become internalized. Your sales presentation is finely tuned and targeted precisely to serving the unique needs of your clients with the unique solutions provided by your product or service.

Certainly, those nagging fears still drop in now and again, but they're way in the background. You know how to handle them. More than that you *are* handling them.

Level #4 is a very heady place to be. You'll like it. Are you ready to enter Level #4? Are you ready to become a one-time closing specialist? Only you know the answer. But we suspect it's a resounding "Yes!" And as the old guy on the radio used to say, "Ah, there's good news tonight." You can achieve Level #4. You can master the art of the one-time close. All you have to do is follow three basic steps.

Step One—Become A Sales Champion

The word "champion" is so important that it became a key element in Tom's first company and it has always been a key element of his training philosophy. A champion is a person who is the best they can be at what they choose to do. Champions always strive to be better today than they were yesterday.

C   Commitment   breeds   competence. Comedian/filmmaker Woody Allen said that half the secret to success is just showing up. Showing up is one of the major commitments a champion makes. Perhaps it is *the* major commitment because without it none of the other stages of success can possibly follow.

H   Honesty in words and action. Words are important. As the talk show hosts say, "words mean things, but without action they are meaningless." You can't be honest with your friends at church or at the civic club and then turn it off when you go to work. Either you are honest or you are not.

A   Attitude is positive at all times. As with baseball great Babe Ruth, the person who hits the most home runs is also the person who likely holds the record for most strike outs. That's just part of the job and a champion must be equipped to handle it. A positive attitude isn't just nice to have—it's essential equipment.

M   Master the material. You can't sell what you don't know. But a champion knows more than just facts and figures. He or she knows the product, the company, the industry, the competitors, the customer and the skills and techniques of a master salesperson. A champion also knows this is a matter of *continuing education.*

P   **Persistence is the key...never give up!** The word quit is just not in the vocabulary of a champion. It's not even in their dictionary or thesaurus!

I   **Imagination will help develop the future.** Right now the future resides within your imagination. What you "see" as the outcome of your efforts, success or failure, will determine that outcome. Every great advance of civilization throughout the history of the world was first developed in someone's imagination.

O   **Organize time, a precious commodity.** In a very real sense you cannot waste time—you can only waste yourself. Time is like fertile ground. You can let it lie fallow or you can plow, plant, harvest and feed the world.

N   **Non-judgmental of others.** A champion is far too focused on creating and improving a well-rounded, thoroughly professional human being to waste time judging others. He or she just doesn't have time for it. (See the item directly above.)

Step Two—Turn Pro

Wherever you go you will find champions of all stripes. Some champions are talented amateurs and others are true professionals. What's the difference? In a word, success. The professional champion earns top dollar in his or her profession. More than that, the professional earns a profound sense of self-worth and the admiration of his or her peers in meeting the needs of others. Here are a few key tips on becoming a pro.

- *Develop a professional's attitude.* Your work is your *profession* deserving your respect and very best efforts.

- *Look like a professional.* From the tip of your highly-polished shoes to the top of your well-groomed head, you always look your best. Whether you are in farm and field or company jet and corporate HQ, people instantly know you're a pro just by your look.

- *Your business looks professional.* Your business is also your "business suit." Is it neatly pressed and in style or looking a little frayed around the edges? You may not notice, but be assured that your prospects and clients will.

- *Organize like a professional.* Your presentation materials are well-organized, up-to-date and readily available. Fumbling for a chart, a document or some other material not only detracts from your presentation, it makes (and proves) the impression that you are sloppy in your attention to detail.

- *Use the language professionals use.* You can talk "down and dirty" without getting down to the lowest common denominator and talking dirty. Your speech or writing should always be appropriate to the situation and the client, but the use of foul language, slang, poor grammar or technical jargon is just unforgivable. Plain English is a universal and quite eloquent language.

■ *Follow your profession.* It's important to know what's going on within your company, but it is equally important to know what's happening within your industry. Keep up or follow in the wake of those who do.

■ *Keep on "keeping on."* In other words, as a salesperson it is your job and your duty to *sell*—every day and at every appropriate opportunity. One of the most significant differences between a champion and an also-ran, is the champion's ability to make a call, knock on a door, approach a prospect, answer an inquiry, set up appointments and make presentations while the others sit around the coffee machine and gripe about the economy.

■ *Adopt a professional's standards.* A professional is honest—period. The highest ethical standards of conduct and behavior are an essential part of the professional's very being. These rigorous standards apply 24-hours a day, seven days a week. There are no exceptions.

■ *Have fun.* Selling is a demanding profession with great rewards, but it is something you should enjoy, really enjoy. A lot of people are delighted to go to the job every day because the "job" of selling is more like a hobby than the traditional sour view of "work."

Step Three—Follow The Four "Ps"

Those famous "Breakfast of Champions" commercials in which the pro athlete and/or the announcer states "You better eat your Wheaties" can be taken on two levels. The obvious one is that it's a wise and healthy idea to eat a good breakfast. The other level is more subtle and at the same time more dramatic. It pertains to an entire set of things the champion must accomplish to claim his or her position in the winner's circle. We call these the Four Ps. The Four Ps aren't a singing group from the sixties. They're guidelines to becoming a master of sales, especially one-time closing.

Prepare—Practice—Perform—Perfect

Prepare. The one-time closing specialist is ready to meet the expected and the inevitable unexpected challenges inherent in this business. The need to prepare was dramatically and tragically illustrated in the book YEAGER by General Chuck Yeager and Leo Janos (Bantam Books). If you haven't read or seen "The Right Stuff," Chuck Yeager was a World War Two flying ace, the first man to break the sound barrier, and a true legend in aviation in his time. Yeager says that the skills and abilities that make a good fighter pilot do not automatically transfer to another field, such as test flying new, unproven and very dangerous jets. Nerves of steel, fast reflexes, and brilliant flying skills need to be balanced with other factors—preparation for each flight, for example. He notes the unnecessary loss of another great ace and test pilot, Richard Bong, who "flamed out" just 50 feet off the ground, too low for a successful parachute escape. Bong hadn't studied his pilot's manual and a simple mistake cost him his life. "Dick wasn't interested in homework," said Yeager. Lack of preparation in sales may not cost you a life, but it could cost you a sale, a job or even a career.

The one-time closer takes his or her homework very seriously.

Practice. Knowing what to do and doing it are entirely different things. Certainly you would practice your piano prior to performing a concerto in public, wouldn't you? You'd practice for a weekend game of softball, an archery contest, or for a presentation to your civic club, right? Then for goodness sakes, why don't you practice your sales presentation? Use a mirror and give a presentation to yourself. Use a home video or audio tape recorder or practice with your spouse or a friend. Become thoroughly familiar with your presentation. Make it so much a part of you that you don't even think about it. The old adage "practice makes perfect" is almost right. But what if your practice isn't up to par? Suppose you practice poorly? Therefore, we'd like to amend the adage to say, only perfect practice makes perfect. And if you don't achieve perfection, at the very least you'll be a lot more prepared than if you jumped into a presentation with "Hi, I'm Bob. Sign this."

Ask Bob. He's now working part time making sandwiches down at the House of Spam.

Perform. Sooner or later you have to get in there and "mix it up" with your prospects and clients. Don't wait until you think you know enough or are good enough or you probably just won't begin. After all, regardless of our level of expertise or performance, we can all improve. We are never "good enough" because there's always something more to learn. Make your presentations to the best of your ability. Give it everything you've got. You'll win some and you'll lose some, but you will continue to improve because you will...

Perfect. A one-time closing master never stops learning, especially from his or her own experiences. Take mental notes on every presentation. Evaluate your performance and take the time to consider how to improve your weak areas. Make a serious study of yourself and your presentation and then practice the Four Ps all over again: Prepare, Practice, Perform and keep on Perfecting!

If you're going to be a champion in any field, why not become a pro? If you are going to be a pro, why not be a champion? One of the things the authors truly love about sales is that it is a field open to all. Whether you are male or female, young or old, a beanpole or pleasantly plump, regardless of your race, education, culture, prior level of experience, or whatever, *you can be a champion in sales.* That fact has been proven so many times that it is indisputable.

Real success in sales doesn't require any special God-given talent. You already have the talent. You don't need the body of Shaquille O'Neal, the voice of Barbra Streisand, or the belly button of Britney Spears. You don't need Tinkerbelle's magic dust, a spell from Merlin the Magician, or the wave of a magic wand from anybody. All you need is drive, commitment, discipline and heart. We think that last item is most important. You can't measure the heart of a champion. It's just too big. Once you have the heart of a champion, all the other items in the list will inevitably follow.

Sales Skills Are Transferable

We have often heard a version of this statement, "Why should I work so hard? I'm not going to stay in sales forever." We offer two answers. One, anything, anything at all that you do you should do to your best ability. Two, the skills you learn in sales are transferable to any other occupation. If you're going into politics, you will still need to "close" with the voters. If you enter corporate America as an executive, you'll still need to make presentations to your boss(es), clients or customers. (Or, are you planning the rest of your career without ever asking for a promotion?) Even if you're just planning retirement, you'll need your sales skills to "close" your spouse on that summer-long tour of America's bass fishing havens or the 28-State Crock Pot Across America Experience.

Sales skills are transferable. You can take them anywhere you go and put them to work building a better life in that arena.

Let's Face Facts

And freeze-out fear. Once you have begun the continuing process of preparing, practicing, performing and perfecting, you can begin to forget about your fears. Like those trouble-making cousins at the family picnic, they'll always be hanging around. But once you have mastered the Four Ps, you can pretty much ignore them. They just aren't much of a factor in your life anymore.

Forget your fear of loss. Loss will happen and it will happen to everyone except those timid souls who lack the courage to reach for the brass ring. Loss is a natural by-product of the sales process and a necessary step on the road to gain. So, when you occasionally lose, accept it, learn from it, *let it go,* and move on.

Forget your fear of the past and move on and into a bright, shining and successful future. You no longer need to be held back by feelings of guilt, regret, or loss over whatever "might have been." You can leave whatever happened before where it belongs—in the past. Just because it happened once doesn't mean you are doomed to repeat the experience. When you learn from your past negative experiences, you know how to avoid those same pitfalls. Even better, you know how to turn them into positive outcomes the next time.

Forget your fear of the unknown. We all face a certain amount of fear of unknown. That means you're not alone. More than that, once you master the art of the one-time sale, knowledge will defeat fear. Your experience and skill will allow you to put yourself in your customer's shoes to discover the best way to serve his or her unique needs. The unknown will always be with us, but you will be able to control the situation because you'll be focused on the known system for lowering sales resistance and increasing sales acceptance.

Forget your fear of failure. Failure is nothing more than just another part of the game. A newspaper editor fired Walt Disney for a "lack of ideas." Thomas Edison's teachers thought he was too stupid to learn. As we noted earlier, Babe Ruth also holds the record for most strike outs. Those very public failures didn't keep him from becoming the Home Run King, did it? The one-time closing specialist accepts failure when it occurs, evaluates what happened, learns from the experience, and moves on as a better salesperson for it. In other words, he or she tries again…and again…and again!

> **Tom says…**   You have not failed until you stop trying.

Forget your fear of the future. That's where we're all going to be living, so why not do your very best to make that future as exciting, as productive and as satisfying as possible?

Forget your fear of making a mistake. You most certainly will make your share of mistakes. We all have. We all do. We all will. And, that's perfectly okay, provided we learn from them. The fear of making a mistake can freeze a salesperson into inactivity. It can also push someone into a flurry of *misdirected* activity just to avoid working with customers. A champion doesn't fret over past mistakes or get stressed out over the possibility of future ones. He or she knows mistakes are excellent learning experiences and a natural part of the sales process. To paraphrase a famous quote, good salesmanship is built by way of experience and experience is built by way of making mistakes. Go on. Get out there and earn your share. Start learning now!

Let's learn a thing or two about fear from a fearless American hero of the Revolutionary War, John Paul Jones, who said, "If fear is cultivated it will become stronger. If faith is cultivated, it will achieve the mastery. We have a right to believe that faith is the stronger emotion because it is positive whereas fear is negative."

Now, go out there and face your fears.

And be sure to eat your Wheaties!

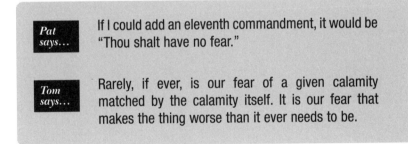

Pat says... If I could add an eleventh commandment, it would be "Thou shalt have no fear."

Tom says... Rarely, if ever, is our fear of a given calamity matched by the calamity itself. It is our fear that makes the thing worse than it ever needs to be.

3

The Prospect's Mind

When preparing for the challenges of the one-time close, your chances of success multiply when you know and understand the mind of your prospect. Yes, instinct is important, even essential, but it is not enough in and of itself. Remember the unfortunate experience of Dick Bong from the previous chapter. Instinct alone cannot replace knowledge. The one-time closing specialist is serious about doing his or her homework.

Back in the 19th century, a brilliant man named Freud created an entire new field of medical science when he devoted his considerable energies to studying the various types of human personalities. The new science was dubbed psychology. Freud focused primarily on two types of people, the introvert and the extrovert. Simply stated, an introvert is someone who's interest is primarily within himself or herself. An extrovert focuses attention primarily on others. Neither one is inherently good or bad or better than the other. They are just two sides of the same human coin. One or the other will dominate your personality. Again, that's neither good nor bad; it's just what you make of it.

Actually, the study of human personality reaches much further back into history. The four basic personality types and temperaments were recorded as early as 400 B.C. by Hypocrates. All the studies since then have helped mankind understand man. That information is available to help salespeople understand prospects and customers, too.

One-time closing requires insight, not necessarily expertise, into the personality of your potential customer The more you know, the better prepared you will be. More important than that, you must develop a keen insight into your own personality. Whatever your own temperament, you must know how it will be received by other personalities. A champion is equally effective with the clients he likes and admires as he or she is with the folks with whom he feels ill at ease or even in conflict. Remember, while we all want to make friends, our goal is first and foremost to meet the needs of our future client.

Continued study of human personalities is essential for real, long-term success in sales. After all, that's a fundamental element of your work. You do sell your product to people, don't you?

Two types your studies will reveal are Type A or Type B Personalities. You probably have heard people remarking, "Well, he's a Type A. What else would you expect?" A Type A is a more aggressive and assertive personality. This is the proverbial hard charger. A Type B is more laid back and introverted. "Nothing ruffles her feathers" or "he just takes it as it comes" might be said of this type. Again, neither is better or worse than the other, just different. And you must know how to recognize and work well with each.

The more you study, the more breakdowns and definitions of personality types you will encounter. For the purposes of this book, we will investigate the one-time closing process with the "big four" types of personalities.

Meet Pa, Hoss, Adam And Little Joe

The chart on page 44 shows the wide variations of personality types you will encounter. You will have to work with each type again and again throughout your career. Salespeople aren't allowed to pick and choose the nature of their clients. That's why it's so important to recognize personalities and be adaptable. The time you invest in learning as much as you can about them will pay off again and again with one-time closes throughout your long and successful career.

Distant
Thinkers
Task Driven

Reserved	**Analytical**	**Driver**	Fast
Slow	Motivated by respect	Motivated by power	Tellers
Askers	and being right	and control	Extrovert
Introvert			Talkers
			Assertive
	Amiable	**Expressive**	Aggressive
	Motivated by approval	Motivated by recognition	
	and support	and pleasure	

Emotional
Enthusiastic
Friendly

You don't have to dig into a deep, theoretical text or sign up for a psychology course at the community college to understand the various types of human personalities. Just think of the differences in terms of people you already know. For example, those of you not old enough to have seen the original television series Bonanza, will surely have encountered it on reruns. After decades, it's still on the air, cable or satellite dish. The program featured four strong men running a ranch back in the days of the Wild West. Each main character represents a distinct type of personality. So travel back with us to the days of yesteryear for a closer look at each.

Pa was a **driver.** Clearly, he was the brains and the power of the ranch. Although a loving father to his three sons, he ran the Ponderosa with an iron hand, often employing aspects of "tough love" to see that his will was carried out. He was a strong character, always building for the future. Even with three fully grown men, and presumably co-owners, around, Pa was the force that kept things moving in the right direction.

His son, Adam, was an **analytical** personality-type. He was the "smart one" of the boys. So smart was the character that the reason given for the actor playing him leaving the show was that Adam went to France to study. Adam used his knowledge to better the Ponderosa, the lives of his family and friends, and the community. When it came to intellectual matters, he earned respect through careful thought leading to the right decision—which was ultimately agreed upon by Pa.

Hoss had an **amiable** personality. Everybody liked "the big lug." His physical strength, matched by a strength of character, was legendary. Although he never started serious trouble (although there was that episode with the leprechauns), he wouldn't back down from a fight. Still, he'd much rather win the support of others by just getting along with folks.

Little Joe was an **expressive** personality-type and always wore his heart on his sleeve. The audience never had to wonder what Little Joe was feeling. He enjoyed a good time and, being the youngest, was often motivated by a need for recognition. Perhaps that explains why someone in the Old West had hair like Elvis Presley.

A one-time closing professional will know these types *and* how his own personality should best interact with that of his or her customer to progress to a decision that's in their best interest—the one-time close. For example, if you are a driver, you will have a tendency to mold your sales presentation into a format that fits your profile. This may work well with about half of the other drivers you approach. What about that other fifty percent, who feel *they* should be in the driver's seat?

(DRIVER) YOU: Morning, Mr. Cartwright.

(DRIVER) BEN: Morning. What brings you out to the Ponderosa?

YOU: I'd appreciate your opinion on something.

BEN: That' be...

YOU: This here wagon I'm driving. It's a new model and I need somebody who knows a maverick from a mossy to give me a working man's appraisal.

BEN: Looks fine. Is it sound?

YOU: Sound as a dollar. Best bracing I've ever seen. Take a look at the axles for me, if you would.

BEN: They appear to be quite sturdy. How do they handle?

YOU: Turns on a dime. It's real handy on those narrow roads up in the timber country, like your logging roads.

BEN: Blasted nuisance. We broke another two axles last month.

YOU: So I heard. Hop up and let's take 'er for a short ride so you can get a feel for it, okay?

BEN: Sure. Head out through those trees and show me how short this thing turns.

YOU: Sure thing.

BEN: Say, how much weight can this old wagon carry?

YOU: I'm glad you asked, Mr. Cartwright.

By understanding the different types of personalities, including your own, you can adapt your style to meet the unique needs of each situation. This is not to say that you become another person. You can't. Just realize that the needs of your potential customer come first, far ahead of your need to appear to be running the show, and act accordingly.

Conversely, an amiable personality might have to become a bit more assertive when working with another amiable who is trying to get along so well that the presentation is going nowhere. Forewarned is forearmed. Whatever the personality mix at the time, your knowledge of personality types will allow you to step out of your own needs, to better meet the needs of your customer.

(AMIABLE) YOU: Morning, Hoss.
(AMIABLE) HOSS: Morning. What brings you out to the Ponderosa?
YOU: I could use your help, Hoss. I surely could.
HOSS: I'll do what I can. What 'cha need?
YOU: I need you to help me help your pa.
HOSS: What kind 'o help you think Pa needs?
YOU: Your timber operation's been busting wagons left and right. Now, I got a new kind of wagon that'll handle those heavy loads up in the high country without breaking an axle every other trip.
HOSS: Pa'd like to hear that.
YOU: That's where I need help from a friend like you.
HOSS: Why don't you just go tell Pa yourself?
YOU: I will, but if you'd check this out and make a recommendation first...
HOSS: I don't know.

YOU: Mr. Cartwright is a mighty busy man, ain't he?
HOSS: Shore is.
YOU: He might be too busy to take time out for a look at something he really 'oughta see, don't you think?
HOSS: Yeah, but I still think you should just go in there and talk to pa yourself.
YOU: I really need your help on this, Hoss. So does your pa, if you think about it.
HOSS: It does look like a good wagon.
YOU: Why don't you take a quick ride and see for yourself?
HOSS: I don't guess that'd hurt none.
YOU: Hop on up. Let me tell you about these axles.

Let's look at one more example. This is the episode where Ben Cartwright assigned Little Joe the task of buying a new wagon. Being an expressive, he's down at the used wagon lot checking out the small, fast, sporty model. He's seeing himself rip roaring along the roads to and from the Ponderosa running errands for Pa. Adam, who is still working on that mill, wants a larger, heavier wagon. Being an analytical, he's considering turning ratios, weight bearing capabilities, repair and replacement costs. Unfortunately, the decision isn't his, so he has to "sell" his wilder brother on the slower, heavier wagon.

ADAM: Little Joe!
JOE: Hey, what brings you down from the Ponderosa?
ADAM: Just thought I'd see if you need any help.
JOE: I have the situation under control.
ADAM: I know you do. But if you need a good hand, I'm your man.

JOE: Sure. I'm looking real close at this one, here.

ADAM: It's a good one, I'm sure. Have you thought about the big one over there?

JOE: Yeah. It's too big, if you ask me.

ADAM: You know best. Say, I notice you've been picnicking with Cindy Lou lately.

JOE: Prettiest girl in town.

ADAM: You sure can pick 'em, Little Joe. But why are you two always riding horses. Wouldn't a wagon ride be more, well, cozy?

JOE: Her old man doesn't like us sitting too close.

ADAM: I just had a thought. If we had that big wagon over there, you could use that and put the picnic basket between you. It'd be like the walls of Jericho to the old man.

JOE: What's the good of that, big brother?

ADAM: After you go over the hill, little brother, put the basket in the back.

JOE: Hmmmmm.

ADAM: And the walls of Jericho came tumbling down.

JOE: Let's take another look at that big wagon.

ADAM: Like I said, you're the boss.

See what we mean? Regardless of your own personal style or the style of your prospects and customers, *you can adapt to fit the situation.* Again, you don't become a separate and false person to manipulate an unsuspecting customer. You just changed your delivery to meet the personality of a specific individual so that you can best serve his or her specific needs. Bonanza was one of the longest running, most successful television shows ever. By entering your prospect's mind, you can have the same kind of enormously successful "run."

Why You Shouldn't Go Fishing With Strawberries

There's a wonderful example of the need to put the needs of our customers ahead of our own in Dale Carnegie's "How To Win Friends And Influence People." He writes about a salesman who didn't enjoy performing a particular part of the sales process. He preferred to jump ahead to what he considered more important areas. He was asked if he ever went fishing. He said, "yes" and in fact, he loved the sport. He was then asked what bait he used. "Night crawlers," he said. Later in the conversation our fishing salesman mentioned that he was particularly fond of strawberries. At this point he was asked if he ever used strawberries for fishing bait. "Of course not!" he said. "Why not?" was the immediate question. "Because the fish don't like strawberries!" And his own answer made the questioner's point. Just because you like something, doesn't mean the other party likes that same thing. Or vice versa.

It is critical that we comprehend the likes and dislikes of the person to whom we are making a presentation so we can determine if our product or service is truly good for them before we ever attempt to close them.

As long as we're back in the olden days of network television, let's leave the Ponderosa and drop in on a bigger spread that is Lost In Space.

Danger! Danger! Young Will Robinson!

If you will think back to this sci-fi version of the Swiss Family Robinson, you will remember the family's "pet" robot would warn of the episode's impending doom by shouting a repetitious "danger!" We're not claiming to be Robbie the Robot, but we'd like to offer a warning of our own.

OBSERVE ALL WARNING SIGNS

Smart drivers pay attention to the speed limit and other warning signs on the highway because they know that it is not only obeying the law, but it is also the safest and overall the fastest way to their destination. Prospects post their own warning signs and it is just as important to obey the "laws of the road" in sales. Pay attention to the demeanor of your prospect and adjust yours accordingly.

It's a bit like acting on the stage. You play to the audience. If you're making a presentation to a laid back "audience," an overly-energetic "performance" with a lot of action and fast-paced speech could lose them. Conversely, if you have an upbeat, enthusiastic prospect, a mellow presentation could turn them off before you can really get started.

The ideal approach is to observe your prospect's demeanor. Mirror the rate and pitch in his or her voice. Subconsciously, this sends a message that, "Hey, we're alike." Additionally, your prospect will automatically understand you better. If someone is a very slow speaker, adjust your rate so that it is just slightly faster. Do not, however, mimic someone's accent. Even if you're a terrific actor on the community stage, you'll never fool a prospect. He or she will be insulted and you'll be injured by your own poor judgment.

Also, while you will use different words, phrases and references with different audiences, never talk down to anyone.

*"Don't become so wrapped up in winning the battle of selling that you lose the war of selling **now**."*

Yes, it is important to know and understand the different personality types you will encounter. It's important to know and to plan out how your own temperament will interact with others. Yet, having said that, we don't want you to fall down the slippery slope of paying too much attention to personality only to leave yourself no time for the business of working toward the close. That's a very real and serious danger-danger.

Completely changing your presentation based on each new client's personality would make the one-time close quite tough, if not impossible. But you don't have to do that. Ideally, you've mastered a proven presentation, something that is effective for you and your product. The presentation might even be something carefully designed and fine tuned by your company for very specific reasons. Changing it rapidly would disrupt the flow of your time with your client and might even achieve the exact opposite of what the company had in mind.

Rather than structuring your presentation around the personality of the future client, you must be prepared to adjust your style and delivery to your customers' mindset. In other words, if they're open and interested, you'd match that mode. If they're hesitant and somewhat holding back or even fighting you a bit, you'll have to give the presentation a bit more methodically to win them over. You don't want to use up so much time customizing or changing your presentation that you run out of time for one-time closing. Believe us, it happens. The sales situation is moving along nicely; the conversation is flowing both ways; and the salesperson strikes the wrong chord. Somehow, despite all that planning, he or she manages to say the wrong thing. Out of nowhere the aliens land, Dr. Smith, the wimpy crewmember from Lost in Space, crosses over to the invader's side, and you have to blast off seeking better prospects on another planet.

It may be unfortunate, but it is still a reality—we one-time closers don't have the luxury of unlimited time. Neither do we have the luxury of multiple visits that allow time to recover from a faux pas, regroup, and come back from another angle. Because of the ever-changing dynamics of sales and human personalities, the one-time closer must make all plans, prepare strategies and potential adjustments to the prospect's mindset. There are only two to choose from. Then, it just becomes a matter of changing gears, as necessary—smoothly and effortlessly. So you need to have a solid understanding of how things work ahead of time—enough of an understanding to be able to adapt on the fly.

That's not an impossible task. In fact, it's relatively straightforward when you follow the principles in this book.

Our system is successful for a very simple, yet powerful reason. When you place your prospects and customers into any sales situation, they will react in a manner that is universally consistent. Now, their individual personality types are just not that big a factor. And that fact doesn't contradict the preceding pages. You still need to know the different types and how to interact with them. We have just eliminated the necessity of investing too much time on that process.

In other words, this process lets you *sell it today, sell it now.*

LEVEL THE PLAYING FIELD
WITH THE LEVEL OF YOUR PRESENTATION

As we've said, you never talk down to anyone. Of course you will adapt the words, phrases, expressions and references to each prospect. A young kid with a GED deserves just as much attention and respect when he or she walks into your showroom as a Summa Cum Laude CEO. Without talking down to either, you will obviously adjust your presentation according to the needs of each. Know enough about your prospect going into your presentation so that you can talk on his or her level.

What does that mean?

Let's look at two different couples walking in to buy a new refrigerator. Couple number one is a retired man and wife who want to replace their 20-year old unit. What do you say to them? The words "fixed income" probably come to mind. We'll assume you've asked a few qualifying questions to determine their specific needs which are likely to center around economy. Therefore, you'll want to discuss such topics as dependability, low energy costs, longer food storage capabilities which stretch a food budget, and perhaps a service plan that can eliminate unexpected repair costs.

Couple number two is young and just starting out. Would you use the same approach? No. You would accent the features and benefits that apply to their specific situation. The features on the unit may be the same, but you will present the benefits in a different light, one viewed from their perspective. For example, they may be cost conscious, like the older couple, and want to look at lower-priced models. You even may refer them to the same model the other couple chose, but you will handle it differently as they may be more interested in features such as outside water and ice dispensers.

continues

continued

You may even win them over to a larger model with a higher investment when they realize the longevity of the higher quality brands. The slightly greater investment they make now will likely be offset by the replacement cost they'll avoid down the road. In truth, the larger unit may be the most cost-effective decision.

In other words, a one-time closer speaks a lot of different "languages." You speak old folks. You speak young family. You speak CEO and you speak GED. The language all depends upon the needs of the individual prospect. If you want to test this, try talking in normal business terms to a five year old. He or she will lose interest almost immediately. But then try speaking on the child's level and just watch the happy animation appear on that tiny face as he or she realizes you have just entered the five-year old world. It's like magic. And the same technique will work magic in sales.

The Prospect Mindset

When put into the sales scenario, the prospect's mindset *subconsciously* asks important questions which must be answered before the individual is comfortable moving ahead with the sales process. Because this is a subconscious process, we know that it is always at work. We can count on it. We depend on it. More than that, we can make it our ally.

How often have you found yourself, or heard others saying the words, "I'm just looking" when approached by a sales person? It doesn't matter what the prospect's individual personality style may be, this is a universal reaction because of the mindset change we all undergo when a sales scenario starts.

We are thinking, "I don't *need* you, your product or service;" "I don't have any reason to *trust* what you have to say;" "I don't need any *help* to determine if you have a product or service of interest to me;" and "I'm in no *hurry* to make a decision." So, basically, "let me shop by myself, thank you."

The insights we will cover on those four thoughts, which, we remind you, are consistent in every selling situation, will help you quickly lower sales resistance and increase sales acceptance, thus reaching the goal of a closed sale today.

These four words, and the questions they bring to your customer's mind, control every sales situation. Here's how.

NEED

"I feel no need." Your goal as a one-call closer is to help them change their mindset to one of "I feel some need."

TRUST

"I feel no trust." No one will let you persuade them into anything if they don't trust you. So, you must work toward helping them think, "I feel some trust."

HELP

"I want no help." No one ever wants to admit they're helpless, of course. However, you can certainly help someone see that you can provide answers in areas where they may not be as educated as you are. After all you are a trained professional in your field. So, you need to change their mindset to one of "I want some help."

HURRY

"I feel no hurry." Unless there's water running uncontrollably at their home, no one is going to be in a hurry to purchase plumbing supplies. Your job is to help them see that by taking care of the buying decision today, they'll be better off than if they wait. They need to think, "I feel some hurry" in order to take action.

All Sales Are Controlled By Need-Trust-Help-Hurry

That's it. When you master the concept of Need-Trust-Help-Hurry you are well on your way to mastering the art of one-time closing. It is extremely important that you learn how these four very specific words help define your potential client's sales resistance. They are the primary barrier between no sale and sale. They are the main line of "defense" they will keep you from providing the prospective client the very product or service they agreed to talk over with you and/or need the most. These four words are powerful enough to keep your future client from making a purchase *right now*. And right now is the time frame that concerns us most.

Viewed from the perspective of a professionally trained salesperson, it is your *duty* to overcome the walls put up by those four words. Mastery over Need-Trust-Help-Hurry will allow you to alter the prospect's mindset, thus helping him or her make a decision that's truly good for them—today. Not only will you be a conscious competent, but you'll have a head start on becoming an unconscious competent— a master closer.

The Four Horsemen Of The Apocalypse Now

Think about this. *You only have four obstacles between "no sale" and "where do I sign!"* All the sales resistance in the world can be boiled down to four simple words. No matter who you approach, the size of the company, the title of the person on the door, you only face a maximum of four obstacles. That should bring you an incredible sense of relief. And power.

It's similar to the situation a football coach faces. No matter how big the organization behind the team may be, there are never more than eleven players on the field, no more, no less. That simple fact alone eliminates a lot of unnecessary stress. The disadvantage is that he or she never knows exactly where those players will be after "one-two-three hike!" Of course, the opposing coach has the same challenge, so things have a way of balancing out.

Mastering the art of the one-time close gives you the edge because you will already know *all* the defense's options. We have given you a look at the opposing team's playbook and all you have to do is run your own well-planned game.

Speaking of running, let's look at your enviable position from the point of view of track and field. There you are in your running togs and your feather-light shoes. The gun sounds. Pow! You're off and running your heart out. One hundred yards later you spread your arms, smile, and pose for the winning photograph snapped by the local newspaper reporter. But wait a minute. Something's terribly wrong here. The other runners dash right past you and keep up their pace. Someone forgot to tell you what kind of race you're running. Clearly its' not a 100 yard dash. Is it the 880 yard run, the mile run or a 26 mile marathon through downtown Boston? Makes a difference, doesn't it? Even the best runner would be severely handicapped not knowing the distance to be run before the race. How could you pace yourself? Evaluate the other runners' strategies? Know when to hold back and when to sprint for the finish line?

That's why it's so important to know what type of race you are to run before you take that first step out of the blocks. The way the one-time closing specialist does that is to enter the mind of the prospect. You will determine your potential client's personality type. Is he or she an analytical, a driver, an amiable, or an expressive (Pa, Adam, Hoss or Little Joe?) Then, after planning and preparing your presentation for the prospect's mindset, you will plan and prepare your presentation by adapting your personality to meet the needs of the other party's personality. If a driver is required, regardless of your own personality, you will become a driver or an amiable or whichever type is required to serve their needs. They will react with the "Prospect Mindset" and you will then proceed with the sales situation in accordance with the system outlined here smoothly, flawlessly and almost effortlessly.

Now that you're off and running, there's even more good news. You don't have to worry about what kind of race you're running—in sales there are only these two: prospect initiated and salesperson initiated. We'll take a more in-depth look at them in the next chapter.

4

The Two Formations of Personality Obstacles

The Race Gets Easier

The more we examine the four key defense measures of Need-Trust-Help-Hurry, the easier our race becomes to run. *The four defenses can be arranged in only one of two formations.* You are never in the position of the football coach or the runner who still must guess at the opposing strategy. You know you face the same strategies every time you go out. All you have to do is open your playbook, and adjust your presentation to the challenge at hand.

What Determines These Two Defense Formations?

That's an excellent question. We'll answer with another.

Who initiated the sale?

There can be one of only two answers:

1. The prospect initiated the sale or
2. The salesperson initiated the sale.

As Porky Pig would say, "that's all folks." Knowing who initiated the sales process is one of the most important aspects of designing your presentation. And that one's not that hard to figure out, is it?

A prospect initiated sale means the prospect has already taken some steps toward becoming a client. He or she has left the comfort of the easy chair, the distractions of the media, and the other concerns of the day. This potential future client may be a walk-in to your showroom, an inquiry on your web page, a letter or a phone call. What form the inquiry takes isn't as important as the fact that your prospect believes it's time to consider buying something. At this stage of the game he or she is already feeling some NEED.

There's already at least a bit of TRUST because he or she took the first step and it was toward you, right? Clearly, this person recognizes a need for some HELP and may even be in a HURRY to get it.

"My car broke down last night and I have to be on the road tomorrow. I NEED some help. My cousin said I could TRUST you folks to HELP me with a rental in a HURRY."

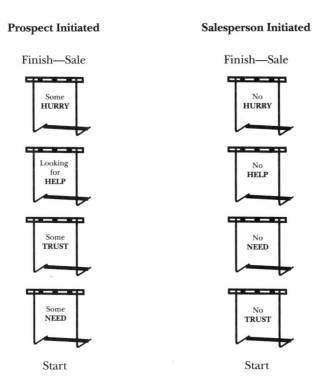

Prospect Initiated

Finish—Sale

Some HURRY

Looking for HELP

Some TRUST

Some NEED

Start

Salesperson Initiated

Finish—Sale

No HURRY

No HELP

No NEED

No TRUST

Start

A salesperson initiated sale is quite different. Here the seller makes the first inquiry with a cold call. You may walk-in, call up on the phone, or just approach someone who is "just browsing, thanks." In these situations the prospect is feeling NO TRUST, NO NEED, wants NO HELP, and is in NO HURRY. Do you get the impression that you will not exactly be greeted with open arms? But you knew you had your work cut out for you when you initiated the call in the first place, so there's no surprise there anyway.

Notice that we have repositioned the words *need* and *trust* between the two examples. That's because your prospect has changed his or her mindset. This is important because the prospect's thought patterns have become more important than the personality you are approaching. The prospect slides into a defensive mode the second you start your presentation, even earlier. Often you can see a physical change from across the showroom floor as you walk over or even catch it in their tone of voice as the person on the other line realizes the reason for your call.

Don't worry. Remember, you are a master of one-call closing.

Meanwhile Back On the Ponderosa

Changing your style and delivery to meet the needs of the four personality types will change your closing ratios for the better. Let's refer to an earlier illustration of these four types.

Distant
Thinkers
Task Driven

Reserved	**Analytical**	**Driver**	Fast
Slow	Motivated by respect	Motivated by power	Tellers
Askers	and being right	and control	Extrovert
Introvert			Talkers
			Assertive
	Amiable	**Expressive**	Aggressive
	Motivated by approval	Motivated by recognition	
	and support	and pleasure	

Emotional
Enthusiastic
Friendly

This is normal behavior. Pa is balancing the books. Adam is making plans for that new sawmill. Hoss is helping the school 'marm with the kids. And Little Joe is trying rather unsuccessfully to tell everybody that it was really another Michael Landon who starred in I Was A Teenage Werewolf. When the sales process begins, everything changes. Two different, but highly recognizable mindsets will emerge.

Again, the benefit of this way of looking at things is that you know what you're in for. You know the length of the foot race or the number of players on the opposing team. You know the potential strategies, the options and the obstacles you face and you are thoroughly prepared. After all, there aren't that many to handle in the first place, right?

Just knowing those basic facts should eliminate all or at least most of your fear of the unknown. Every time you use this bit of information you will get more and more proficient. You will become more confident in your approach and presentation. Your self-esteem will grow as will your desire to better serve your customer. And you will inevitably master the art of the one-time close.

Jumping the High Hurdles

Some of the most exciting events in track and field are the high hurdles. Not only are the runners in a fast-paced race, they have to jump obstacles every so many yards. Getting to the one-call close is a lot like that. So let's look at the mindset of your potential client in terms of a 100 yard high hurdle race.

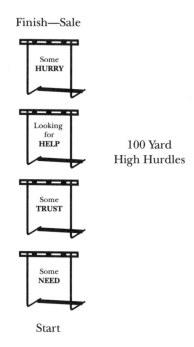

Prospect Initiated

Finish—Sale

Some **HURRY**

Looking for **HELP**

100 Yard
High Hurdles

Some **TRUST**

Some **NEED**

Start

Hurdling The Prospect-Initiated Sale

The first hurdle is your prospect's need for your product or service. He (or she), obviously, feels some need or you wouldn't have received the e-mail inquiry, letter, phone call or walk-in visit. You will encounter various degrees of need. "My Internet provider just crashed. Again! I need to get back on line today or I'll be out of business." Obviously, you will handle the needs of this individual a bit differently from the person who drops by to browse and who has no immediate need to swap recipes online with Cousin Francie back East.

The second high hurdle is trust. Again, some trust has already been expressed by the call or visit. The prospect has heard of your company through advertising, word of mouth or the recommendation of a trusted friend and they've shown up at your door. A major part of your job description is to start proving the value of that trust and to make it even stronger. Start building trust immediately. Do it with every question, every statement, and every gesture you make. Examples:

"We carry the finest line of vacuum cleaners recommended by Consumer Digest magazine."

"We've been helping families like yours take charge of their financial futures for over 20 years."

"Our company takes great pride in its high customer satisfaction rate. Let me show you some of the comments our clients have made about our service."

"A reputation for professionalism is important when seeking out someone to help you sell your home, isn't it?"

Next, you have to jump the hurdle of help. The prospect is knocking on your door, so there's already some hope that you will be of help in resolving his or her challenge. Your task is to find out how, show how, and then prove the wisdom of your prospect's trust in you and your organization.

The last hurdle is hurry. There will be variables here. The prospect facing a major business loss has a significantly greater sense of urgency to get online than Francie's favorite cousin and his recipe for blueberry pie. We want to encourage and enhance that sense of urgency. Even if it is just a tiny seed, we need to help it grow. The cousin may not be in any particular hurry, but you can change that. Show him the limited-time price reduction, the end-of-the month special, the factory rebate, the dollars-off coupon or offer to "talk with the manager" for some special arrangement. Point out that blueberry season is almost over back east, for goodness sakes! You can easily and legitimately create a sense of urgency even when one does not initially exist.

Here are a few examples of how the prospect-initiated sale works.

1. A Top Restaurant
Need—I feel hungry. Don't you?
Trust—Upscale's Restaurant has great food, don't you think? Of course.
Help—Their menu offers great food at reasonable prices. And it's not in French.
Hurry—Let's beat Frasier, Niles and the rest of the after-the-concert crowd.

2. A Grocery Store
Need—I'm throwing a big party.
Trust—A&P is a good store.
Help—Their deli has a variety of party food.
Hurry—Party trays are 15% off with our coupon that expires this week.

3. A Clothing Store
Need—A new job demands a new suit.
Trust—Dillards carries my favorite name brands.

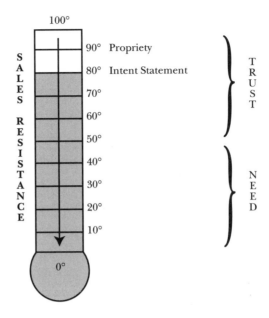

Following up your proper and appropriate approach with an intent statement automatically "lowers the temperature" of your prospect's sales resistance.

Next, I'll show you the product demonstration and after that I'll discuss the details and the amount of your investment.

Summarize: Now folks, I represent my company and this fine product that is used successfully by many happy clients. However, I'm not a high-pressure salesperson. I just don't believe in it. And I realize my product isn't for everyone. It may or may not be for you. I just hope you'll keep an open mind and at the end of my presentation, you will tell me if this product is for you. Okay?"

The above example is most effective in a seller-initiated sales situation. It is offered when an incentive has been offered to the prospect for investing his or her time. A condensed version can be used in any sales situation once the actual presentation starts. Whatever the situation, letting your prospect know your intentions and to imply that "it's okay to say no" should be part of every intent statement.

Breathing Space

A one-time closing specialist always builds pauses and silences into the presentation. They allow the prospect time to consider important information, formulate appropriate questions, or just to catch his or her mental "breath." Authors do the same thing. So, we'll take a break now, let you absorb all the information you've just received, and then complete steps three, four and five in Chapter Six.

6

Building trust is essential from the prospect's point of view.

Tom Hopkins

*If we compare sales to an automobile trip,
then trust fuels the journey.*

Pat Leiby

The First Defense—Trust

Part II

As you will remember from Chapter Five, the five steps to gaining trust are:

1. Propriety
2. Intent Statement
3. Commonality
4. Credibility
5. Competency

At this point, we're assuming you've gained a clear understanding of and made adjustments to your personal grooming habits to meet each potential future client with Propriety. We'll also assume you've mastered an effective Intent Statement so the potential clients knows what the agenda is and is relieved to know there's no pressure to own your product or service.

The last three steps to increasing trust, which reduce sales resistance are so important, they have their own nickname. We will identify them from here on simply as the "Three Cs."

Seek The All Too Uncommon Common Ground

Athletes, the really professional ones anyway, always warm up prior to a game, match or performance. They'll stretch, hop, skip, jump, and run through a few paces to get limber and loose for the upcoming event. Salespeople should run through a few paces with their potential clients and customers just before the "big event" too. Anyone who's been in sales for any length of time knows the value of this "warm up." It's basic.

Of course, *you don't have to make a friend to make a sale,* but making an enemy won't move you any closer to that "salesperson of the month" award either.

People buy from people they like and trust. Finding common ground is an essential part of a salesperson's presentation and you must discover it early in the process. You can find common ground with anybody, any time and any place if you'll just look hard enough. After all, you and your client are both human, right? During some of history's most tragic wars, bitter enemies found common ground.

Here's one famous example. During one of the most brutal battles of World War I, the fight stopped one evening. It happened to be Christmas Eve.

One side heard a Christmas carol floating on the cold air across the contested ground. The language was different, but everyone knew the tune and soon both sides were singing together. Before the evening was over the men emerged from their muddy trenches, met in "no man's land," and exchanged greetings and even humble Christmas presents with their enemies.

If battle-hardened men who were in the midst of trying to conquer each other's territory can find common ground in no man's land, then certainly we salespeople can do the same thing on the showroom floor, at the executive desk, or the dining room table.

Step #3—Commonality

Finding that common ground is what Step Three is all about. During this early segment of the sales process you should search for areas of interest you share with this new person you've just met—your future client. The supply of topics is limitless. For example, their family, the weather, sports, hobbies, or current events are natural choices in consumer sales. If you're in business-to-business sales, you can always ask questions about their company or industry as well.

Because of the potential for highly-charged emotions, we recommend that you always avoid seeking commonality in two areas: religion and politics, unless that's how you and your prospect met. For some people, there just is no common ground on these subjects. You either agree one hundred percent with their view or it's "back to the trenches" and "fix bayonets." Those are battles you should choose not to fight because you can't win them.

In those rare cases where you just can't seem to find commonality, create some. Humor is an excellent tool for this purpose. Don't be afraid to use a light-hearted approach, even if your customer is showing a good bit of tension—especially if your customer is showing a good bit of attention. Here's an easy-going ice breaker for a visit with a couple.

"How did you two meet?" Sometimes just the question itself will start a thaw. The answer to that question, for example, is almost always a humorous one. *"Oh, I picked her up in a bar. Ha-ha."* This would probably be followed by a mock-surprised *"You did not!"* and a mild slap on the "offending" party's shoulder. Someone else might say *"Oh, he showed up at the back door and mom said I could keep him."*

Without realizing it, the customer has helped you break the ice and start the warm up. For example, the how did you meet question often leads to brief comments about their dating and courtship. That friendly chatter usually brings up all kinds of warm feelings. The comfort level between salesperson and prospect grows right along with those feelings. They open up a part of their lives. *Because you make the effort to find or build commonality, your customer opens up personal "turf" that few other salespeople ever see.* With very little effort you're suddenly a friend of the family!

Never forget, customers want to like you. They want to trust you. Do your part and they'll always do theirs to meet you halfway. When trust builds, sales resistance crumbles.

A Common Commonality Mistake

One of the most important things to remember during this early stage is to *avoid asking sales questions.*

We can't count the number of times we've observed or heard about inexperienced sales people virtually attacking a customer with sales questions the moment they enter the room. They come on like whirling dervishes—legs pumping, arms flailing, eyes wide and tongues wagging. Would you want something like that coming your way? Neither would a customer. So many good sales have been blown to pieces before they ever had a chance to develop because the salesperson failed to develop commonality.

Think initially in terms of *social* and not sales situations. What type of conversation would you initiate at your friendly neighborhood sports pub, the church social or in that shared cab ride from the airport? Which of the following questions will promote commonality and which will douse your warm up with ice water?

"Are you from around here?"

"That's an exquisite brooch. Is it an heirloom?"

"Did you catch the game last night?"

A good way to open a conversation with executive level people who are more likely to want to get down to business would be to ask general questions about the organization.

"Isn't the pace of business today amazing?"

"Tell me a bit about how your company has developed."

"How long have you been with the company?"

None of those questions are inappropriate in the appropriate context. There's that "propriety thing" again.

Ask a question that will get your customers talking. At this point you're not trying to close a sale. You're initiating a relationship. Listen to their answers and build your next question on those answers. That's all.

Time Creates Obligation

Have you ever met a stranger, become engaged in a conversation, and then discovered that somehow a significant amount of time had passed unnoticed? Sure, we all have. What happened was a bonding process in which two people found a common interest. The conversation and budding relationship quickly, easily and naturally flowed out of that bond. People often say, "You know, it feels like I've known you all my life" after such a conversation, regardless of how brief.

How does that happen?

Well, in sales it happens because the salesperson made it happen. The first step is to find a subject in which the other person is interested. Don't assume that just because you discover an area of particular interest, skill or knowledge that it's a subject they want to discuss. After all, the greatest chef in the world may just not want to get into the niceties of making sausage. Look for something they want to talk about. For example, our chef may be the world's worst player on the golf course, but also an avid fan. As a salesperson, you'll do much better if you encourage a conversation about golf links rather than the frying kind.

If you're familiar with the subject, golf for example, then you've made the connection. Proceed! If you don't know the difference between a tee or a green and green tea, you'd better move on. Don't try to fake it. The customer will see right through it and you'll drive your chances of building common ground right into a self-made sand trap. Just keep politely asking more questions on more topics. At some point, you and the prospect will share a common interest.

There is an excellent alternative to faking it, though. If your customer seems really interested in a topic that you are totally unfamiliar with, go for it. Admit your lack of knowledge and start asking questions. Get him or her talking up a storm about that fascinating subject. As long as you are sincere, the other person will be flattered by your attention. Conversation flows and commonality is established. In fact, learning something new is one of the real benefits of earning a living in sales. Every day there's something different. How many occupations can boast that perk?

Here's the beauty of this situation. *If your potential clients are reasonable persons, all the time invested in talking about themselves and their interests creates an obligation on their part to listen to you when it is time to make your presentation.* Human beings are wonderful that way. Respect and interest earns respect and interest.

Here are a few subjects to give you an idea of how building common ground can begin.

Job Related:
- Tell me a bit about your job.
- Tell me what you do for a living.
- What's your occupation?
- What do you like most/least about your work?
- How long have you been doing this?
- What's the most interesting part of your job?
- What gives you the greatest amount of satisfaction at work?

Kids Related:
- Do you have any kids?
- Do you have any children?
- What are their names?
- How old are they?
- I bet you're proud of him/her/them.
- What interests are they developing?
- What do they do for fun?

Family Related:
- Are you married? (you might be meeting someone wearing gloves, okay?)
- Been married long?
- Where do you folks live?
- Did you go on a honeymoon? Oh, where?
- Where does he/she work?
- What do you folks do for recreation?
- Do you share any hobbies?

Location Related:
- Are you from around here?
- Where are you from?
- What do you like most about living in your town?

- Have you traveled much?
- What is the most fun thing to do in your area?
- What three things would you recommend a tourist to see first?

All of this information isn't gathered just to be discarded. You'll use much of it later when it comes time to cover your customer's needs. We'll discuss that later in the book.

We could go on and on with this, but you get the idea. You want to be friendly and to encourage the other person to be friendly. *Don't treat these questions as a checklist you have to march through like "Sherman to the sea."* Sure, General Sherman achieved his objective and shortened the Civil War, but he's still not too popular a figure down Georgia way. Your goal is conversation not conquest.

Also, avoid the trap of droning on about any given subject. Getting overly involved in the topic of conversation will cut out valuable time you'll need for getting down to business and making your presentation. Just find the commonality. Establish it. Make sure your customer is comfortable with it. And at the appropriate moment, move on.

Speaking of moving in, let's see where all that common ground leads.

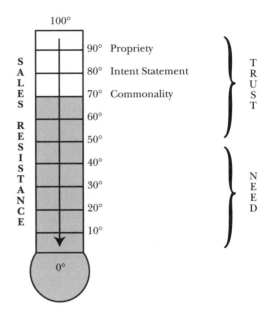

*The trend continues. From a high of 100 degrees,
your persistent and courteous efforts at propriety,
your intent statement, and establishing commonality
have reduced your customer's sales resistance down
to 70 degrees and you're just getting started!*

Step #4—Credibility

"Okay," you ask, "now that I've captured the common ground, what do I do with it?" The answer is "move on." And your destination is the next step, which is to prove your personal credibility to your customer.

The amount of time you invest establishing credibility varies according to a number of factors. Among these are:

- your product
- your product's required investment

- your industry
- your company
- you
- your customer
- your customer's level of need
- your customer's budget

We could add "etc." or keep the list going for several pages, but you get the idea. Even a variable such as available time itself can have a dramatic effect. For example, you'll have a lot more seconds, minutes and hours in a four-hour flight from Dallas/Ft. Worth to Phoenix than in a four-floor ride on an elevator. Of course, there are two key factors regarding time: (1) respect your customer's time and (2) use it wisely.

Sharing A Timely Tale Of Time Shares

The importance of credibility was proven rather dramatically a few years ago when the once-booming timeshare industry entered some serious bad times. A lot of those bad times were well-earned. Poor management, unscrupulous marketing practices, bad management, poor property management, and a "customer be darned" attitude took a heavy toll on profits and public relations. Things were much worse than the implication in the title of the spaghetti western "The Good, The Bad And the Ugly." The timeshares offered were either "The Good," "The Bad," or "The I Want My Money Back!" As always, the good folks in the business got hammered right along with the bad. Things became so rough there was serious talk that the entire industry could collapse.

Fortunately, wise heads prevailed. Good management was brought back, serious self-regulation began, and some big name companies entered the field. Things began to change for the better and now timeshares are a well-respected, international, multibillion dollar business. What carried the industry through those rough times was the simple fact that the public liked the idea of vacation ownership and enjoyed the lifestyle it provided.

Over time, enough credibility had been built up to keep the concept alive during the dark days. A lot of very smart salespeople did everything they could to enhance that credibility. During this period of low sales, they provided forms of reinforcement to gain and hold the confidence of a prospect. These items included:

- documented articles from respectable publications
- letters of endorsement
- referrals
- positive word of mouth
- and working *really* hard to earn it.

We chose timeshares to illustrate the point because good salespeople went to great lengths to prove credibility in every aspect of the business. That's something we admire and encourage you to emulate.

And we can almost hear your comments coming. "Sure, but I sell furniture. We just don't have those kinds of problems." "I'm an automobile salesperson. We've been in business more than half a century." "My insurance company is one of the largest in the world."

"The appliances (jams and jellies or tires and tie-rods or pens and paper) in my store practically sell themselves." True. Contrary to some of the "comedians" on cable and television, a company or an industry may not be the true source of evil in our galaxy. However, *you* still face a credibility problem even if your product or company is a household word that can stand proudly on its own.

As a general rule, *the salesperson is an unknown element.* Personal relationships and referrals are exceptions, but in most cases customers won't automatically like and trust you because they just don't know you.

Yet.

Picture This

One of your authors was cursed and blessed with a rather young-looking face early in his career. In fact, walk-in customers or people meeting him for the first time at his real estate office would say, "Hi, sonny, is your dad around?" The trouble was, even though he certainly was credible, he didn't **look** credible to some prospects. Instead of resenting the situation or getting belligerent, he did something else. He overcame the challenge. He had a good quality portrait of himself taken with his wife and kids. This was displayed prominently on his desk so new arrivals could quickly see that "sonny" was indeed an established member of the community with a growing family. Over the years, that one picture eliminated hours of explanations and efforts to overcome an apparent credibility issue.

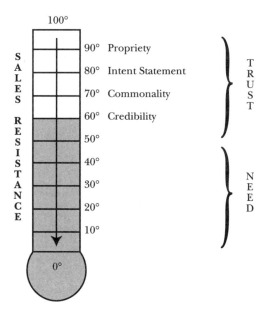

*As your growing credibility lowers the temperature
of sales resistance, the prospects of your
one-time closing heat up.*

You can use this same technique to "picture your-self" to your prospects and customers. Create an advertising "flyer" on yourself. This can be a real advertising-style flyer or just a mini-scrapbook. You can do this with your home computer or even with a careful hand, a pair of scissors, some glue and a clear plastic sleeve or two. Just pop in a couple of photographs of you and your family, you accepting that Woman Of The Year Award, or anything that is appropriate. Include any appropriate business certi-fications, awards or citations. Don't drop anything in as "filler." Everything must build your professional reputation. The idea is to *show* your credibility. Don't try to recreate War and Peace or even War Cry Comics. Include just enough material that you can present in no more than a few minutes to prove that you are the absolute best sales counselor for that potential client to believe in.

You *are,* aren't you?

Then, show it.

Step #5—Competency

Visualize competency as clay. Unused it's nothing more than something sticking to the bottom of your shoes—useless, unappreciated and something that will just drag you down on a slow road to failure. Slapped between a couple of logs on a cabin it can protect you against the wind and rain and secure your shelter on a cold night. Formed into bricks it can become the building block of a skyscraper, a city or even a civilization.

The question is, what will you do with your allotment?

Look at it from your client's point of view. When she wants, needs or desires a product or service, how much time does she want to *spend* with an incompetent salesperson? The obvious answer is "little or none." How much time do you think she'll *invest* with a competent one. That answer is just as obvious—"all the time it takes."

How competent are you at your work?

How well do you present your company's product or service?

Are you serving your company well?

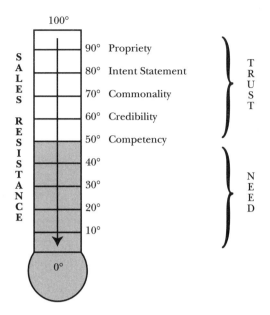

*By taking the five steps to gaining trust one
at a time and in proper order you will soon
reduce the sales resistance "temperature" by half
and eliminate the NO TRUST hurdle!*

Are you serving your clients well, too?

Do you know your new potential client's real needs?

Are you as good as you were last year? Better?

Are you working at peak performance right now?

Which is more important, your monthly quota or your customer's challenge?

If any of these questions, or those most likely popping into your mind right now, are bringing up some feelings of doubt, then it's time to start working on building your competence.

Even if the answers have sent you into a spiraling depression, relax. There's good news. *When you properly complete the first four steps of the trust segment of the one-time closing sales presentation, your prospect will perceive you to be competent.* Looking competent isn't as vital as being competent, but it is important. As Dr. Laurence J. Peter, author of the multimillion-copy-selling "The Peter Principle" and "The Peter Prescription" reminds us, "Competence, like truth, beauty and a contact lens, is in the eye of the beholder." The customer's eye is going to be on you so make sure that customer sees what he or she expects to see—a salesperson practicing a high level of competency.

The creation of that vision is all up to you. It's your job to make it a reality.

The Three Cs
Just Do The Math

You can improve your odds in winning the "numbers game" of sales when you look at things through the eyes of your client. What does he or she really want and need from the process? Your needs are not irrelevant, but they should take second place to those you serve. Don't worry about your sales quota, your mortgage or that long-awaited vacation in the Bahamas. Take care of your clients and the quotas, the bills, the vacations and a lot more will take care of themselves.

It really boils down to a mathematical equation. A plus B always equals C. In this case, Three Cs.

Question Yourself

By that we do not mean to question your motives, your thoughts or reasons for being. We mean for you to put yourself in your client's mind and formulate a list of questions to ask the salesperson—you. If you develop a good match, your potential clients will feel that you are professional and credible. Competency is then automatic. We're back to doing the math.

Propriety + Intent + Commonality + Credibility = Competency

Like all math equations, if the elements are correct and in the correct order, you always get the correct and desired result. Numerous factors will dictate how you vary your questions. Among them are:

- Is it a seller-initiated sale?
- Is it a customer-initiated sale?
- What is the investment range?
- Is there an investment range?
- How much latitude do you have to negotiate the sale?
- What's going on in your industry?
- What are your company policies?
- How is the current economy affecting their business and yours?
- What is the projected economy and how will it affect this sale, if at all?
- And the ever popular category called "other."

The key is to put yourself into the mind of your potential future client. What do prospects and clients really want to know? If you're new to the profession and have some difficulty developing your questions, ask a veteran salesperson to help you get started. As with any other skill, once you give it a couple of good tries, you'll learn and eventually become a master. Here are a couple of "idea starters."

- How long have you/your company been in this business?
- Who are you folks and what are you all about?
- Can you provide me with any recent testimonials?
- What kind of warranty do you provide?
- Tell me about service after the sale?
- Is there someone who can do the installation for me?
- How much does it cost?
- Are a lot of colors available?
- What are the extras?
- When can I take ownership?
- When can I take possession?

You get the idea. The simplest way to draw up a list of questions is to think just like what you are when you're not selling—a consumer. What would *you* like to know before making your next purchase? (Commonality) Chances are that's pretty close to what your own customers are wondering. (Credibility)

Answer Before You're Asked

An excellent way to put your potential client at ease and begin building trust is to answer three or four of the most important questions right up front. Get them out of the way. This provides a measure of genuine relief for your customer. "Gee, they're a lot more flexible on pay plans than I thought!" "Whew, this isn't going to ruin my morning after all." "Gosh, I didn't realize so many options were available." You will answer the rest of the questions, and probably a couple you may not have considered yet, during the remainder of your presentation.

Most of the time your customers will bring up questions that really aren't all that pertinent to the sale or very relevant to their real interest. It could be that they are nervous, trying to come up with better questions or just stalling for time. It is your job to find and address the real questions. One way to gauge the true importance of a question is to ignore it—once. Just respond with something like "Good question. I'll address that specifically, later in my presentation, if that's okay with you?" Of course, it's okay. If the question is legitimate, you've told them you'll provide the answer. If you forget or don't cover it well enough, they can always bring it back up again. And if it's not relevant, then you can just forget it. Rarely will a customer restate an unimportant question. It just doesn't come back up because you guide the process into the relevant areas.

Say Goodbye To B.R.I

Your enemies at this early stage of the sales process can be labeled B, R, and I for:

- **B**oredom
- **R**esistance
- **I**mpatience

These enemies can be dispatched quite early in the battle to serve your customer. When you:

- establish the correct *propriety,*
- deliver your *intent statement,*
- ask casual warm-up questions for *commonality,*
- show reasonable documentation of your *credibility,*
- address and answer the Three Cs,
- you will have achieved *competency* and will have the level of trust necessary to continue with your presentation.

Once you have correctly used The Five Steps To Gaining Trust, your customer psychologically grants you that permission. In fact, mentally they're encouraging you to "get on with it." They're interested and even getting a bit excited about the prospect of owning your product or service. That's a very good place for both of you to be. It's called a win/win situation.

Once you achieve the desired level of trust, your prospects and customers will listen to you with a sense of respect and acceptance *and you can say goodbye to boredom, resistance and impatience.*

> *The worst death of all is to be bored to death.*
>
> Will Rogers

Now that we've said our goodbyes to BRI, let's move ahead and say hello to the next line of defense—your customer's need.

CHAPTER

7

Necessity is not an established fact, but an interpretation.
Frederick Wilhelm Nietzche

The Second Defense—Need

Part I

Nietzche got it right. A need is an interpretation. Your customer doesn't really need a new car. He or she needs reliable transportation to get to work and back. She doesn't really want a new life insurance policy. She wants to leave something for her grandchildren. They say the company needs a new steam turbine for the power plant. You interpret that correctly to mean they need greater efficiency, lower cost per kilowatt, happier customers, or higher fourth-quarter earnings.

Ralph Waldo Emerson said, "The finest poems of the world have been expedients to get bread." In other word's we do *this* to get *that*. It's all a matter of proper interpretation.

What Is *"That"*

We all know by now that the success of our sales presentation depends upon serving the *needs* of our customers. We also know that the entire sales process starts before we can possibly know those all-important needs. In a way it's like stepping into a large office building ready to make your presentation, but without knowing exactly where you're going. Is your appointment on the first floor or the fifty-first? Should you meet in the mezzanine, the coffee shop or over at the security desk? Perhaps you should check in here at Acme, Inc. Or was it Ajax? Or Apex? You're surrounded by opportunity, but where precisely is this moment's opportunity? Defining the illusive "that" is like finding the office directory on the first floor. Sometimes all you need is a good look to get headed in the right direction.

No one should offer solutions to challenges not yet discovered or agreed upon.

The one-call closing specialist begins the sales process from the first second of the initial meeting. He or she doesn't jump the gun and start offering solutions because he or she doesn't even yet know the challenges. They will initiate instead the discovery agreement process. This process can be surprisingly brief or it can require a considerable investment in time. How much time depends upon who initiates the sale and the prospect's level of need. For example a need can be:

- non-existent ("No thanks, I'm just looking.")
- slight, but real ("No thanks, I'm just looking.")

- real and immediate ("No thanks, I'm just looking")
- real and "help!" ("No thanks, I'm just looking"—with sweat beads)

So, our goal is not only to determine the real challenge so we can offer a real solution, we also have to determine the level of that need.

"Cold Reading" Heats Up The Sale

Professional "mind readers" often use a technique called cold reading. It's a way of getting more information from a member of the audience than that audience member realizes. It involves (1) asking questions, often in a "shotgun" approach, to get basic information, (2) extreme active listening to pick up on the answer, body language, inflections, and other "hidden" bits and pieces of information, and (3) feeding the information back to the audience in a way that surprises, excites and entertains.

One-time closing salespeople do the same thing to make certain they are serving the real needs of their clients. When the potential client initiates the sale, there is some level of curiosity. *Something* brought these folks to your doorsteps or caused you to come to theirs. Often there is also an absolute level of need for your product or service. In these situations the psychological sequence of events is much different from salesperson-initiated situations in which we offer some type of incentive. When we first meet the client, we must start the discovery and need process in a more comprehensive manner.

Do Not Put Need Before Trust (In A Seller-Initiated Sale)

We just mentioned something about jumping the gun. Putting your customers' need before building sufficient trust is one of the most blatant and most common examples of leaping over that firearm. Why is this basic mistake so common? Because it seems so natural, that's why.

The customer walks-in. He or she clearly has a need, a desire, and some kind of budget. They're ready to buy, aren't they? Surely this is a prime example of a buyer-initiated sale with the buyer ready, willing and able to be sold, right? Of course not. Without trust you will never be able to close a sale. It just can't happen.

It is a mistake bordering on the criminal (or criminally insane) to attempt selling this way. You make several bad and often sale-destroying mistakes:

- you're desperate.
- you're just trying to make your quota.
- you don't care about their real needs.
- you're already thinking about the next customer.
- you're under pressure from the sales manager to "close 'em now!"

If you put need before trust you'll be taking a long hop, skip and a jump off a short pier and will find yourself up to your neck in lost sales.

Take The Time To Read The Mind

And if you can't actually read minds, you can certainly (and rather easily) find out what's going on in there. The discovery process can begin as simply as *"What brings you folks out to Ajax Autos today?"* It can be as complex and time-invested (not "consuming") as having your customer fill out a twenty-question survey.

Many of the top companies we've trained in the health and fitness field have built into the facility tour a questionnaire/survey that allows the health consultant to isolate the information necessary to find out what is important, really important and not very important at all to the potential member. This valuable information is then used (or not, if it isn't important) to move the closing forward.

Whatever the situation, you must invest all the time required to find out what is going on in your client's mind. You must take care of this important step completely before attempting to prescribe product benefits. There are no exceptions.

Take the real estate industry for example. A champion salesperson would never start showing property without first qualifying the prospect. A significant number of variables will dictate which properties will and will not be shown. For example:

- Family budget
- Expansions—babies on the way?
- Reductions—kids heading off to school?
- Neighborhoods
- Proximity to good schools
- Proximity to jobs for each spouse
- Location of major traffic arteries
- Distance to medical and health facilities
- Peace and quiet or "hubbub" of city life

Without qualifying, you'd be showing starter homes to millionaires and mansions to apartment-seeking newlyweds. Initially, you have a lot of questions with big, long blanks where the answers should be. Start out with a friendly, conversational question. *"What brings you good folks out to our store today?"* Generally, your customers will start filling in the blanks for you right way.

Read That Mind Back To Your Customer

Even as those blanks get filled in, you know there are other empty spaces on the page, so you keep on asking those friendly questions. Slowly, surely and courteously you begin to narrow the focus on discovering their real needs. Additionally, your efforts are enhanced by your professionalism. People considering doing business with you appreciate a professional attitude. It proves you care. They respond positively because they'll begin to see that you are competent, credible and trustworthy.

You see how this works? First things first. One step at a time. A place for everything and everything in its place.

One of those steps is to repeat what you have just heard. This serves two very important purposes:

1. Repetition shows that you are actively listening to your customer, and
2. It makes sure you and your customer are "on the same page."

"Let me see if I understand."

"Let me show you an example so I can be sure I understand exactly what you want."

"If I'm hearing you correctly, you're looking for this, that and the other in blue, right?"

"So I discuss what is really important to you, Mrs. Prospect, let me see if I understand what you've just said."

Of course, there's another way to "read" someone's mind. It's called body language.

The study of body language has been around for a long time. Many of us have studied it. In fact, we consider it to be a "mini-science" of the profession of selling, just as dressing for success or color imaging. These mini-sciences are important because, added together, they give you many more tools to become a highly-skilled professional.

Some of us are aware of a few basics "moves." Unfortunately, most of us don't take advantage of this powerful and effective sales tool. Head down to your favorite bookstore or library and pick up one of the many books on the subject. Once you study, observe and begin to put the theory into practice, you'll be delighted by how soon and by how much you benefit. Here are a few examples to illustrate our point.

Leaning forward means your prospect is interested and is listening. Our experience has shown that when people are presented with new information, they begin that process with their back pretty much against the back of their chair. When they begin to lean forward, this is a positive sign that they're ready for more and means that you should proceed with your presentation. You can even pick up the pace a bit.

Leaning back or glancing away is a clear sign that you are losing your prospect's interest. If this happens while you are in the middle of a long segment of your presentation, pause.

continues

continued

Then, summarize your last couple of sales points and ask a question to bring the prospect back into the process. If you see this happening to a number of people in a group presentation, suggest a short break or initiate a question and answer session.

Crossed arms indicates doubt about what is being said. When this happens, proof is in order. Charts, graphs, diagrams, or testimonials are quite effective in this situation. Just as it is important to "read" the other person's body language, it's important for the salesperson to send his or her own non-verbal signals. What you do can be as important and as effective as what you say. Here are a few examples.

Sit positioned so that you can have good eye contact with all the people at the table. If you were with one person, you could sit by his or her side, but with more than one person you want to be in a position to make good eye contact and observe any non-verbal communication between the prospects.

Use a pen or pointer to draw attention, at the appropriate times, to your visual aids. Notice how magicians use a "magic wand" to direct the attention of their audience to or from something. You can and should do the same thing. Do not be tentative or appear uncomfortable because that uncomfortable feeling will be transmitted directly to your prospect. Like a bad cold, it's catching.

Use open-hand gestures and eye contact. This shows that you are "open" and that you have nothing to hide. Be careful using the palm-out pushing gesture unless you're trying to eliminate a prospect's negative concern. Even then, push to the side and not directly at your prospect.

These few examples give you a brief glance at an entire field of study. The more you study, observe, practice and apply, the more you will see just how powerful this tool is and how big a help it will be in your efforts to become a one-call closing specialist.

Don't Put Your Cart Before Your Horse Sense

Why should we put trust before need in a seller-initiated sale?

At some point during the sale you will be required to ask important, often confidential and sometimes very personal questions. Honest, 100% correct answers from your potential clients are essential to serving their real needs. Inaccurate answers are a waste of time for both parties and will only result in inevitable dissatisfaction for everybody concerned. Putting the cart before the horse creates a lose/lose situation.

You can't get the valuable information about your customer's needs without trust.

Would you discuss your salary with someone you do not trust?

Your plans for the future?

Your family budget?

Your heart condition?

Your aging parent's medication needs?

Yet, these and other extremely serious and personal subjects come up all the time in sales. And, while they *ought* to come up, it should be only *when appropriate.* If they remain hidden in the background during the entire presentation, some salesperson has not built a foundation of trust and there will be no close. The reason for clients to hesitate to provide certain information, at least initially, is because the salesperson skipped the step of trust and jumped into a self-made mud puddle of need. (Then salesperson is in need—the need for a new customer!)

Imagine an attractive young man approaching an attractive young woman at a singles get-together. What are his chances of building a relationship if he addresses her in the following manner.

HE: Excuse me, but I've been noticing you all evening.

SHE: Oh?

HE: Oh, yes. That's a lovely dress. You must know a lot about fashion.

SHE: Thank you. I pay attention to style.

HE: Well, it certainly shows.

SHE: And thank you again.

HE: I think you are very attractive and I would like to ask you out to dinner...

SHE: You would?

HE: ...but first would you mind telling me how old you are?

SHE: What.

HE: And how much you weigh?

SHE: What!

HE: Do you have any unusual medical conditions? Wait! Don't go! What did I say?

We're certainly not romance columnists, but we feel pretty safe in saying that young man has already seen the best moments of his new "relationship." Suppose, however that the young woman was in a medical complex and the young man was her doctor.

"How old are you...How much do you weigh...Do you have any unusual medical conditions?" take on an entirely new context don't they? In fact, these questions seem completely appropriate. Instead of walking away, the young woman would probably provide the answers immediately and without question.

The difference is the different level of trust.

A master at one-call closing gets accurate answers to such questions because he or she establishes trust with the customer. Only then can the questions be answered with any degree of honesty. If you're going to be asking for a good bit of personal information, debt or health matters, for example, you should always preface them with a phrase something like, "We don't mean to be personal, but we can do a better job by asking you these types of questions. Will that be okay?" This is called getting permission to ask personal questions.

"Not to be personal, but to do a better job for you, may I ask you a few questions?"

"To serve your needs to the best of my ability I need to get to know your specific situation and concerns. Do you mind if I ask you a few questions now?"

"With your permission, I'd like to ask you a few questions now. They will help me maximize your time here and make sure that I provide the right solution to your particular need. Okay?"

You see? It's not so difficult at all provided you put your customer's needs first.

When you make the effort to prove that you, your product and company are credible, and that your intentions are directed toward providing unique solutions to your customer's unique problems, the discovery process becomes much easier. Sometimes it flows so naturally as to be unnoticeable as a sales step at all.

The Five Steps For Understanding And Developing Customer Needs

Regardless of your product or service, regardless of your industry, your company, the economy, geographic location or any other factor, there are five basic steps you must take to develop and understand your customer's real need. And remember, we are always talking about a customer's *real need*. He doesn't want a four-on-the-floor Warthog XLF, he wants to pick up girls. She doesn't want a bank loan. She wants to start her own business and call her own shots. They don't want a mortgage. They want to live together happily ever after.

You can help them get there, wherever "there" may be, by taking these steps. They are:

1. Problem Identification*
2. Discovery
3. Qualify
4. Need Acknowledgement
5. Pact Acknowledgement

Step #1—Problem Identification

What usually happens when a prospect enters a retail environment?

A salesperson rushes up with a big grin and a mighty "May I help you?" The salesperson, bless his or

---

*We are well aware that many of Tom's students will recognize the word "problem" as one taught never to say in front of a client. We are identifying a strategy here, which, hopefully, you would never turn around and teach your client, so Tom gives his blessing to its use in this context.

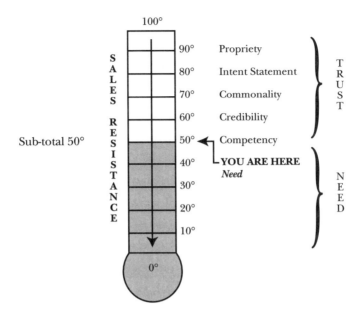

Pretend you're in a visit to Sales Wonderland and you're standing in front of a map of the complex. You've been so busy working your way through Sales Resistance Land that you've lost your place. Not to worry "You Are Here," halfway through. It's been great so far. And the ride's only half over!

her heart, is trying to do the right thing. She wants to be polite, be conscientious and offer her services. Of course, this is usually followed by the equally mighty "Oh, I'm just looking." The potential client has a number of reasons for this response. He, or she, might really be looking, might be killing time waiting for a movie at the other end of the mall, might be too shy to ask for help, or just not ready to divulge his vulnerability at this point. Maybe he just wants to take his time, set his own pace and make his own decision whether or not to proceed.

We see two major challenges with the "May I help you" approach.

The first challenge is the "may" part. That automatically gives control of the situation to your prospect. We respect prospects. We need them and we want them all the rest of our lives, but we know they are not the most capable people to lead someone through the sales process. The one-call closing specialist is far more qualified to see that each prospect gets precisely the product or service he or she needs. Why turn over the bus keys to someone who just stepped on board when you can "leave the driving to us" with a trained professional?

The second challenge concerns the word "help." Your friendly inquiry assumes and implies that your prospect is in need of help. Even people in desperate need are sometimes loath to admit it. If you've ever seen reruns of Tim "The Tool Man" Taylor from television's Home Improvement, you'll realize that some folks are just incapable of admitting a need for help. They'd rather risk sawing Grandma's antique dinner table in half rather than admit to a lack of knowledge of saw blades.

Using the word "help" jumps you over a couple of important steps, as well. All you can expect from such a leap is a very hard landing. You'll be hearing "May I help you—up" from your less-than-impressed sales manager.

A much better opening statement would be:

"Hello. What brings you to Cox's Cabinet Corner?"

Notice how this simple, friendly statement eliminates those two challenges. The prospect can't

10

The Fourth Defense—Hurry

Part I

First Things First

This is the heart of our one-time closing system, the core of sell it today, sell it now. Every step, every phase of mastering one-time closing is important, but of all of them, mastering the step presented in this chapter is central to your success. **This chapter is so important it could have been written first and all in bold face type, but like many salespeople, we would have then been covering it out of sequence.**

The Devil Made Me Do It!

The late comedian Flip Wilson developed a number of hilarious characters. One of them always refused to take personal responsibility for anything by saying "the devil made me do it!" That character has a lot in common with most customers. At this stage of one-step closing you will notice that your customer has a strong desire to relieve himself or herself of all responsibility for the purchase. They are seeking, sometimes desperately, to say "I didn't have any choice...I had to do it...I couldn't help myself."

That kind of attitude can give you a devil of a time, but it's natural and it's all right provided you know how to handle that tricky little situation. When you master the techniques in this chapter, you will.

Send Back Your Be-Backs

A be-back is what happens when a prospect hears your presentation and then says something to the effect of "I'll be back to talk things over tomorrow." Like the old saying goes, far too frequently "tomorrow never comes." Most people would rather procrastinate. They'd prefer to sleep on it, think it over, kick it around for a while, and so on instead of making a decision now. This fact remains true even when the customer's need is high. There's just something about making a decision that intimidates most people.

It's your job to help them over that hurdle.

A little thought on the psychology behind that kind of thinking makes things a bit more clear. People are taught from an early age to save their money, to avoid being a spendthrift, to hold onto their hard-earned cash. We must face the fact that there is a certain amount of guilt involved in spending* money. That's an okay philosophy until it gets in the way of obtaining the goods and services you need. People often express this mentality with statements like the following.

"Yeah, the mechanic told me my car only had six months to live so I traded the old clunker in while I could still drive it into the dealership and get something for it."

"I just had to have a new dress for the board presentation."

"We had to have a bigger house so we could have some privacy from the kids, especially when all their friends come over."

Do you see what's going on here? Those customers are trying to relieve themselves of the responsibility for making a purchase. Some outside factor is forcing the situation. "The devil made me do it."

Hurry Up And Wait

Just like a waiter proud of his craft, you must be in a hurry to "wait" on the needs of your prospects and customers. You have to develop the mindset and the skills to structure your presentation so your customer is relieved from the guilt of making a decision after the purchase.

---

*Of course a one-time closing master doesn't encourage spending. He or she encourages customers to *invest* in enjoying the benefits of your offering.

*Relieving your customer of his or her purchasing "guilt"
leads directly to more sales, more sales today, and more
sales now.*

This "hurry" part of the sales presentation is
perfectly suited for this task. All you have to do is
apply the information gathered during the "need"
process, rely on the universal mindset of your
customer, and turn those be-backs into sales. That way
the only time they'll be-back is when they'll be back
for repeat business.

How To Turn Up The Heat Of Sales Acceptance Without Turning On The High Pressure

The only thing high pressure can do is cause your
customer to blow his or her top. Two critical issues are
involved.

1. Timing is essential. You must always know
   where you are in the presentation and how
   much time is left for you to complete it. Too
   often salespeople continue developing rapport
   and building trust long after those goals have
   been achieved. While you're still trying to make
   a friend, you become as welcome as the character in the Broadway play, "The Man Who
   Wouldn't Leave." Once you've achieved a goal
   in the sales process, move smoothly on to the
   next step. If you try to build your customer to
   100 degrees of sales acceptance with a rapid
   boil of high pressure, you'll only succeed in
   making your presentation uncomfortable or
   even offensive. Instead of heating things up,
   you'll just cool them down.

2. Reaching 100 degrees must be done in small increments, one small step at a time. Steps of 10% or 20% at a time are ideal.

Let's take a closer look at how this is done.

The Three Reasons Customers Choose to Own Your Product or Service

People give all kinds of reasons for buying a product or service, but when you pin them down to "seriously, now, why?" the answers fall into three categories:

- Ownership solves a challenge they were having.
- Ownership satisfies a need.
- Owning this product or service is a goal aspired to.

Despite how it may be expressed, "I wanted to surprise her...We just couldn't pass up a deal like that...he really had his heart set on it...we gave up on the old one before it gave up on us..." and so on, every reason will fit nicely into the three listed above.

BUT, (and you knew that was coming, didn't you?) we one-time closers are concerned with something else. We want to make our presentations based on why people get involved **today** and why they take owner-ship **now** *because that's when we want to close them—to get them involved.* Customers go ahead **today** and **now** for another set of three reasons:

- They buy for need.
- They buy for desire.
- They buy for urgency.

We have already taken you through the need
portion of the presentation, now we'll show you how
to create enough logical urgency to bring out the
emotional power of desire. This logical process will
also help you combat the inevitable onset of "buyer's
remorse" all buyers feel. Buyer's remorse sets in the
instant the purchase is made, the papers are
approved, or the check changes hands. Immediately,
the customer is filled with fear that he or she has done
the wrong thing. "I shouldn't have done that!"
"I should've banked that money." "I spent too much."
"Am I out of my mind?" We one-call closers know this
effect is coming and we prepare ourselves to help our
customers over this rough spot as we do with all the
others along the line.

A Needed Word About Desire

There are two types of desire, also recognized as
greed: inappropriate and appropriate. Inappropriate
desire or greed was showcased in the film "Wall Street"
in the character Gordon Gecko*, played by Michael
Douglas. Gecko made a lofty, noble-sounding speech
to a group of stockholders on the subject of "greed
is goooood." Of course, at the same time he was
busy buying and breaking up companies, ruining businesses and destroying the lives of innocent working
people. That's inappropriate desire. When a salesperson victimizes customers by foisting some unwanted
product on them, that's inappropriate.

---

*In case you think Hollywood has lost its taste for obvious symbolism, a
gecko is an insect-eating lizard with a big head.

Appropriate greed is what those shareholders *thought* Gecko meant in that speech. Appropriate greed is a legitimate desire to own a product or service. You want it and that's perfectly okay. We're here to help you get it!

Urgency Sales Acceptance

Hurry is the most important of your customer's four defenses. And, this section is the most important in Mastering the Art of the One-Call Close. Every previous step in the process has led to this one. It is time to create 100 degrees of sales acceptance without resorting to high pressure sales tactics. Equally important, we'll show you how to do that without even creating the *impression* of using high pressure sales.

Customers can be a suspicious lot. You have to perform something like a high wire act in which you walk a fine line between pressuring your customers and serving them through a sense of urgency. Don't worry. As long as your heart is in the right place, with your customer's best interests, you'll always make it to the end of the line.

The Sound System

The system we present here is a sound one and one that has been proven year after year after year. Somewhere out there some conscious competent salesperson is proving it right now. Our system is foolproof and that is no exaggeration. And because it is a system, anyone can use it. You don't need special talents, special skills or decades of experience. All you need is a desire to learn and to serve your customer.

Our system is based on two sound principles and they are infallible when it comes to working with a sales prospect or client. We won't say you can't possibly go wrong 100% of the time, but to botch the presentation you'll have to work at it—really work at it.

Principle #1—use the individual features of the product that the prospect is most interested in to create the sales acceptance. Those are the reasons they will want to make the purchase *now.*

Principle #2—by using these individual features to create the necessary urgency a little at a time, your prospect will quite easily become a satisfied customer. Ten or twenty degrees at a time, you will slowly "turn up the heat" until your customer reaches 100 degrees of sales acceptance. He or she will accept the process naturally and in a positive way.

So, how do we do that, you ask. Well, we're *glad* you asked. Here's how.

The Five Steps To Hurry

The Five Steps To Hurry create a natural and positive sense of urgency:

1. **Product Demonstration** in which you showcase the features and benefits of your product as they relate to each customer.

2. **Three-Option Close** for eliminating "I'd like to shop around" style objections.

3. **Break The Pact,** which was mentioned in an earlier chapter. Here you break up the

agreement made by your customers not to make a purchase today.

4. **Summary (Trial) Close** in which you summarize the key points of your presentation and test to see if the customer is ready to consummate an agreement.

5. **Investment Close** during which the financial aspects are disclosed only after the salesperson is absolutely certain that it is the appropriate moment for the close.

We will address Steps #1 and #2 in this chapter and will finish the remaining three steps in Chapter Eleven.

Step #1—Product Demonstration

Make a solemn pledge to yourself, right now, that you will never make another product demonstration again without following this procedure. We're serious! Raise your hand, cross your heart and take the pledge, brother. This is *the* system that will help turn you into a one-time closing champion.

The first step is to break down your product demonstration into segments highlighting each individual feature of your product or service that you know will benefit this individual client.

The second step is to present each of those features in the following manner, and only in the following manner.

State the FACT.

Show the BENEFIT.

Facts and benefits create the sale. Urgency and feedback make it happen *now*.

Create URGENCY.

Ask for FEEDBACK.

The first two, fact and benefit, are pretty easy. After all, the facts will be obvious or at least readily available with a little research. "I recommend this property for immediate purchase because it is on the announced route of the new freeway." Additionally, you should quite easily elaborate on specific benefits associated with those facts. "This will make it more convenient for you." One will fall naturally and logically right after the other.

Urgency about each feature is something that the salesperson must create. It's not there until you make it so. It's not being pushy or trying to force your customer into a quick decision. Creating urgency requires effort and creativity to assure that your customer feels a genuine need to make a purchase today and now. "This means that you will double your investment within three years."

Asking for feedback serves two purposes: it provides a way to monitor your progress and to see if your customer is ready for the next logical step.

Use the FACT-BENEFITS-URGENCY-FEEDBACK formula by breaking down the features of your specific product or service. To give you a better idea of how the process works, we will provide a number of examples using different products. Read them, study them and imagine how the system will work with your product and your customers.

You Auto Buy This

FACT: "This powerful V8 engine is the largest stock gasoline engine made in the U.S."

This fact is obvious. You can simply lift the hood and show it. Even if the facts aren't that visual, anti-lock brakes or a roadside assistance plan, for example, one of your product brochures will list them and more. Our point is, that facts are easy to come by.

BENEFIT: "This engine will allow you to pull your boat with ease and it's a standard feature with this model."

To discover the appropriate benefit, just put yourself in your customer's mind and ask "what's in it for me?" In this case, the customer is concerned about the ease of pulling a boat from the house out to the lake. Power is obviously in it for him. Gas mileage, acceleration, braking, and turning ease could also be important benefits. After achieving trust and need, facts and benefits may do the selling, but urgency and feedback will do it now.

URGENCY: "This particular engine will not be an option on next year's truck and even with the smaller engine there will be a higher sticker price on the new model. So next year you'd be paying more for the same model, but with less power." Without using any high pressure or being pushy, the salesperson has merely pointed out the significant advantage to making a purchase right now over procrastinating until later. Buying now is clearly in the customer's best interest according to the customer's own definition of need.

FEEDBACK: "Because next year's model will look and ride exactly the same, which one do you think would fit your needs and pocket book the best?"

The customer's answer will lead directly to the next appropriate step in the sales process.

Let's see how the system works on a few other products and services.

Pooling Your Efforts

Here's an example using a swimming pool in a resort property.

FACT: "Here we have a full-sized pool, Jacuzzi and kiddie pool with an expansive deck."

BENEFIT: "As an owner here, you can relax by the heated pool any time of the year. We also have water aerobics, water volleyball and many other activities for adults and children alike."

URGENCY: "This is our first pool. We now have five more. In fact, our developer is investing millions of dollars on additional amenities impacting the future value of the property and vacation lifestyle of our owners."

FEEDBACK: "At this point, I don't know if you are interested or not, but if this were something your family could use, when do you think would be the best time to get involved?"

A DVD Is S-O-L-D

Our salesperson can give himself or herself a "high five" after using the system to turn a potential challenge into a reason to own.

FACT: "This particular unit is a state-of-the-art DVD system."

BENEFIT: "It is the highest quality DVD available at this time and will give you better picture and sound reproduction than anything else on the market."

URGENCY: "I have just two of these units in stock. One was returned because it was a gift and the person receiving it already had one. The package has been opened, but the unit has never been used. But because it's been opened, I can give it to you at a lower amount with the same guarantee."

FEEDBACK: "Although the unit is new and has never been used, or even plugged in, the carton was still opened. Technically, we can't sell it as new. Is having that carton opened something you can live with if it would save you money?"

Lawn Down On the Job

Here our example is a lawn service.

FACT: "I stopped by today to offer my services. You may have noticed that I mow and trim your neighbors' lawns across the street and next door."

BENEFIT: "Because I have a dozen customers in this neighborhood, as well as your next door neighbors, I can offer you a more economical fee than someone from across town. In addition, since I have to bring all my equipment each time, I can throw in trimming your shrubs at no extra charge."

URGENCY: "The flip side however, is that I can only handle two more accounts in this area because that will fill up my time on this side of town."

FEEDBACK: "I can have a quote prepared for you tomorrow or would Wednesday be better?"

Clipping The Hedges

Use the preceding examples to spur some thought as to how the process will work with your product or service. We have seen how a fact, even something as simple as a swimming pool or the size of an engine, can be turned into a benefit to move the process toward a successful completion. We can use outside influences, such as other residential developments or an opened carton, to help us create the urgency necessary to close the sale *now*.

You should not and must not be perceived as someone using high-pressure sales tactics. Getting the proper feedback throughout the process is essential. If you wait until the time for the close to get feedback, your customer will start hedging on you. He or she will stall, back-peddle, and start making excuses for not making the purchase now. Something you said earlier in the presentation may have triggered a negative reaction. If you don't generate feedback, you may never discover the concern(s) until it is too late to effectively address them. You have to "clip" these hedges when they first develop or they will grow out of control.

When you get proper feedback throughout your demonstration, your close becomes much easier because your customer would be contradicting himself by refusing to go ahead. Your customer is not an opponent to be overcome, but a partner to be helped. Even negative feedback is valuable because it lets you know where your customer stands on a particular issue or feature.

Negative Feedback: "Sure, the V8 engine has a lot of power, but I bet it's a real gas guzzler."

Positive Reaction: "I'm glad you brought that up. Specifically because the V8 engine is so powerful, it does not have to run beyond its capabilities when pulling a heavy load, such as your boat. A smaller engine has to work much harder and less efficiently to pull the same load. It actually uses more gasoline while towing."

Without that negative feedback this gas mileage issue could have remained dormant until the close when it would suddenly appear in the form of a major obstacle. Feedback, even the negative kind, provides you with a golden opportunity to address important issues the moment the customer thinks to brings them up, rather than after you have shown the investment and asked for the sale.

Make sure your presentation doesn't get "clipped" on the way to your one-time close. Product demonstration is basic. It's simple, but it's not as easy as falling off a log. You have to do your homework, study, and practice the techniques. You also need to research your client's real needs, wants, and concerns. Beyond that, you have to apply your own creative resources to put the entire system together in terms that provide the unique solution to your client's unique situation.

When you use the system properly, the "math" will astound you.

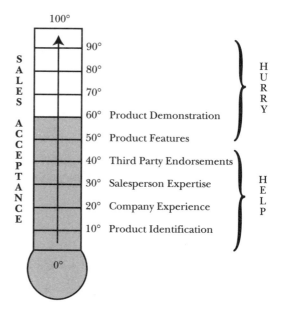

*Combining customer research with your own creative abilities
causes a natural reaction that raises the "temperature"
of sales acceptance closer to the desired 100 degrees.*

FACT + BENEFITS + URGENCY + FEEDBACK =
SOLD TODAY, SOLD NOW

Repeat this mantra over and over, "I will never give a product demonstration again without presenting the features in this manner:

State the facts,

Show the benefits,

Create urgency and ask for feedback."

Step #2—The Three-Option Close

"Well, we'd like to look around a little more before we make a final decision."

"I'd like to take a look at a few more options before making a firm commitment."

"This is great, but we'd just like to see what else might be available."

"I would like to shop around first."

"Shop," "around" and "more" are three of the most dreaded words in sales. They form the basis of one of the biggest enemies of one-time closing, but there is an effective and proven way to overcome that most powerful of opponents. We call it the Three-Option Close. It works and it works really well because you use your customer's own psychology to allow him/her/them to help you provide the unique product or service they really want and need.

This technique allows your customers to do their "shopping around" **during** *your presentation.*

Here's how it works in four easy steps.

Step One: During the early stages of the hurry phase you narrow down your prospect's need and price to a definable category or range. It's a standard part of every sales presentation. The further along the road you travel with your customer, the better the picture you get of the ultimate destination.

Step Two: Review your product inventory and select three items that fit, generally, the parameters your customer has established. The items don't have to precisely match. Two of the three items can actually be out of those parameters, but they should be close. For example, if your customer is a young middle-class couple wanting a slightly larger house to make room for a family, you wouldn't show them that multi-million dollar mansion out on the lake.

You wouldn't show them a tiny one-bedroom apartment either.

Three items are the optimum number to present. Fewer options don't offer enough choices and more options tend to confuse the customer.

We'll stay with that young couple throughout this example. One of the three homes you have selected will be the one you believe is the ideal home for their needs. *Do not show this best option first.* Show them the two comparable homes first and then wrap up with the ideal selection as your last presentation.

Let's suppose that the three comparable houses you have selected are priced at $185,000, $205,000 and $225,000. Which one would you show first? Your best option is to start with the lowest priced house, even if you think they'll choose a higher priced model—especially if you think they'll choose the higher priced model. The $185,000 home will not meet their expectations or standards and that's exactly the reaction you want. When you show them this home, introduce it by saying:

"Let me show you this particular home so that it will help me get a better idea of exactly the type of home you are looking for."

After politely looking the place over and conferring silently among themselves, the couple will usually respond:

"This is nice, but we're really looking for something a bit nicer. We can afford a little more."

Take a moment to look at the operative words in that nice win/win situation your customer just described. You as a sales person can earn "more" because you will be providing your customer with something "nicer." Everybody wins.

Next, skip over the middle range house and go directly to that $225,000 unit. Again, they'll probably be impressed and will like it. But as it is at the extreme top of their budget or more likely just outside of their range, they'll respond with something along the lines of:

"This is really nice, but we just can't afford that price."

Now the process is nearing completion, but you don't slap your hands together, put a big grin on your face and say, "well, folks do I have a deal for you now!" That smacks of high pressure sales and ultimately the only one who gets smacked around is the salesperson. You should appear a little disappointed, but not angry or bitter. Take the position that sales process has about lost its energy. Then just when it seems there is nowhere else to turn, phrase a response something close to this:

"There is another home I'd like to show you. After investing this time with you, and getting to know you and your needs a bit better, and getting your feedback, I think this model really might be just what you're looking for. It's got the features you want and it's within your price range. Let me check with the office to be sure it's still available." Call in and then respond with, "Yes, it's still on the market. It has all the features you want and at a reasonable $205,000. Would you like to see it?"

Of course, they'd like to see it. That's why they're investing all this time with you. So, now you head out to see the home you had in mind all along. If this sounds a bit like manipulation, it isn't. If you had taken your potential clients to the $205,000 house first, they still would have wanted to see more options. They would have a need to "shop around" some more, right? Well, by showing those other options you are giving them exactly what they want. The major difference with our system is that *you allow your customers to do all their shopping around as part of "your" presentation.*

Regardless of the price, regardless of the product, every customer should leave the sale believing he, she or they have gotten a bargain. Of course, you and your organization need to make a profit on each sale as well. Even if the customer is making an investment at the listed price, your presentation can stress how much value the customers are getting so they still feel as if they are getting that bargain. Sometimes an added gift will accomplish the same thing. The important point is that you want your customers walking away with the firm belief that they have gotten more than expected.

All you have done is helped prepare your customer for a decision. More than that, you have helped prepare them for a positive decision *now.* As long as you are acting in good faith with the best interests of your customers at heart and are providing them a fair opportunity, you are not manipulating the situation or the people. You are just doing what you are supposed to do—helping that nice young family move into their dream home.

Ending A Driving Reign

Picture a young family in their mid-twenties with two young children. This husband is a hard-working carpenter earning a modest living. His wife is focused on raising her children and creating a picture perfect happy home. Their budget allows for one vehicle and that's a small truck. The husband must use it to travel from job to job all across the community. His wife is beginning to show signs of cabin fever. A second car would put an end to the fever and would certainly make her chores significantly easier. They have even discussed acceptable makes and models, features and options, and even colors. Fortunately, they are due an income tax return which, combined with some of their savings, will get them into a "new" used car. The check and the savings total $9,000. They can't afford a penny more and certainly no additional monthly payments.

One day our carpenter gets rained out of a job. On the way home, he decides to drop into a local automobile dealership to kill a little time and to see if there just might be a good bargain available. As he steps out of his truck and under the large metal canopy over the cars he notices a salesman leaning on the hood of a car. The man smiles and nods. He looks as if he believes he is the king of the car lot, reigning supreme over all he surveys. He is the "pitch man," the "answer man, " the "man with the plan," and the giver and taker of all good "deals." He continues leaning on the hood of the car. When the carpenter approaches, the salesman asks, "May I help you?"

Our hard working young carpenter explains his family's needs and the parameters he and his wife have discussed. At last the king speaks. His voice is as boisterous as his "over the top" manner. "Well, heh heh, my friend this is your lucky day. Why here's the little gem you are looking for right here. Go ahead, kick the tires, slam the doors, why it even still has a bit of that old 'new car' smell. This is exactly what you are looking for."

Ask yourself a serious question. What has this salesman done to earn the carpenter's business? Has he really listened to his needs? Has he tried to provide a unique solution to a unique problem? Has he put his customer's interests first? Has he helped prepare his customer to make a financial decision?

Certainly not and he'll probably record the incident as another no sale. "The guy just wasn't ready to buy," he'll say. Well, our carpenter wasn't ready to buy because he wasn't prepared to make a purchase. Get that? He wasn't *prepared* to make a purchase by his salesperson.

Putting A Customer In The Driver's Seat

Let's look at the same situation, only this time our salesperson doesn't view herself as the absolute ruler of the car lot. Instead, she believes she actually works *for* the customer. Our carpenter drives into the lot. The young saleswoman approaches.

"Hi, my name is Mickey, what brings you by to see us today," she asks.

Charlie discusses the situation and lays out all the parameters of the purchase that he and his wife have discussed. Mickey then tries a much different approach than the "king."

"Charlie, if you don't mind I'd like to show you a couple of cars just to get a better idea of what you're looking for. Is that okay with you?"

"No problem. I'm just shopping around, though."

Mickey escorts her customer to a very nice car which, in a general way, fits the parameters they have just discussed.

"Nice car. How much does it cost," asks Charlie.

"It's in the twelve thousand dollar range. I'd have to check the price list to get the precise figure."

"Don't bother. There's no point. As I said, we can afford nine thousand and that's it."

"Okay, Charlie, let me show you something over here."

She takes him to look at a car that has obviously seen better days, much better days.

One look tells Charlie this isn't the car for his family. "This isn't really what I'm looking for. I don't want my wife and kids riding around in something that might fall apart any second."

Mickey nods knowingly, but says, "Well, it's only five thousand dollars."

"Yes, but I told you I can afford nine thousand," he says. "I need something a little better than this."

At this point, Mickey looks a bit disappointed and with sincerity says, "Well, Charlie if I had a lot of gems like the one you're looking for I could sell a hundred a day. They are hard to come by these days."

Charlie now believes that the sales process is winding down to an unsuccessful completion.

They start walking through the lot back toward his truck. After a couple of minutes, Mickey says," I was just thinking, Charlie…"

"Yes?"

"We took in a trade last night that might just fit the bill. It has not been priced yet, but I would guess it will hit the lot at around ninety-five hundred."

"Yeah, but as I said…"

"Before you say no, let me explain something to you."

"Okay."

"First of all, the good news is that it is in great shape and has low mileage. I took my kid out for ice cream in it last night just to check it out. It runs like a top."

"And the bad news?"

"Well, Charlie, the man who drove it last didn't much care about how the car looked. I don't think he ever waxed it at all. It also needs a new spare."

Charlie's interest perks up. Now he is aware that a positive offering might just be coming his way.

"The car is scheduled to go into our shop," says Mickey. "It's slated for detailing and a new spare. If it goes into the shop, they'll charge the sales department at least three hundred dollars for a good clean up and a spare. The reason I'm telling you this is, if you were willing to do the clean up yourself and get your own spare tire, we might be able to get the price down to where it fits your budget. Would you like to see it?"

At this point Mickey walks right over to the car she was standing by when Charlie drove in. It's the same car as in the earlier scenario, but this time a one-time closing specialist is on the job. We have a different story, a different presentation and a different conclusion. We have a sale.

The Three-Option Close is one of the most powerful ever used as Mickey has just proven. She was professional. She listened. She prepared her customer for making a decision. And she created a situation that allowed Charlie to do all his shopping around during her presentation. If the car is even close to what his wife wants, Charlie is going to give serious consideration to making a purchase today and now. He'll probably borrow the phone to make a call to say, "Honey, guess what I found?"

Our Three-Option Close increases sales acceptance with dramatic results and it gets you closer to a one-time closing right now. This is especially true for big-ticket items, but it will work equally well in all price ranges, even shoes, for example.

Finding The Shoe That Fits

If you've ever paid attention to a presentation in a quality shoe store with a conscious competent, you will never see the salesperson come to the fitting part of the presentation with only one pair of shoes in hand. Being fully conscious and competent he or she knows much better than that. Presenting just one pair of shoes forces your customer into the most restrictive of choices—"yes" or "no." We think you'll agree, that's not much of a choice.

When the salesperson brings at least three pairs of shoes, the customer's world of choices opens up.

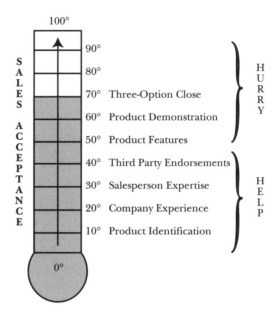

The Three-Option Close proves the old adage that
"the third time's the charm!"

The customer can compare prices, colors, designs, materials, workmanship and so on. Not only does presenting choices increase your chance of closing today and now, it can also result in selling multiple pairs to your customer. "I just can't make up my mind, so I'll just take 'em all!"

With the Three-Option Close you aren't limiting your customers to your selection, you are allowing them to make the purchase on their own. The technique will even work on items far less expensive than shoes.

"I can offer you a single roll of thread, a box of twelve, or this handy two-pack which saves you fifty cents. Which fits your needs best, Mrs. Prospect?"

Once you've created a situation in which your customer makes the desired choice, you still face a powerful obstacle. It's called The Pact. Breaking that pact and the other three steps to mastering the hurry step are discussed in Chapter Eleven.

11

The Fourth Defense—Hurry

Part II

The Five Steps to the hurry phase of the sales process are:

1. Product Demonstration
2. Three-Option Close
3. Break The Pact
4. Summary (Trial) Close
5. Price Close

We covered the first two stages in the previous chapter. Now let's continue where we left off with a way to address one of the most serious obstacles customers can place in your path.

Break The Pact

As you will remember The Pact is an agreement between two or more prospects that they will not become customers that day.

"No matter what he says, Marge, we're not buying anything today, right?"

"That's right, Herbert, not today."

Their resolve can be anything from weak and tepid to "mighty, indeed!" Whatever the level of resistance, it is your duty to break that pact. As long as it remains in force you cannot serve the best interests of these people—they won't let you. It's a curious, but true fact that one of the biggest obstacles preventing customers from getting the goods and services they want and need are those very same customers. The old phrase that sometimes we're our own worst enemy is certainly true when it comes to The Pact.

Mickey Has A Breakdown

Let's forget about Marge and Herbert for the time being and return to Charlie and Anna who have returned to Mickey's dealership to look at the car they can get for just $9000 plus a tire and a clean up. During Mickey's presentation she has discovered the existence of a pact. As we go through this example, mentally replace the cast with players drawn from your own customer experience and imagine yourself handling the situation with your own product.

After her presentation, Mickey asks, "Anna, how do you like this little gem, overall?" She then waits for a response.